AMSTERDAM

INSIGHT *City* GUIDES

Edited by Christopher Catling
Editorial Director: Brian Bell

APA
PUBLICATIONS

AMSTERDAM

First Edition

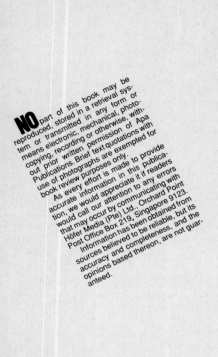

Printed in Singapore by Höfer Press Pte. Ltd

ABOUT THIS BOOK

Descartes said of the city of Amsterdam: "Where else in the world could one choose a place where... all the curiosities one could wish for are as easy to find as here?"

What was true when Descartes lived in Amsterdam (1628–49) remains true today. Amsterdam is a whirligig, a city at the cutting edge of the arts, a place of experiment. These characteristics are manifest in the positive delight that Amsterdammers seem to take in the quirky, the eccentric and the freakish. That is why it is so difficult to pin down this city – although long familiarity with Amsterdam qualifies many of our contributors to tackle this task.

Human companionship

Christopher Catling, the book's project editor, first visited Amsterdam in 1987. He was editing Derek Blyth's excellent *American Express Guide* to the city at the time and this made him want to go and see the city for himself. Arriving in the depths of winter, he dived into the nearest brown café and found not only the warmth of a glowing stove but also of human companionship. The next winter he was back again, this time on an assignment to write about the city from a business traveller's angle for the *Economist European Cities* guide, and he has since visited the city so often that he now considers it almost a second home.

Stuart Ridsdale, who contributed most of the Places section, commuted between London, where he worked during the week, and Amsterdam for the weekends. The reason? A romantic attachment both to the city itself and to a lady who lived there. A new assignment has since taken Ridsdale to Hong Kong, but he hopes to live in Amsterdam one day. In the meantime, his frequent sojourns have made him very knowledgable about the city.

Tim Harper is an American journalist who writes on European business, politics and economics for leading US publications such as *Time* and the *International Herald Tribune*. Since relocating to London from New York, he has frequently visited Amsterdam to report on social initiatives and to indulge his passion for antique maps. In this book he investigates the freewheeling character of the Amsterdammer.

Michael Gray is a freelance journalist used to challenging assignments. After all, he is a regular contributor to *SPUR* (which, we hasten to add, is a glossy magazine for thoroughbred racehorse breeders and not the sort of thing that sells in Amsterdam's Red Light District). We asked Gray to find out what it is like to live and work in Amsterdam and, true to form, he came up with some intriguing answers.

Mike Cooper is an Amsterdam resident, the son of Dutch and English parents. As a young tearaway, he remembers being chased by the police while demonstrating against the construction of the controversial Amsterdam Metro. Now he earns his money writing punchy features for *Holland Herald*, the inflight magazine of the Dutch national airline, KLM, and enjoys living in this festive, artistic city of characterful brown cafés – all of which he describes here.

Joan Corcoran-Lonis is perhaps better known to the readers of the UK *Daily Telegraph* and *Sunday Telegraph* as Joan Clements, the by-line she writes under as their Netherlands correspondent. She came to

Catling

Ridsdale

Harper

Gray

Cooper

Amsterdam in the late 1970s and stayed – first because she became enamoured of a sit-up-and-beg bicycle, then because she met Constatijn, her Dutch school-teacher husband. Corcoran-Lonis has written about the terrible tragedy of the war years, and about Anne Frank, whose memory draws thousands of visitors to the city annually.

Yvonne Newman lives in Oxford, a city that is twinned with the Dutch city of Leiden. Through her participation in the twinning programme, she regularly visits the Netherlands via Amsterdam and here she shares with us her love of the city's cuisine, in all its cosmopolitan variety.

Susie Boulton's knowledge of Amsterdam stems from two quite different experiences. On the one hand, as a researcher and writer for the Consumers' Association magazine, *Holiday Which?*, she has compiled reports on all aspects of the city, from the salubrious to the sleazy. On the other hand, as a History of Art graduate, she specialised in the paintings of the Golden Age and spent many long hours in the Rijksmuseum. These two contrasting focuses on the city enable her to guide us painlessly through the rich art collections of the Museum Quarter, and to pinpoint the city's best hotels, restaurants, shops and cultural attractions in the Travel Tips section.

Through the lens

Without the stunning photography, this book would be a duller affair, despite the best endeavours of our writers. **Paul van Riel**, one of our principal photographers, was born in Amsterdam and has lived there all his life, sallying forth all over the world on assignments for leading fashion, travel and business magazines. Of his native city, van Riel says: "Returning from Tokyo, Paris or New York, it never ceases to surprise me how cosmopolitan Amsterdam really is. On the other hand, I hate the filth on the streets, the result of our excessive love of dogs."

Eddy Posthuma de Boer, also a native Amsterdammer, started his carrer as a newspaper photographer and now travels the world doing photo-features for the KLM and Sabena in-flight magazines. As well as publishing numerous photobooks, de Boer's witty exhibitions, on themes as diverse as barber's shops, carnival and the nature of photography itself, are a regular highlight of the Amsterdam cultural scene.

George Wright is a freelance photographer living in Dorset, England, who works internationally for magazine and book publishers. His first assignment in Amsterdam was for the *Observer Magazine* in London. He admires Amsterdam's vitality and the unconventional way it appears to operate. Like all our contributors, he singles out the dog mess on the streets as its worst feature.

Other photographs have come from regular Apa contributors; **Christine Osborne**, who both writes and photographs her own books and is a noted specialist on the Middle East; **Lyle Lawson**, an inveterate traveller who runs her own travel firm, taking amateur photographers to unusual locations, as well as finding time to be an author, editor and photographer; and **Bodo Bondzio**, a German who can always be relied upon to get good shots of people and faces.

This book was expertly steered by **Jill Anderson** through a variety of Macintosh computers, and **Kate Owen** was the eagle-eyed proofreader and indexer.

Newman

Boulton

van Riel

de Boer

Wright

Amstel Bieren
Tarief
CIRCUS VAN PEKING NAAR CARRÉ
Straks maar weer gewoon naar Locki en Philips kijken.
CIRCUS VAN PEKING

CONTENTS

HISTORY AND FEATURES

AMSTERDAM IN HISTORY

AMSTERDAM TODAY

MAPS

TRAVEL TIPS

de Gouden
6
VER. H DE KEYSER
Algemeen Dagblad
De Telegraaf
de Volkskrant

Snuif
de Silveren
RESTAURANT
4
Ola
KRONE
Gladstone
MILD
REEMTSMA
REEMTSMA
R6
R6
INTERNATIONAL
INTERNATIONAL

THE CHARACTER OF AMSTERDAM

Amsterdam, the city of water and brick, is unique for the way it balances past and present. Perhaps no community has ever had such a glorious explosion of wealth and culture as Amsterdam during the 17th century, the city's Golden Age. While the legacy of that period is pervasive, the city is hardly like some others where the present is devoted to worship of the past. Instead, modern Amsterdam, from the titillation of the Red Light District to the vitality of the contemporary arts, from the energy and awareness of the entrepreneurs in their small shops to the fast-growing immigrant fringes of the city, offers a range of experiences that are the result of a remarkable human heritage.

In strolling around Amsterdam—one of the best walking cities anywhere—you are also reminded continually of how the city was built and how it thrives: on hard-headed business acumen and on a sense of community that combines several all-too-rare qualities. Foremost among these, paradoxically, is the desire to be left alone, and the willingness to leave others alone—that is, unless they need help. For while Amsterdam is, and always has been, a city of people pulling themselves up by their own bootstraps, it is and always has been a city that believes in spreading its wealth among the young, the old, the poor and the sick as well. Making money and being comfortable is important, but so is a happy and healthy society.

Amsterdam is one of the most intriguing of cities in several respects. Largely because of its small size, in terms of both population and geography, it is intimate and accessible. The fact that so many Amsterdammers routinely speak up to half a dozen different languages—few people plunge into conversation with strangers as readily as the Dutch—provides visitors with an extraordinary opportunity to look beyond what they've read or heard about the city. Or, indeed, what they know from previous visits.

For Amsterdam, apparently so solid and unchanging, as it sits astride its miles of canals, is really a city that is changing constantly. What's the latest trend in art? Where's the best place to go late-night dancing *this* week? Who's saying what about the future of NATO and the European Community? When is the next big environmental demonstration? How are the authorities getting along in their efforts to clean up the squatters and the drug addicts?

Amsterdam is a city of character, and of characters. It is a freewheeling city, so feel free.

Preceding pages: warehouse turned into chic apartments; Café Hoppe, Spui No. 20; De Silveren Spieghel restaurant and newsagent's shop, Kattengat; the Christmas twins, Amsterdam entrepreneurs; anti-pollution measures have brought wildlife back to the canals; reflections, Prinsengracht. Left, Amsterdam's hospitable face.

DECISIVE DATES

12th century AD: First communities of herring fishermen settle on the banks of the Amstel.
***circa* 1220:** The first Dam, or sluice, is built to hold back the tidal waters of the Zuider Zee.
1275: Floris V, Count of Holland, grants the people of "Amstelledamme" freedom from tolls on their goods passing through the county; the first documentary record of Amsterdam.
1300: The Bishop of Utrecht grants Amsterdam official city status.
1334: Work begins on the Oude Kerk, Amsterdam's oldest church.
1345: A dying man regurgitates the Communion host which, thrown on the fire, remains undamaged. A miracle is declared and pilgrims flock to the shrine of the host.
1350: Amsterdam becomes the export centre for local beers and an entrepôt for Baltic grain.
1395: The first city hall is built in Dam square.
1400: Work begins on the Nieuwe Kerk.
1452: Fire destroys much of Amsterdam's timber-and-thatch buildings. New laws ordain that new buildings shall be built of brick and tile.
1480: Walls are built to defend the city.
1519: Charles V, King of Spain, is crowned Holy Roman Emperor. Amsterdam, as a result of war, treaties and marriage alliances, is now part of the mighty Spanish empire and nominally Catholic. Amsterdam remains tolerant of Protestant minorities (persecuted elsewhere in Europe).
1535: The situation changes when Anabaptists invade the Town Hall to proclaim the Second Coming. The occupiers are arrested and executed. Strict Catholicism is reimposed on the city.
1566: The Iconoclasm (*Beeldenstorm*). Calvinists protesting at the lack of religious freedom storm many of Amsterdam's churches. As a result they are given a church of their own.
1567: Philip II of Spain sends the tyrannical Duke Alvarez to restore Catholic control of Amsterdam. Many Protestants are executed and others flee to England.
1572: The Dutch Revolt against Spanish rule begins in earnest, led by William of Orange.

1576: Amsterdam, loyal to Philip II, is besieged by Prince William's troops.
1578: Amsterdam capitulates to Prince William. Protestant exiles return to the city. Calvinists take over all the churches and the reins of government in a peaceful revolution known as the Alteration (*Alteratie*).
1579: The seven northern provinces of the Netherlands sign the Treaty of Utrecht providing for mutual assistance in the event of attack but otherwise allowing for self-determination. The southern provinces remain under Spanish Catholic control and Protestant refugees from Antwerp, Amsterdam's main trade rival, seek asylum in Amsterdam, laying the foundations for the city's Golden Age.
1595–97: Ships from Amsterdam sail east via the Cape of Good Hope to discover the Indonesian archipelago.
1602: The Dutch East India Company is established to co-ordinate trade between the northern provinces and the lands east of the Cape, financed by an innovative public share flotation.
1609: The Bank of Amsterdam is formed, placing the city at the forefront of European finance. Hendrik Staets draws up the plan for Amsterdam's Grachtengordel, the three concentric canals ringing the city (work starts on the first section in 1613).
1621: The Dutch West India Company is founded and benefits from a monopoly on trade with the Americas and West Africa.
1626: Peter Minuit "purchases" the island of Manhatten and founds the colony of New Amsterdam (taken by the English and renamed New York in 1664).
1632: The Atheneum Illustre, forerunner of Amsterdam University, is founded.
1642: Rembrandt paints *The Night Watch*.
1648: Under the Treaty of Münster the seven northern provinces are recognised as an independent republic. Work begins on Amsterdam's new Town Hall.
1650: Amsterdam now has a population of around 220,000, making it the largest city of the new republic.
1652: The first of numerous wars with the English for maritime supremacy.

1685: Huguenot refugees flood into Amsterdam after the Revocation of the Edict of Nantes, reversing their rights to freedom of worship.
1688: William III of Holland is crowned as King of the United Kingdom, having married the English princess, Mary Stuart. William's wars against the French do much to strain the economy of the Netherlands and the Republic begins to decline as a trading nation.
1697: Peter the Great visits Amsterdam to study shipbuilding.
1702: William III dies without heir. Amsterdam and the northern provinces suffer further inroads to their trade when the Austrian Emperor Charles VI sets up a rival East India Company based in Ostend.
1744: France invades the southern provinces.
1747: William IV is elected hereditary head of state of the seven northern provinces, now unified under one leader and called the United Provinces.
1751–88: The United Provinces are torn by civil strife between conservative supporters of the House of Orange and liberal reformers, called Patriots, demanding greater democracy.
1795: France invades Amsterdam and, in alliance with the Patriots, establishes a new National Assembly. The United Provinces are renamed the Batavian Republic after the Batavi tribe that rebelled against Roman rule in AD 69.
1808: Napoleon reverses the constitutional reforms and establishes his brother, Louis Napoleon, as King of the Netherlands, with Amsterdam as its capital.
1813: After the defeat of Napoleon, William VI is welcomed back to Amsterdam from exile.
1814: William VI is crowned King of the Netherlands. The Austrians give up their claims to the southern provinces and north and south are united under one monarch.
1831: After years of unrest and revolt against rule from Amsterdam, the southern provinces achieve independence and are renamed the Kingdom of Belgium.
1845: Riots in Amsterdam calling for democratic reform lead to the establishment of a constitutional committee under J.R. Thorbecke.
1848: The new Dutch constitution comes into force, providing for a directly elected parliament.
1870–76: A period of rapid developments that lead to the emergence of socialist principles of government; improvements are made in education and public health, the Dutch railway system is established and the new North Sea Canal revives Amsterdam's position as a port and centre of shipbuilding.
1914–20: The Netherlands remain neutral during World War I, but food shortages lead to strikes, riots and growing support for the Dutch Communist Party.
1928: Amsterdam hosts the Olympic Games.
1930s: During the Great Depression, thousands of Amsterdam's unemployed work on job creation schemes, including the construction of the Amsterdam Bos recreation park.

1940: Germany ignores the neutrality of the Netherlands and invades on 10 May.
1941: 400 Jews are rounded up in Amsterdam on 22 and 23 February. City dockworkers lead a two-day strike in protest at anti-Jewish measures on 25 and 26 February.
1942: Anne Frank and family go into hiding.
1945: After a bitter winter Amsterdam is finally liberated.
1949: Indonesia achieves independence, the first of the former Dutch colonies to do so.
1963: Amsterdam reaches the peak of its population (868,000) and housing shortages lead to the formation of numerous organised squats.
1965: The Provos, dedicated to shaking Dutch complacency, win representation on the Amsterdam city council.
1966: Protestors throwing smoke bombs disrupt the wedding of Princess Beatrice and Claus von Amsberg.
1975: Protest in Amsterdam reaches a peak as police battle with demonstrators over plans to demolish areas of Nieuwmarkt to build the new metro system and the Opera/Town Hall complex.
1986: Despite strong opposition the Muziektheater and Stadhuis complex is completed.
1989: The government is brought down because its proposed anti-vehicle laws are not considered tough enough. New laws are aimed at eventually making Amsterdam traffic-free.
1990: Van Gogh Centenary exhibition.

VILLAGE IN THE BOGS

The herring fishermen who established a community at the mouth of the Amstel river in the 12th century must have been fairly desperate. As elsewhere along the North Sea coast, they pieced their huts together on top of mounds anchored by wooden stakes. They piled up the mounds with seaweed and anything else dredged from the tidal flats that couldn't be put to a better use. Along with a few craftsmen, these early settlers had to devise a more reliable existence than living at the whim of the unpredictable tides that surged in from the Zuider Zee.

Yet the Amstel community hung on and grew, and the scattered collection of huts became rows of timber-framed houses built on top of the dykes alongside the river. Three of the old dykes are still distinguishable today as Warmoesstraat, Nieuwendijk and Kalverstraat.

Below sea level: With the excess soil from digging drainage canals, the level of the houses was raised about 27 inches (70 cm) above NAP or Normal Amsterdam Level. NAP is the standard "zero" measurement for the nation, like sea level everywhere else. In Amsterdam, and all of western Holland, sea level would mean knee-deep or even neck-deep in water, hence the different base measurement. Examples of the NAP, showing how so much of the Netherlands is below sea level, and what happened when the country was devastated by the flood tides of 1953, can be seen in a permanent exhibition on the ground floor of the new Stadhuis (city hall) in Waterlooplein.

The first dam, intended to hold back the highest tides, was built about 1220, most likely near the present Central Station or further up the Damrak. It was probably nothing more than a sluice gate across the mouth of the Amstel. The gate would halt the inundation from the big tides and at low tide could be opened to allow the Amstel river to flow into the sea.

By 1275, the peat bogs surrounding the hamlet, known then as "Amstelledamme", had gradually attracted farmers, refugees and tradesmen who bolstered the population to the point where it might, with generosity, be called a town; even so, it was still very small by comparison with higher and drier European capitals.

First public buildings: According to contemporary woodcut, which gives us an idea of the scene at this time, the forerunner of the Oude Kerk, or Old Church, had been erected near the site of today's church, on Oude Kerksplein, along with about 600 houses. Surrounding the little burg was a moat, the remnants of which can be traced in the Oude Zijds Voorburgwal and the Nieuwe Zijds Voorburgwal canals; the latter was not filled in until 1884, some 600 years after it was originally dug.

Amstelledamme, or Amstelredam (it did not become Amsterdam until the mid-16th century), then began making great strides—quickly enough, in fact, to find itself the prize in a battle for provincial fiefdoms between the Bishop of Utrecht and the Count of Holland towards the close of the 13th century. In the first recorded reference to the city, Count Floris V granted the people of Amsterdam freedom from paying tolls on goods shipped along the waterways in his county of Holland. As the city's trading status grew, the Count was trying to curry favour with residents who technically fell under the domain of the Bishop of Utrecht.

To a point, Floris was successful. But the local nobles did not want to be anybody's pawn. Led by Gijsbrecht, a group of city barons ambushed and murdered the count in 1296. Gijsbrecht van Amstel was later turned into a hero of a classic 17th-century play by the poet and playwright Joost van den Vondel, now known as the "Shakespeare of the Netherlands".

Preceding pages: *Woman Spinning*, by Maerten van Heemskerck, 1529 (Rijksmuseum); J. R. Thorbecke (1796–1872), father of the modern Dutch constitution. Left, Dutch landscape: *The Mill at Wijk*, by Jacob van Ruisdael, 1670 (Rijksmuseum).

City charter: In 1300, Amsterdam was officially granted city status, receiving its charter from the Bishop of Utrecht. By this time the old conflict between the Bishop and the Counts of Holland had been resolved; in typical medieval fashion, the heir of the assassinated Count Floris V defeated the old bishop and installed his brother as the new Bishop of Utrecht. When the Bishop died, the Count of Utrecht inherited his brother's fiefdom, including all of Amsterdam and the surrounding Amstelland.

Shipping and trade: About this time, the series of weirs and drainage ditches that had kept residents relatively dry were proving too great an obstacle for the shipping that the city was attracting, and the moats *cum* canals were proving equally restrictive for population growth. Locks were constructed to enable smaller vessels to move into the interior of the city, where they often sold their wares directly from the canalside. Shops and stalls sprung up alongside the dykes and on top of the big dam (the Damrak today). An agricultural market and town square evolved around the Waag (or weighing house) which lasted until Napoleon's brother, appointed King of the Netherlands, removed it for blocking his view in 1808.

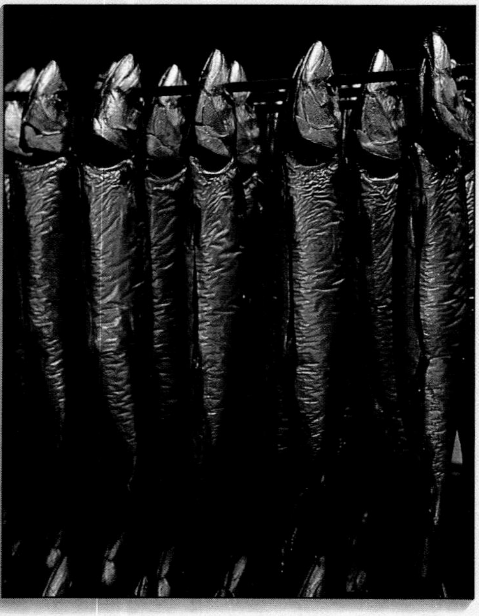

Expansion would prove to be an eternal dilemma for the growing port. The first solution was to widen the *terra* most *firma*: the tops of the dykes and embankments. These became the main streets. Next, rows of warehouses and homes were extended over the water. Narrow alleys and tiny canals, sluices really, connected the principal canals to the drainage system of the Amstel.

The easiest remedies exhausted, the next step was to dig more canals parallel to the dykes on either side of the river. This symmetrical process led to more pairs of canals on both the old and new sides.

This process was repeated through the 15th century until the city fathers decided they had enough space. Following popular urban planning practices of the day, they constructed an encircling series of canals and walls. The city boundary can still be traced in today's canals and streets; it ran approximately from Gelderskade, just east of Central Station, north through Kloveniersburgwal and around the city via the Singelgracht canal. The round, squat turret in Nieuwmarkt, on the edge of the Red Light District, is one of the best-preserved and visually striking remnants of the old wall.

Built on piles: Residents of Amsterdam had also become ingenious builders. The soft, porous top soil, usually a mixture of sand, peat and clay, meant that the buildings needed deep foundations to keep them from sinking. Long pine tree trunks, almost like modern pilings, were imported from Germany and Scandinavia to anchor the foundations. They had to be driven up to 40 ft (12 metres) through the sand into firmer soil. The same practice is still followed today. Long rear annexes were built to take advantage of every inch of soil. Warehouses and homes were often narrow at the front but extended back a long way. Homes were taxed according to the width of their facades, traditionally pierced by large windows.

By 1500, Amsterdam was the largest city in the Netherlands and 50 years later had a population of 30,000 people. Given the crowded conditions, and with timber the predominant construction material, fires were inevitable. After a series of conflagrations in the mid-1400s, one of the earliest fire codes in history was adopted. New facades had to be built of stone or brick and roofs had to be of slate or tile. Thatch was prohibited.

Fuelling all this growth was commerce, particularly with the coastal towns of the Baltic. Salt became crucial for cod and herring fishermen, who, by gutting and salting the catch, could preserve it and stay at sea longer. Salt came from Portugal, and Amsterdam was the perfect halfway point between southern Europe and the Baltic, especially since the city benefited from the favourable tax status granted by its benefactor, the murdered Count of Holland.

The wool trade: Clothing sweatshops were also well established in Amsterdam, according to city records, as much as 600 years ago. Wool from England initially went to workshops in nearby Leiden and Haarlem. Increasingly through the 1500s Amsterdam, too, produced and manufactured quality cloth and eventually became the leading centre in the Netherlands for this product.

Though the city grew prosperous on this trade, not everyone benefited equally. According to one city historian, the oppressed workers rose up in protest at the conditions they worked under. Several times during the 15th century entire groups of labourers would protest by leaving the town *en masse*, giving new meaning to the word "strike".

Early breweries: Amsterdam's beer trade was equally vital to the medieval economy, especially since water in that era was of dubious purity. The Count gave Amsterdam the sole right to import large quantities of hop beer from Hamburg. Eventually, Dutch brewers in Haarlem, Gouda, Delft and Amsterdam abandoned their own grout-flavoured brew and began making a similar style of stronger-flavoured hop beer. These local breweries proved so successful that they were soon exporting their products through the free port of Amsterdam.

Grain for beer and bread also passed through the Baltic to Amsterdam. Spices, pitch, fur, timber and iron ore kept city warehouses full, and the principle of entrepôt was born. This meant that goods entering the city but ultimately destined for another port could be stored without incurring tolls, taxes or duty. This principle, maintained through the centuries still exists today in the form of bonded warehouses.

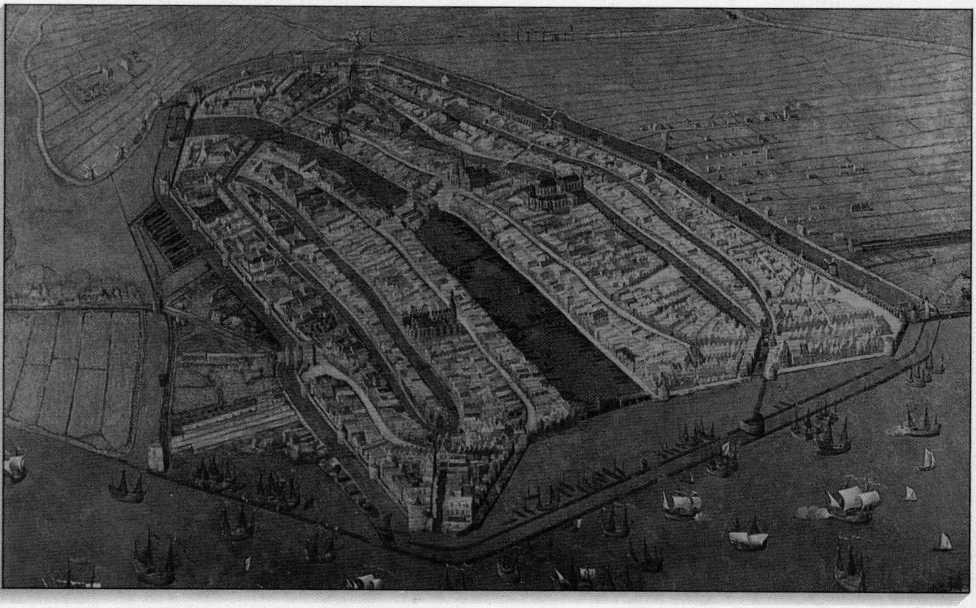

Left, herrings: the basis of Amsterdam's early prosperity. Above, Cornelius Anthoniszoon's 1538 map of Amsterdam.

PROTESTANTS AND ICONOCLASTS

Sixteenth-century Amsterdam was a potpourri of religious convictions. Even so, not everyone could practice their beliefs openly and the fine line between religious orthodoxy and heresy was often drawn along political, rather than religious, grounds.

Until the turbulent 1500s, Amsterdam was 98 percent Catholic. The city even had its own miraculous host, housed in a healing shrine that made Amsterdam an important pilgrimage resort.

The Miracle of the Host occurred in 1345 when a dying man was given his last communion rites, but he could not keep the host down. The vomit was thrown on the fire, as was customary then, but the host did not burn. A small shrine was built on the site of this miracle and over the years other magical acts were attributed to the host. A century later, when the chapel burned down, the host was again miraculously spared. This only served to confirm the special properties of the host and the whole of Amsterdam, swelled by pilgrims from further afield, would turn out for the annual procession in which the sacred relic was carried round the city for veneration.

Tradition revived: Interrupted by the Reformation, the winter procession was revived again in the 19th century, but was conducted in silence and at midnight so as not to offend the non-Catholic residents of what was still officially a Protestant city. Today's silent night-time procession, held on 17 March, still attracts thousands of worshippers.

The 15th-century church built in Nieuwe Zijde on the site of the miracle, however, does not survive. It became Protestant after the Reformation and continued this way until 1908, when the Catholics wanted to buy the old building. Protestants refused to sell and the church was ultimately destroyed.

Spanish and Catholic dominance of northern Europe began to fragment after the Augustinian monk Martin Luther nailed his 95 points, condemning church abuses, to the

Nieuwe Kerk, founded in the 15th century.

chapel door of Wittenburg Castle in 1517. But more popular in Amsterdam were the teachings of a French Protestant theologian, John Calvin, which leaned heavily on the doctrine of predestination.

The Catholic Church urged strong punishment on the heretical followers of Calvin, but little was done in Amsterdam. The civic fathers were not going to shatter their prosperous co-existence with the Calvinists at the behest of Catholic bishops based in Brussels who, technically, held pastoral authority over the Netherlands.

Prophets of doom: This lax attitude was blamed for the Anabaptist uprising of 1535.

These early charismatics were followers of a furrier named Melchior Hofmann, who imagined himself to be a doomsday prophet. In May that year, about 40 Anabaptists who had worked themselves up into a religious ecstasy tore off their clothes and stormed the Town Hall, imitating an earlier coup attempt in Münster. The revolt, which was intended to shock Amsterdammers into renouncing their worldly ways, succeeded briefly only because it was an annual Catholic feast day—the civic guards and officials were, as one record put it, "far gone in drink". The next day the guards retook the Town Hall. Many rioters were executed and their heads placed on pikes at the city gates.

Strict Catholics replaced the unvigilant leaders who had allowed the Town Hall to be stormed and a period of religious repression followed. Naturally when something is forbidden, curiosity to know more about it increases exponentially. Calvinism was no exception; it gained support from many wealthy city merchants, including several liberal Catholic burgomasters.

Summer of discontent: By the 1560s, Protestant services were being held outside the city gates and out of the jurisdiction of the Catholic police. Religious tensions boiled over in the summer of 1566. In another episode of copycat violence, this time with inspiration from Antwerp, a mob of Amsterdam Calvinists smashed their way through the altars and statuary of the Oude Kerk, a protest which became known as the "Iconoclasm". In the following months the rioters also turned their destructive attentions to the city's priories, hitting the wine cellars when they ran out of works of art to break upstairs.

Again, in typical Amsterdam fashion, the city fathers chose to placate rather than confront the mob. In return for profitable peace they allowed the Calvinists to hold services openly in one of the Franciscan churches they had earlier looted.

Spanish repression: But the vandalism had earned Amsterdam the harsh attention of King Philip II of Spain. The northern front of the Eighty Years' War extended as far as Amsterdam shortly thereafter. Repression at the orders of the Iron Duke, Fernando Alvarez de Toledo, was ruthless. Unlike the rest of Holland, however, Amsterdam remained loyally Catholic, not switching allegiance to the Protestant Prince William of Orange, leader of the Dutch revolt against Spain, until 1578, by when it was obvious that the Spanish were in retreat.

What followed is politely known as "the Alteration". All Catholic city officials were peacefully replaced with good Protestant merchants and overnight the city's churches became Calvinist. Wealthy Calvinist merchants fled from Catholic southern Holland and the southern provinces of the Low Countries (modern Belgium)—still under Spanish rule—and moved to Amsterdam. As Amsterdam grew into a major trading capital, many of these men were to finance the Dutch merchant fleets and trading companies that fuelled the expansion.

Many Amsterdammers remained Catholic, however, and with this reversal in their fortunes it was they who now had to worship secretly, in barns or in the attics of city homes. (While traces remain of other attic churches, only one, the Amstelkring, is completely preserved, as a museum.) An unofficial "pacification" evolved by 1630 under which the Catholic minority was tolerated but barred from public office. The attic churches then became an open secret, even though for the next 200 years Catholic worship was officially prohibited. Police in search of bribes often "raided" services.

Economic (and in the case of the Jews, religious) migrants quadrupled Amsterdam's population to 220,000 between 1600 and 1650. Portuguese and German synagogues began to appear alongside churches for German Lutherans and French Walloons and Huguenots. Still fearful of papal influence, however, the Amsterdam authorities would not allow Catholic churches to become "visible".

Pragmatism rules: The Calvinist principle of "freedom of conscience" evolved, once

Left, the Anabaptist uprising of 1535. Above, Anabaptists: portrayed as licentious communists in contemporary engravings.

the Catholic threat was removed, into an ethos of religious tolerance for which the Amsterdam city fathers became widely damned—or praised, depending on your view. Pragmatic citizens often chose their religion at the time of marriage, influenced by the power of different denominations to offer a secure guild job or large dowry.

Preoccupied with commerce, the city was practically the only one in Europe to have no form of censorship on publications. The city pastor even published a book denouncing his own church for its superstitious belief in witches and black magic. The church dismissed him, but the city burgomasters continued to pay his salary and held the official position vacant until his death.

A free press: This freedom of conscience was not without economic benefits. Over the next century, Amsterdam became a haven for intellectuals unable to work in their native land, including philosophers such as René Descartes and John Locke. Writers and, symbiotically, Amsterdam printers used the city's liberal ethos to create publishing empires, the remnants of which are still important to the city's economy.

This heady, liberal climate, which placed the city at odds with the rest of the conservative Netherlands, did not extend beyond the Christian denominations. Portuguese Sephardic and High German Ashkenazic Jews enjoyed good relations with officialdom but they suffered economic discrimination. Citizenship had to be purchased anew each generation and could not be inherited. Intermarriage with non-Jewish citizens was prohibited by religious as well as city law. With the exception of surgeons, brokers, printers and booksellers, Jews were prohibited from guild membership. This left street trading and diamond cutting, which had no guilds, as the particular preserve of the Jews.

When aftershocks from the French Revolution hit Amsterdam in 1796, the religious make-up of the city reflected the previous two centuries of tolerance. Only 22 percent of the population was now Catholic, compared to 98 percent three centuries previously. The remainder was Calvinist (50 percent), Lutheran (16 percent) and Jewish (12 percent). Already the city had developed a mixed character and was shortly to change again, as migrants arrived from the far-flung parts of the mighty Dutch empire.

Above, attic church (Amstelkring Museum). Right, Hare Krishna child.

STRANGE SECTS

Amsterdam today is home to many fringe religions. As you would expect, the most highly organised practices are the most visible. The late discredited guru, known worldwide as the Bhagwan Rajneesh, was the titular head of a large organisation whose fortunes in Amsterdam peaked in the mid-1980s.

In those glory days, the Bhagwan organisation owned Zorba's, the hottest disco in the city. With up-beat music and a drug-free dance floor, Zorba's attracted hundreds of young people a night to its bar in the Red Light District and no one was ever pressed to enlist. The Rajneesh Mystery School on Troostplein is still around and can be rented for yoga and other therapeutic classes.

The robed and nearly bald Hare Krishna followers still maintain a high profile in the city despite declining numbers. Together with their more conventionally dressed supporters, they run a restaurant and a food distribution charity for Amsterdam's homeless, collecting unsold produce from the city's 26 outdoor markets, preparing it in Hare Krishna kitchens and distributing it to the needy around the Central Station.

The city's most unusual and infamous "church", for lack of a better word, is the Satan Church in the Red Light District. Because of its location, it is widely assumed to be nothing more than a sex club. But "church" officials insist that the organised "love" sessions are an integral part of their religious devotion. Under Dutch law, all organisations registered as churches are exempt from taxes. The legal battle continues.

Religious observers in the city are concerned that the *laissez-faire* reputation of Amsterdam acts as a magnet for young people across Holland, Germany, Ireland and Great Britain. Many of them arrive penniless and lacking either strong will or a knowledge of what they want in the city. "They often make one of two choices", one observer reports. "They choose drugs or (having experimented and rejected them) make then contact with the Hare Krishnas or other cults."

While fundamentalist Christian groups grow all over the rest of the Netherlands, Amsterdam itself has become increasingly irreligious. In surveys carried out at regular intervals since 1971, over half the population claims to have no religious beliefs at all, a factor which accounts for the unusually high number of vacant or converted churches in this Babylon of a city.

On the other hand, the 1980s saw a large increase in popularity among Amsterdammers for "New Age" philosophies—humanist principles without the supernatural elements of conventional religion.

One of the most popular new beliefs, called anthroposophy, is best described as a mixture of oriental philosophies and western humanist values that place man rather than God in the foreground. The followers, typically intellectuals, have their own restaurants, stores, schools and even doctors.

The anthroposophic director of NMB-Post-Bank, the fourth largest in the Netherlands, built the new bank headquarters in Bijlmermeer according to these principles. The unusual four-storey edifice resembles an Inca pyramid. A Japanese garden lies inside. None of the outer walls meet at right angles. When it was built in the mid-1980s, it was said to be the most expensive building in the country (see photo, page 77).

Reasons why Amsterdammers are drawn to unconventional practices are as diverse as the beliefs. "People are searching for themselves and they can't find the answers in the usual places any more. The popularity [of these practices] in general is very good when the world isn't going very well," said a manager at Kosmos, the oldest shop of its kind in the city, specialising in New Age books and paraphernalia. "They come in to buy incense, which is always the start."

But, despite the good intentions of many, the profit motive has crept in. "Alternative religion has become big business as well," the manager said sadly. "Established publishers are now starting to churn out expensive handbooks for this market, just like they did cooking and gardening books a few years ago."

Amsterdam now regards itself as Europe's fourth city, behind London, Paris and Rome. But in the 17th century, Amsterdam was pre-eminent. Then, as now, it was much smaller than its rivals. Nevertheless, during that brief shining moment in history known as the Golden Age of the Netherlands, it was the commercial and cultural capital of Europe.

Art in demand: The rapid growth of the Dutch trading empire provided the prosperity at home that led to an unprecedented period of development in art, architecture and many related crafts. Besides the paintings of the Dutch Masters and the attendant "Little Masters", Amsterdam was the focus for developments in silver, porcelain, furniture, engraving, printing and various skills related to building. Sculptors such as Artus Quellen and Rambout Verhulst made their marks but sculpture was never as popular in Amsterdam as it was in the Italian Renaissance cities, perhaps because there were no princes to commission grand stone monuments in the hope of keeping their family name alive through the ages.

Art historians credit the Dutch artists of the Golden Age with launching the era of realism in painting, particularly with their landscapes and seascapes as well as what one critic whimsically calls "cowscapes", after the detailed portraits that some farmers commissioned of their favourite bulls and cows, often complete with a fresh cowpat beneath the animal's hindquarters. In 1976 the critic Eugene Frometin said: "Dutch painting was not, and could not be, anything but the portrait of Holland, its external image, faithful, exact, complete, lifelike, without any adornment."

New realism: Frans Hals (1580–1666) is regarded as the founder of the Dutch School of realistic painting. Often called "the first modern painter," he introduced to fine art the emotion of the moment, a glance or a grimace that might be seen anywhere on the streets but nowhere in the posed, stilted portraiture of the past.

Jan Vermeer (1632–75) painted only in Delft and produced perhaps only 40 paintings in his life but he, too, is regarded as one of the Masters. Gerard Lairesse (1641–1711) was "the Dutch Raphael". Among those less well known today, but extremely influential in 17th-century Amsterdam, was Jan van Goyen of Leiden (1596–1656) who led the way in making landscapes the whole purpose of the painting instead of a mere background.

Rembrandt's rise: Few, however, would doubt that the Golden Age painter with the greatest reputation, then as now, was Rembrandt van Rijn (1606–69), who started painting in his native Leiden but spent his most productive years living and working in Amsterdam. Like other leading members of the Dutch School, he broke new ground in realism. One of his most daring, and most costly, paintings was his 1642 masterpiece *The Night Watch*, a study of the members of one of Amsterdam's volunteer civic guards.

Left, Rembrandt's house, Jodenbreestraat. Right, *The Night Watch* (detail).

The large painting now has pride of place in the Rijksmuseum, but was apparently not well received at the time because it was regarded as too casual and haphazard; in particular, critics of the painting did not like the fact that not all the faces of the guards could be seen clearly, demonstrating an insensitivity to factors which modern critics most admire—Rembrandt's realism in creating a crowded scene.

The Night Watch condemned Rembrandt—who had, up to that point, been extremely popular and grown quite rich—to a period of relative unpopularity. Fewer commissions meant that he could no longer support his extravagant (and in that way un-Dutch) lifestyle. He was forced into bankruptcy and out of his fine house at Jodenbreestraat 4–6, where he lived from 1639 until 1658.

The house is now a museum featuring many of his etchings as well as the furnishings that were typical of the comfortable Amsterdam home of the 17th century. It is worth visiting the Rembrandthuis for the toilets alone, where the master's whimsical drawings of a man standing in a familiar pose of relief and a woman squatting in some bushes is displayed.

Also recommended, even for those who are not art *aficionados*, are Rembrandt's often ruthless self-portraits, reflecting his moods and the process of ageing as he moved inexorably towards frailty and senility. The experts say there has never been an artist so popular for so long; there are certainly few artists of the 17th century so popular that they are known familiarly by their first name.

Art for all: Did art become so popular in Amsterdam because it was home to so many good artists, or did Amsterdam produce so many good artists because art was so popular? In either case, the wealth of the commercial middle class allowed the Dutch to indulge their appreciation of art. For the first time, ordinary citizens could afford to commission and buy paintings.

Instead of being tied to a few rich patrons who demanded grand religious and historical works, artists in Amsterdam were able to sell to the highest bidder. It was the first truly open market for art. And the Dutch buyers, as much interested in their own enjoyment as in posterity, commissioned paintings of themselves, their friends, their families, their homes, their shops, their ships, their farms and even their prize cattle. Bankers, bakers and even common farmers had paintings on their walls, much to the amazement of less fortunate foreign visitors.

Certainly the Dutch appreciated art, but the middle-class families of 17th-century Amsterdam frequently had equally down-to-earth reasons for collecting paintings. For one thing, a painting allowed them to display their success to their neighbours without being seen as trying, too obviously, to keep up with the van Joneses. And paintings, along with ceramics and silver, were a hedge against inflation. As one critic has shrewdly pointed out, the Dutch fledgling art market exploited "the need for sound investment and conspicuous display in a rapidly expanding economy."

Practical value: The modern Dutch disdain for self-aggrandisement has its roots deep in the 17th century. Even during the Golden Age, the emphasis was on enjoying a comfortable life, not on ostentation. The quality of goods, of workmanship and artistic talent was highly valued but the Dutch liked to be able to show the symbols of their prosperity in belongings and property that had practical value and could be used in everyday life.

In this way, people could show their wealth without being accused of putting on special airs. Their salt shakers, for instance, were typically silver and often carried luxuriant floral designs. Plates, beakers and knife handles were engraved. The walls of the formal reception rooms might be covered in hand-tooled leather, and the veneering and marquetry, often renderings of floral patterns, were of a quality that has rarely, if ever, been excelled.

The ultimate lasting expression of the Golden Age in Amsterdam is the city itself, particularly the 17th-century design and construction of the concentric rings of canals linked by radial canals—a model much studied and admired by other cities. It is doubtful whether such a project could have been planned, much less completed, without the medieval-style city-state administration that prevailed in Amsterdam.

Left, *The Young Bull*, Paulus Potter. Above, frieze detail, Koninklijk Palace.

Far-sighted plan: Because Amsterdam was its own master in the loose alliance with other Dutch city-states, known in the 17th century as the United Provinces, the commercial middle classes were the city's driving force. They had no king or prince or ruling family over them, and the other provinces had little say over the internal affairs of the city. Consequently, the usual vetoes were absent for such an ambitious and far-sighted project as the expansion of the city by building the three new canal rings outside the old 1481 city walls: the Herengracht, Keizersgracht and Prinsengracht.

Designed by Hendrik Staets, the municipal carpenter, the Herengracht is 2.2 miles (3.5 km) long, the Keizersgracht 2.5 miles (4 km) and the Prinsengracht 2.8 miles (4.5 km). The three ring canals were built 7 ft (2.1 metres) deep and 82 ft (25 metres) wide to accommodate four lanes of medium-sized ships (20 ft/6 metres wide). Ships frequently moored directly in front of a merchant's home and the cargo was unloaded directly into the fourth-storey storeroom/warehouse via the crane-hooks that still survive in the gables of most canal-house facades.

Shops and factories: The combined 15.6 miles (25 km) of quayside on the three main canals provided room for 4,000 ships to be moored at once, which resulted in a forest of masts that often obscured the views from the houses. The fine houses were all to be on the three ring canals, while smaller homes and shops would be fitted in along the radial canals. The Jordaan area was added from 1612 for artisans and small factories, which included sugar refineries, potteries, print works, ropeworks and glass factories.

The straight-sided sections of the big canals made it easier to lay out regular building plots for the fine houses, but precluded the sweeping canal vistas of cities such as Venice, Pisa and Leningrad. Many commentators have noted that the physical layout of the ring canals means that they must be "enjoyed as scenes of individual vignettes", and that the only way to get an idea of the massive scale of the design is to walk the canals and their numerous side streets.

Leafy banks: Further diminishing the potential grandeur of the design were the thousands of trees planted along the 36-ft (11-metre) wide quays on either side of the three main canals. Originally, the quays were planted with elm trees and those that survive are diligently looked after by municipal tree surgeons. It is worth noting that Dutch elm disease got its name not because the disease originated in the Netherlands, but rather because the most comprehensive studies have been carried out here.

This town plan, which has effectively left modern Amsterdam perched on 90 islands linked by 500 bridges, also provided the

model for future municipal zoning. The city paid for the construction of the canals, which took most of the 17th century to complete, by selling off canal-side housing plots. Owners had to agree to conform to a set of strict rules, including a requirement to pay for maintainance of the quayside and footpath in front of their homes.

Sale terms: Although a few exceptions were made for the most influential and wealthy, especially the six "Magnificat" families, most of the lots were sold with 100 ft (30 metres) of canal frontage. Speculators sometimes bought two adjacent plots and then re-sold them as three 67-ft (20-metre) plots. Zoning laws also limited how deep the houses could be, and insisted on a certain amount of clearance between the backs of houses on adjacent canals.

The rules specified that certain types of brick and stone should be used in the construction, and left only minor differences in the facades and gables as the main opportunity for owners to express their individualism—sometimes these were embellished with flourishes and sometimes with a sculptural relief to indicate the owner's occupation, such as cannons on a gunmaker's home. The result is a city of essentially similar buildings, but with charming individual details. "Architectural good manners," today's critics call it.

Trippenhuis, on Kloveniersburgwal, is an example of one of the very few Amsterdam houses that can be said to rival the palaces of Venice. It was built in 1662 by Justus Vingboons who, along with brother Philip, designed many of the big canal houses, often marked by their trademark pilaster gables. Across the street from the palatial Trippenhuis is the narrowest house in Amsterdam. According to the story, the Trip family coachmen was overheard complaining that he wished he could afford a canal house even if it was only as wide as the door of his master's home; so they built him exactly that at No. 26—a house as wide as its front door.

The Golden Age also produced most of Amsterdam's best-known public buildings and monuments, particularly the churches. The most prominent building, of course, is the Town Hall, now the Royal Palace, completed on Dam square in 1662. Jacob van Campen, a Haarlem painter and architect, was given the job of designing the grandest town hall in all of Europe, and he did—but only after overcoming the technical difficulties of putting a building that size on virtual swampland. The building was finally constructed on 13,659 pilings 60 ft (18 metres) deep; virtually every Amsterdammer knows the number of pilings because of a formula, drilled into them in schools, that goes: "take the number of days in a year (365) and add a '1' at the beginning and a '9' at the end."

Left, Golden Age splendour (Museum Van Loon). Right, East India import: cloisonné spice jar.

Modern critics still marvel at the astonishing wealth of decoration on the building. There are a number of specifics for visitors to note, including the plan of the building, constructed around two courtyards, with a huge central hall. The bronze gates are fitted with gunports for muskets, and the narrow staircases and hidden entrances were designed to allow officials to defend the building easily against mob attack. On top, the weathervane represents one of the thousands of Dutch merchant ships that roamed the world and came home laden with riches.

Empire Builders

The Golden Age of the Netherlands, spanning most of the 17th century, is today best known for its art and architecture. But the Golden Age would probably never have occurred, and certainly would not have carried the same sheen, without the extraordinary boom in world trade that paved the way for Holland to become the financial and artistic hub of Europe.

The increase in trade provided immediate benefits in the form of unprecedented wealth, particularly in Amsterdam. It also established the far-flung Dutch empire, extending from South America and the Caribbean to the Far East.

War with Spain: The Dutch empire grew out of an 80-year conflict with Spain, beginning with the 1568 revolt against Spanish rule led by William the Silent, whom the Dutch revere as the father of their country. The 1579 Treaty of Utrecht created the United Provinces, which provided the foundation for the modern Netherlands, a loose alliance of seven northern provinces—as distinct from the southern provinces, which had remained subject to Spain and eventually evolved into modern Belgium and Luxembourg.

The decades of strife with Spain are commonly characterised as arising out of a religious dispute—the result of the refusal by Dutch Calvinists to allow Philip II of Spain to impose Catholicism on them as part of his anti-heresy Inquisition. But there were—as there always seem to be with the Dutch—underlying economic factors. Spain not only wanted to control religion, but also wanted centralised control of the Dutch economy. In the face of attempts to limit their religious freedoms and restrain their economy, the Dutch reacted in typical hard-headed fashion. They outlawed Catholicism and did everything they could to expand their economy, which included competing with Spain for trade and colonisation across the globe.

The first Dutch ships landed in the East Indies (now Indonesia) in 1595, and the East India Company was formed in 1602 with a government-guaranteed monopoly on all trade east of the Cape of Good Hope. In an innovative move for that time, the East India Company sold shares—in effect allowing any daring Dutch investor to help finance voyages and reap the profits. This gave a much broader section of Dutch society a personal interest in the spread of the empire.

Spices and profits: In 1611, by which time the United Provinces had supplanted Portugal as the leading spice importer in Europe, the East India Company paid a dividend of 162 percent. Annual dividends for the next several decades typically ranged between 12 and 50 percent—a tidy little return that certainly helped to build and furnish quite a few imposing canal-side houses.

Dutch ships ranged as far as China and Japan. Occasional shiploads of Ming porcelain, arriving in Amsterdam, caused great excitement along the docks and the demand

Preceding pages: Amsterdam's flower market *circa* 1670, G. A. Berckheyde. Left, Neptune, Nederlands Scheepvaart Museum. Right, East India House, Oude Hoogstraat.

led to the foundation of a domestic pottery industry that made Delft famous.

Eventually, the eastern Dutch empire included parts of Ceylon, Tasmania and South Africa, but the heart of the Company—and, indeed, of the whole empire—was the Dutch East Indies. The East Indies totalled nearly 8,000 islands stretching over 3,000 miles (4,800 km), and included many of the islands of modern Indonesia: Bali, Timor, Java, Sumatra, Borneo and Western New Guinea.

Pirates: The West India Company was founded as the 1609–21 truce with Spain—the only formal break in the decades of war—came to an end. The West India Company was modelled on its East India predecessor, except that making a profit was secondary to fighting the Spanish. The West India Company's captains won some famous victories over the old enemy, notably the capture of the Mexican silver fleet in 1628. But the West India Company, virtually an organisation of sanctioned pirates, was never as financially successful as its East India counterpart.

Nonetheless, the Dutch holdings grew to include Tobago, Cayenne, Bonaire, Curaçao, St. Eustatius, St. Martin, the Dutch Antilles, Aruba and Dutch Guyana (now Surinam). Trading settlements were also established, or taken over from the Spanish and Portuguese, in Venezuela and Brazil.

At home, the Bank of Amsterdam was formed in 1609, and quickly established fiscal policies that made the city the financial centre of Europe. Mortgages and loans, almost impossible to obtain in most other capitals, were readily available in Amsterdam, and at interest rates of 3 to 4 percent compared with 6 percent in London or Paris. The Amsterdam Stock Exchange, founded in 1611, is one of the oldest in the world.

Trade: Accounts of Amsterdam at the height of the Golden Age describe a bustling

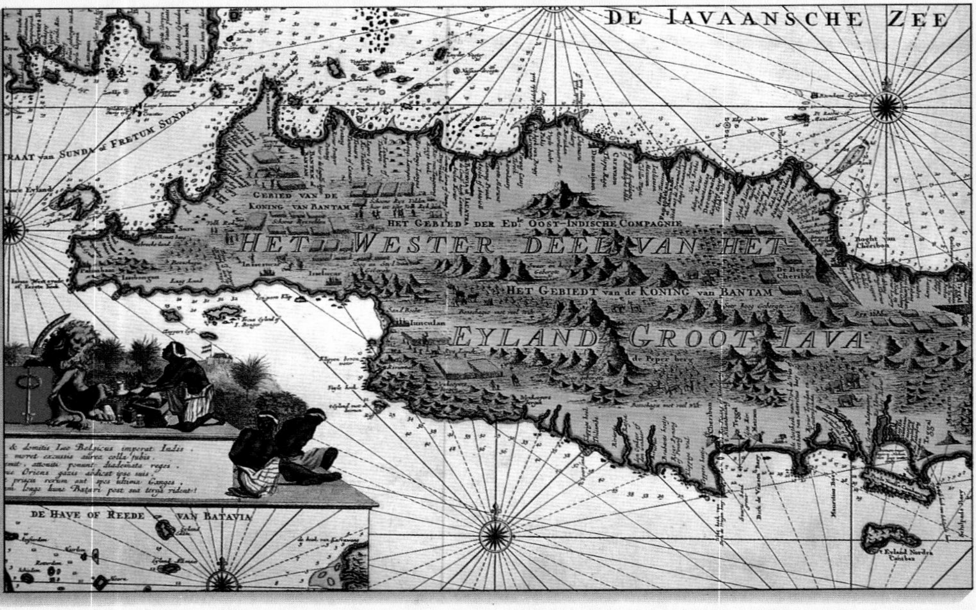

city—the population grew from 40,000 to 200,000 during the 17th century—with business being conducted everywhere. "What impressed contemporaries about Amsterdam was that it was a city entirely dedicated to making money," writes social historian Mark Girouard in his book *Cities and People* (Yale University Press, 1985).

There were no major universities or huge cathedrals or places where the public might gather except for some commercial reason. Dam square, in the shadow of the imposing Town Hall (now the Royal Palace) was the main public space in the city, but it was partially given over to a weighing house and a fish market. The major buildings seemed to be warehouses, where Dutch traders stockpiled their goods, often until they had created scarcity in the market and could then drive prices up. Smaller ships sailed right up the canals, and goods were winched straight off the decks into the attic-storehouses in the solidly comfortable canal houses of the merchant owners.

Cosmopolitan: As the streets of commerce became busier, Amsterdam became the most cosmopolitan city in Europe. Besides the Dutch themselves, with their widely varying manner of regional dress and speech, the harbour and the shopping streets were crowded with Germans, Poles, Hungarians, French, Spanish, Muscovites, Persians, Turks and Indians, all coming to buy and sell. As the empire expanded and the Dutch intermarried and took on natives as partners and employees, so the common mix grew to include Malays, Arabs, Chinese, Papuans, Caribs, Creoles and Africans.

The decline: The empire was not destined to last, however. The home-loving Dutch were never very good colonists. They liked to arrive, conduct their trade and then go back to their native provinces rather than settle in faraway countries. As a result, they never put down the roots that were the key to the longer-surviving European colonies in the New World. The failure of Dutch farmers to settle the West Indies is one of the reasons cited for the importation of untold numbers of African slaves to work the colonial Caribbean sugar plantations.

The Dutch did not impose slavery in the East Indies, but nonetheless ruthlessly exploited both people and natural resources. When the European spice market collapsed in the early 18th century, the Dutch successfully introduced coffee, which remains a key Indonesian crop today, but then proceeded to wring a higher and higher percentage of the profits out of the islands.

The United Provinces became an independent republic as part of the Treaty of Münster in 1648. The treaty was part of the Peace of Westphalia, which ended the Thirty Years' War, the wide-ranging conflict that had diverted the attention and resources of other European powers while the Dutch were quietly building up their empire and selling everything from spices and tiles to

Left, Dutch East Indies, 17th-century map. Above, *Amsterdam Harbour*, W. van der Welde.

guns and marine insurance, to friend and foe alike. The peace among the other major powers, however, allowed them to turn their attention toward the traders (and pirates) of Amsterdam for the first time in decades.

New York: England wasted little time in initiating the first of several wars with the Dutch (1652–54) that resulted in the loss of significant chunks of East Indies trade. In the West Indies, war with Portugal cost the Dutch their holdings in Brazil. Another war with England erupted in 1664 over the New Netherlands in America, and its strategic harbour at New Amsterdam (now New York). New Netherlands was founded in 1612, but there was no permanent settlement at New Amsterdam, the capital of the colony, until 1625. By 1626, when Peter Minuet, the Dutch governor, "bought" Manhattan Island from its American Indian inhabitants for the proverbial $24 worth of beads, the population was still fewer than 300. After the English finally seized New Amsterdam in 1664 and renamed the colony New York, the Dutch gave up their claims to the New Netherlands in exchange for English promises not to take away Dutch Guyana.

By the mid-17th century, the lustre of the Golden Age was fading. The Zuider Zee had begun silting up, and it became difficult for ships to reach the Amsterdam docks. Perhaps more significantly, many of the citizens living in their fancy new canal houses no longer wanted ships sailing up to their front doors and unloading cargoes into the attic.

Gentrification: The second and third generations of the merchant families did not share their ancestors' zest for chasing the guilder to the ends of the earth. As the concentric canal design neared completion, the monied classes in Amsterdam seemed more interested in spending money than in gathering more. The merchant fleet was depleted, the national debt grew and peasants who had been wearing leather shoes went back to making wooden ones.

The Dutch, nevertheless, managed to hold on to a good part of the empire when the Netherlands emerged from French rule at the end of the Napoleonic era. Trade in colonial products such as tin, quinine, coffee, timber and rubber remained an integral part of the Dutch economy until World War II. After that war, the East Indies came out of Japanese occupation with a new determination to seek independence. The Dutch were reluctant, but finally yielded in the face of protests led by Sukarno who was later to become

Indonesia's first president. These protests sometimes turned violent but were supported by the United States and most of Europe. Independence was finally granted in 1949 and the Dutch East Indies became Indonesia, now the fifth most populous country on earth.

Close relationship: Over the past decades, since Suharto (the current president) took power in 1969, the Netherlands and Indonesia have conducted an unabashed long-distance love affair highlighted by cultural exchanges. It is impossible for anyone visiting Amsterdam today to miss the consequences, from the many Amsterdam citizens with island ancestry (there have been hundreds of thousands of Indonesian immigrants) to the Indonesian restaurants that serve some of the best food in the city.

Several of the smaller Caribbean islands remain part of the Dutch realm, but the western colonies have had much less cultural impact on modern Amsterdam than Indonesia—perhaps because of slavery, lower profits and relatively disinterested rule.

Mass migration: By the time Surinam gained independence in 1975, Dutch roots were so shallow that many of the country's educated and professional-managerial classes were Javanese, or the descendants of Javanese, who had been trained in the East Indies and moved in by the Dutch to work as managers. At independence, 150,000 of Surinam's estimated population of 400,000 exercised their right of immigration to the Netherlands. Though many of those people represented the educated middle class and the majority have become a valued part of Dutch society, many Dutch today admit that the immigrants from Surinam, who are frequently blamed for involvement in illegal drugs and other crimes, have not assimilated as well as the Indonesian migrants.

Amsterdam likes to boast of having more monuments, and more historical markets, than any other city. Given its history, that is entirely possible. And while the Dutch themselves are not overly caught up in that history, the rise and fall of the empire helps put the modern city and its ethnic-cultural diversity into perspective, and goes a long way toward explaining how Amsterdam has become the distinctive city that it is today.

<u>Left</u>, The Dutch army in Indonesia before independence. <u>Above</u>, first Indonesian President, Sukarno (left), and his successor, Suharto.

Always an independent crowd, Amsterdammers are in turn stubborn, friendly, abrasive, opinionated and fiercely loyal to their Queen and country. The city has a vibrant cosmopolitan mix and Amsterdammers have a rude charm similar to that of New Yorkers. Jewish culture has played a major role in shaping the city, and its dialogue is peppered with Yiddish words, while the humour is black, but never bitter.

Refugees: The first Jews came to Amsterdam in the 16th century, fleeing from persecution in Portugal. The Netherlands always had a reputation for tolerance but the Dutch, also excellent businessmen, were aware that many of the Portuguese Jews were rich and would bring their money and vital trade connections with them to the north. The raggle-taggle group of less affluent Jews who were also accepted ended up in ghettos, poor but safe, for a few centuries at least.

One of the remaining relics of rich Portuguese Jewish life in Amsterdam is the beautifully restored Pinto family house, located just doors away from Rembrandt's home in Jodenbreestraat. Rembrandt did not care much for the Pinto family, who were successful bankers. It is not clear why he disliked them but it was certainly not because they were Jews. Rembrandt chose to live in a Jewish neighbourhood because he found the ambience more colourful and stimulating. But he was given to violent dislikes and Pinto became a target.

Quarrelsome neighbours: Amsterdam city records chart an hilarious court case when Rembrandt, who always lived beyond his means, bought lots of expensive wood for repairs to his house and charged it to the banker Pinto. The case was brought to court and the judge ruled that, as Pinto's name was on the bill, Pinto must pay. Rembrandt lost interest and stored the wood in a recently acquired cellar. Months later Pinto needed storage space and rented a cellar nearby. It was full of wood. The cellar turned out to be Rembrandt's—ditto the wood. The artist, truculent as ever, refused to remove it and Pinto was left with a second good reason for breaking an easel over Rembrandt's magnificently talented but stubborn head.

Happy co-existence: Apart from this trivial incident, historical records show that Amsterdam's Jewish population lived peacefully in the city, and the Dutch seemed to

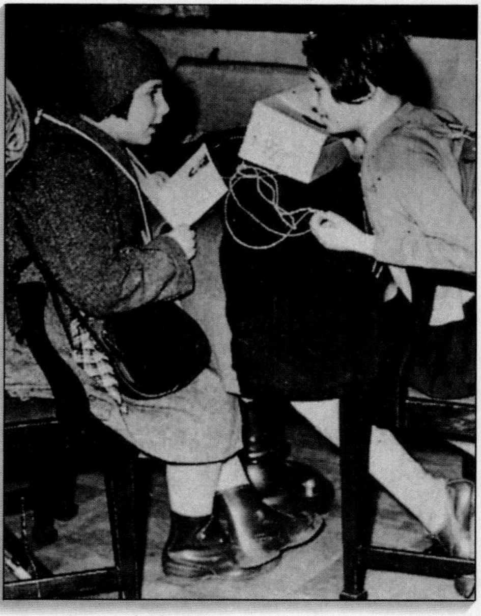

hold no dislike or fear of Jews. Therefore the revulsion felt by the Dutch when the first Nazi deportation of 400 terrified Jewish men and youths from occupied Amsterdam got under way was great. The Nazis started with the men; women and children followed.

The Occupation begins: Amsterdam's Raadhuisstraat, a street leading to the city's Dam square, was lined with hundreds of silent Amsterdammers when the German convoy drove in during the first weeks of May 1940. One tenth of the population—the Jews—stayed at home.

The crowd watched the Germans arrive in

Preceding pages: Bickersgracht in 1893. Left, the Nazis enter Amsterdam. Right, Jewish refugees.

their lovely city with fascinated horror. Many had read the red-bordered proclamation of power issued by the country's new ruler, Dr Arthur Seyss-Inquart, which was displayed around the city. The message was friendly in tone. "I have today taken over civilian authority in the Netherlands… The magnanimity of the Führer and the efficiency of German soldiers has permitted civil life to be restored quickly. I intend to allow all Dutch law and general administration to go on as usual."

No escape: Some people watching the triumphant arrival of the Germans that day actually allowed themselves to believe the message and these glimmerings of hope anaesthetised their sense of foreboding. But the city's Jews knew better; especially the 25,000 German Jews who had fled to Amsterdam to escape German persecution in the 1930s. They now had their backs to the North Sea, with nowhere left to go. All escape routes were cut off, all hope abandoned. It was merely a question of how long it would take the "magnanimous" Führer's evil tentacles to reach them.

They did not have long to wait. But the Nazis had other details to arrange first before the attack on the Jews could get under way. A number of people unfortunate enough to be on Nazi blacklists had to be rounded up, many of them political activists. The Dutch Nazi party (NSB) was finally coming into its own, with many of its members, black-shirted louts and rednecks, being promoted to executive positions.

The party had already, with great efficiency, prepared lists of "troublemakers" for the perusal of their German overlords. A perfect opportunity for settling old scores—the playground bullies had taken over.

Soon certain new signs became a familiar part of the city scene. For Amsterdammers the long-drawn-out agony of tension and rumour was over. German army traffic signs went up, Nazi newspapers appeared on the streets, sold by the hated Dutch NSB members, German marching songs, accompanied by hectoring German voices, and the sound of marching jackboots were heard everywhere. But Dr Seyss-Inquart continued his efforts to convince Amsterdammers that the Führer had sent his troops to watch over them like a kindly father figure. As yet nothing ghastly had been seen to happen, and many people still hoped that their lives would continue as usual.

Passive protest: Then, on 29 June 1940, the

Dutch showed that, though they may have abandoned any thought of taking direct action against the occupiers, they had not abandoned hope. Suddenly thousands of people showed up on the streets wearing white carnations. It did not take the Germans long to realise what was going on. It was Prince Bernhard's birthday and H.R.H., as well as being a robust, brave man, was a romantic who liked to dress well. The Dutch were copying one of his more discerning vanities as a symbol of passive resistance—he always wore a pure white carnation in the buttonhole of his well-cut tweeds.

The Royal Family: The Prince had been ordered by his formidable mother-in-law, Queen Wilhelmina, to accompany his wife and two daughters to Canada via Britain. He was reluctant to do so as he desperately wanted to remain with his people. Wilhelmina was adamant. The royal blood-line must be protected. The Prince, a fervent Nazi-hater, agreed to go on one condition, that he be allowed to return to Britain after depositing his wife and children in Canada. His mother-in-law agreed and in Britain he was made head of the Dutch free forces.

Juliana in exile: The shy, lonely Princess, meanwhile, began coping on her own in Canada. Some of her neighbours whose gardens adjoined her modest villa were amazed to see the young woman, used to being surrounded by servants, doing her own washing as she kept an eye on the two princesses playing in the garden.

The eldest princess, Beatrix, a sturdy, determined-looking child, grew up to be Queen of the Netherlands, for Queen Juliana abdicated for her daughter in 1980. But thoughts of future monarchs must have been far from the family-loving Juliana's mind during those days as she tried to imagine how it must be for those she had to leave behind.

Left, Dr Arthur Seyss-Inquart, the Nazi ruler of the Netherlands, in The Hague. Above, the *razia* (round-up) of Jewish men and youths which took place in February 1941.

Anti-Jewish measures: In Amsterdam the noose was tightening for the Jews. From July 1940, the Germans started to issue more and more restrictive proclamations. Jews could not be employed in the Civil Service and those who already were must be sacked. Jews could not enter cinemas or travel on public transport and all firms owned by Jews must be reported for registration.

Over two days, on 22 and 23 February

1941, the Germans finally made their move. Four hundred Jewish men and youths were rounded up and herded into the Jonas Daniel Meijerplein, a square in the Jewish quarter. Contemporary photographs in the Jewish Historical Museum show them staring straight ahead, hands above their heads, faces full of terror. They were kept in the square for hours before being moved into transport trucks lined up beside the nearby Portuguese Synagogue. The trucks drove off; the men were never seen again.

Protest strike: Today a statue of a burly Amsterdam docker stands on the square commemorating what happened two days later. News of the deportation of the men spread around the city and from 25 to 26 February there was a general strike led by the city's dockers. It was Amsterdam's first open gesture of rebellion, as revulsion for the occupiers began to conquer collective fear.

The two-day strike has gone down in Dutch history as the city's "day beyond praise". The Germans, at first stunned by this show of defiance, quickly moved to stamp it out. German police patrolled the streets shooting at passers-by and notices were posted up ordering everyone back to work. The text, which was signed by General Friedrich Christiansen, read as follows: "There will be no meetings or gatherings of any kind, nor any political party activity. Anyone disobeying will be proceeded against under German military law. Hereafter anyone who strikes, or who agitates for strikes, will receive up to fifteen years and, if the defence industry is involved, death."

People slowly went back to work, morale temporarily boosted by the fact that Amsterdammers had openly dared to resist tyranny. But the euphoria did not last long, as the everyday, mind-destroying ennui of the Nazi occupation began to sink in. There were no more posters urging the Dutch to learn to "trust" their German friends. The kid glove was revealed to be covering a steel fist, and it was being used against the Jews, with the utmost force.

The nightmare begins: Jews watched in horror as the stories they had heard of Nazi brutality in the German ghettos became reality before their own eyes, and on their own streets. The sight of pathetic groups of people, the men clutching suitcases or knapsacks, the women carrying infants, toddlers clinging to their coats, being continuously hustled along by the military or plain-clothes police, became a commonplace and everyday reality that Amsterdam people were unable to prevent.

One man recalls: "On a particularly beautiful autumn day, when the canals were at their loveliest with the reflection of the trees in the water and the beautiful canal houses behind, a group of prisoners passed by, mainly women and children, who had been hiding in a nearby house. They were Jews. I heard later the owner had been shot. One little girl stopped to pick up a leaf. I heard her mother sob in fear as she called to the child. One of the guards butted her in the back with his rifle when she paused to wait for the infant who was about three years old. As they crossed over a canal bridge I saw the child give the leaf to its mother, who surreptitiously tucked it into the front of her blouse. Then they were gone and silence returned to the canal. That was the moment I stopped believing in God."

By now Jews were being forced to wear the yellow Star of David, six-pointed, black-bordered and bearing the word "Jood". Most wore it proudly. Even more restrictions were being introduced, Jews could not use the public parks, could not own telephones nor use public telephones. A curfew was introduced; Jews had to be indoors from 8 p.m. to 6 a.m. and were not allowed to have visitors when at home.

The end of the line: More and more Jews were being "transported"—the euphemism for train transport to Westerbork camp in the province of Drenthe, close to the German border. The trains to Westerbork were normal passenger trains in every respect, except that they were locked from the outside. One woman survivor told how, after months of claustrophobic terror in Amsterdam, she remembered enjoying the journey through the countryside to Drenthe. That is where any enjoyment would have ended, for Westerbork was a transit camp for Auschwitz; from there the long journey east was made, not in passenger trains, but in locked cattle trucks; the railway line ended in front of the gates of the camp where the real horror began.

Left, the first Jewish deportations. Right, Anne Frank's diary.

As it started to dawn on the Jews that they were only being couped up in the city for identification and processing in preparation for the cattle trains to the slaughterhouse, some lucky ones were able to "dive" (*onderduiken*)—to disappear into hiding. Of course, to do this you needed to have very brave friends because anyone caught harbouring Jews was shot without question. Many non-Jews on the German "wanted list", including members of the resistance, also "dived".

Resistance: Organisation of those volunteers willing to take fugitives and to provide their food—which was now only available

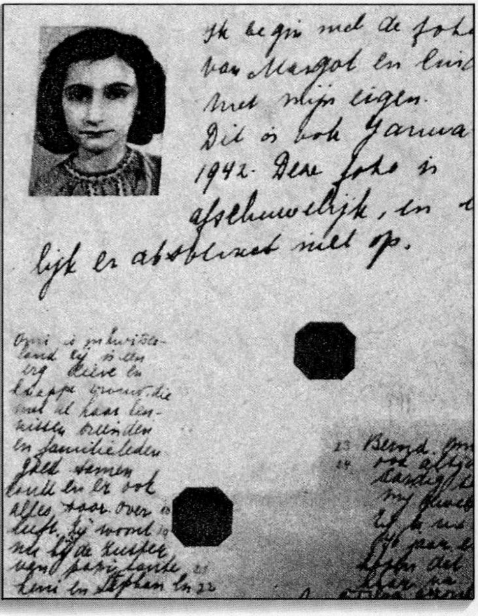

with coupons—lay in the hands of an extraordinarily brave group of people with networks extending throughout the city and surrounding countryside. There were betrayals, too, with catastrophic results, as in the case of the now famous Frank family in Amsterdam. Humans under duress can display the most extraordinary courage and valour, but the horrible chaos of war can also produce monsters.

The Frank family decided to "dive" in July 1942, after receiving a card calling up their 16-year-old daughter Margot for work in Westerbork. They had been planning to go into hiding for some time—in a concealed apartment behind her father's Prinsengracht office (an *achterhuis* or "house at the back").

Anne Frank was then 13, already a clever and natural writer. But the unnatural ambience of eight people (four others joined the family) being incarcerated in a small room for two years, most of the time living in fear of German discovery, brought out her true genius. Her diary is variously a wonderfully sane, funny and perceptive book, and, at the same time, dreadfully sad.

Humane endeavour: Moreover, Anne's story reflects the best and the worst in human behaviour. The best were the people who

looked after the Frank family when they were in hiding, her father's two partners, known as Koophuis and Kraler, and the two office girls, Miep and Elli, who came to work each day, to give the impression that nothing had changed, even though they were terrified of what would happen if the fugitives were found. Then there was the greengrocer around the corner on Leliegracht, one of the city's 105 who supplied "divers" and did not ask any questions when Miep turned up regularly to shop for provisions to feed eight.

Whoever tipped off the police, with the result that seven of the group, including Anne, died in concentration camps, epitomises human nature at its worst. On a Friday, at the beginning of August 1944, the Germans came and led the family away. Only Mr Frank survived, and there were probably times when he wished he hadn't. Anne's last diary entry, written three days before her capture, read: "I keep on trying to find a way of becoming what I would so like to be, and what I could be, if... there weren't any other people living in the world."

Anne Frank finally died of hunger and disease in Bergen-Belsen, as did her sister. In the end so much life was turned into a sad bundle in dirty rags, huddled on the bare boards of the bunk nearest the door, through which icy winds blew each time it opened.

The final winter: Meanwhile, in Amsterdam, as the war dragged on, the city moved into the last and most terrible winter of the Occupation. Food supplies were cut off; there was no fuel, gas or electricity. Thousands died from cold and hunger. There were funerals every day, and bodies were buried in cardboard boxes or paper sacks because there was no wood to spare for coffins.

Hundreds left the city each day on bicycles or on foot on foraging expeditions to farms, trying to barter anything they had for food. Some carried the last bits of family china or linen, some just a skinny, starving child to touch the heart and open the larder of some kind farmer.

All services broke down and the canals began to stagnate. In the end, with the Canadians approaching from the west, the Germans blew up the sluices at Ijmuiden, from where the North Sea Canal runs into Amsterdam. Suddenly there was water on all sides of the city, rapidly rising water, and to add to the misery, the sewage system no longer worked, which led to a plague of rats.

Then, at last, came salvation, with Allied aeroplanes dropping food parcels. Hitler was dead, the Germans were on the run and the Canadians were in the city. The war was over, but the wounds took a long time to heal and, for many who lived through it, the scar tissue is still aching.

Left, the famine of the final winter. Right, Jewish memorial, Waterlooplein.

לזכרון לוחמי המחתרת
בשנות ת"ש-תש"ה
TER HERINNERING AAN HET VERZET
VAN DE JOODSE BURGERS
GEVALLEN IN 1940 - 1945
5700 - 5705

AMRO BANK
AMRO BANK
change
change

ASCOT

Agfa

Not long ago, a business visitor in Amsterdam found himself with a little time between appointments. In need of some exercise, he located a municipal swimming pool, walked in with his towel, bought a ticket and asked which way to the locker room. But it turned out that the man had not bought a ticket to swim; he had bought a ticket to an art exhibition that was being staged at the pool. "The pool is closed for swimming, but you might as well look at the exhibit," the amused ticket seller advised.

The exhibit turned out to be an arrangement of the pool's lifebelts, kickboards, rubber rafts, beach balls and float-ropes, all stacked—in a highly artistic manner, of course—in a small but colourful mountain at one end of the otherwise empty pool. The would-be swimmer and other visitors—they were not carrying towels, so they presumably bought their tickets knowing that it was an art exhibition—walked around the pool's balcony, staring down at the greenish water and the floating foam with its rubber mound of red, orange, white and blue.

Mixed reputation: Such is the freewheeling nature of Amsterdam in the late 20th century, a city where visitors never know what to expect and where surprises such as art in the swimming pool can become routine. Most people come to Amsterdam knowing something of its reputation for sex and drugs and rock 'n' roll. That reputation, to the lament of some but the applause of many Amsterdam residents, has been tarnished somewhat in recent years by efforts to clean up some aspects of the city—including pornography, drugs and graffiti—and to improve its overall image.

Many visitors, though, quickly come to realise that what may seem radical anywhere else in the world is all but routine in this unique city. Amsterdam's willingness to live and let live continues to spark social experiments that, when examined, show themselves to have a logical grounding in good old-fashioned Dutch pragmatism.

Certainly many of the social attitudes in modern Amsterdam grow out of the city's history of religious tolerance, dating back to the late 16th century when Protestants and Jews fled repression in other countries for Holland's freedom of conscience. Then, as now, the citizens of Amsterdam wanted to be left alone, to live their lives as they saw fit, without the interference of officials or disapproving neighbours. To uphold the right to be left alone, they were and are willing to leave others alone.

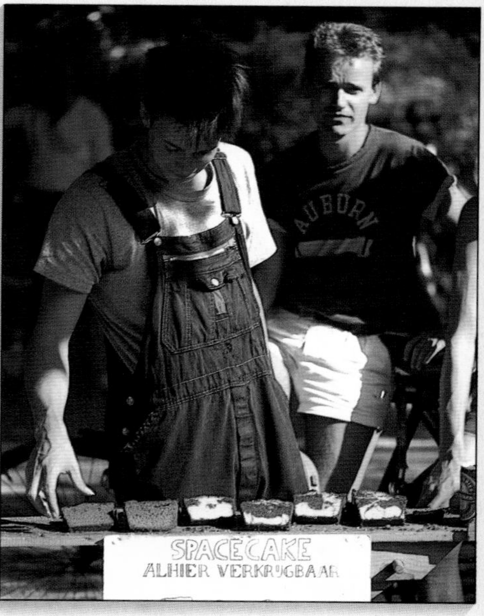

Preceding pages: carnival festivities, Dam square. **Left**, Amsterdam's colourful face. **Right**, space cakes for sale.

Sex for sale: The notorious Red Light District is a direct result of this. Prostitution is not strictly legal in Amsterdam; streetwalkers and hookers soliciting in bars may still be arrested though brothels were legalised as recently as 1990. Most prostitutes who perch in the red-hued windows of their "sitting rooms" do so because of Amsterdam's longheld belief that what people do in their own homes is their own business—whether inviting Catholic neighbours in for a forbidden mass in a hidden room in the 17th century, or inviting strangers in for commercial fornication in the 20th century.

The concept of a legalised Red Light District is nothing new to modern Amsterdam. The English consul in the mid-17th century complained about the many Amsterdam music-houses patronised by "lewd people of both sexes," and there was an informal exchange, modelled on the stock exchange, that operated for prostitutes during the early evening hours.

Strict limits: The Amsterdam prostitutes even then lived and worked without harassment, in an area just south of today's Red Light District. Some accounts report that if prostitutes strayed out of the designated area, where they paid rent to the local bailiff, the bailiff sent his drum-and-flute guard to track them down. The musician-policemen would play loudly outside the house where the prodigal prostitute was ensconced until she returned to the designated area.

Since the mid 1960s, Amsterdam has acquired a reputation for trying to see just how far individual liberties can be allowed to go before society in general is harmed. These experiments have produced some memorable newsreel footage, such as the demonstrations of the late 1960s against autocratic university administrations, or the two-day battle in August 1970 when police fought with hippies who had been living on Dam square and, more importantly, had been scaring the tourists away.

Protest on every front: In the 1970s, drugs became rampant and effectively legal for personal use, and the Red Light District grew, both as a centre for sex and for those same gawking tourists. Dutch feminists, the "Mad Minnies", marched against anti-abortion laws under the slogan "*Baas in eigen buik*" (Boss of your own belly). Beards and long hair were permitted for policemen and soldiers. While the rest of the Netherlands celebrated on the day that Queen Beatrix was inaugurated as head of state in 1980, squatters in Amsterdam rioted over the lack of adequate housing.

Fourteen years earlier, the wedding between Beatrix and Claus von Amsberg, celebrated in Amsterdam, was marred when young protesters threw smoke bombs at the wedding carriage. Many of the protesters said they were anarchists, but the newspapers called them "provocateurs"—Provos, for short. Active over the next several years, the committed Provos probably never numbered more than a few dozen people, but they had many spontaneous sympathisers who readily joined in mass street "happenings". They protested against all manner of local and national government policies as well as against other symbols of popular institutions and culture, from art to marriage, that they considered part of "The Establishment".

Humour: In protesting against US involvement in Vietnam, or just against everyday Dutch capitalism, they employed whimsical humour in much the same manner as America's Yippies. Once, when police showed up at a happening brandishing nightsticks, the Provos waved sticks of rhubarb back at them. The whimsy aside, the Provos did achieve some political successes. Several Provos and members of a splinter group called the *kabouters*, or "gnomes", were actually elected to the Municipal Council, where they smoked dope during meetings and put forward zany proposals, such as planting rooftop gardens on all city buses.

One Provo proposal that sounded wonderful in theory but failed miserably in practice was the so-called "White Bike" programme, under which the city was supposed to provide hundreds or maybe even thousands of white bicycles and distribute them around Amsterdam. The idea was that the bikes belonged to no one, and could be used by anyone. If you needed a ride, you simply grabbed the nearest white bike, rode to your destination and left it there for the use of the next pedestrian in need of wheels. Unfortunately, the experiment lasted only a few days—the amount of time it took for non-registered drug addicts to steal the bikes, paint them a different colour and sell them for money to buy drugs.

The drugs problem: Besides prostitution, drugs represent Amsterdam's best-known, out-in-the-open sin—from the clinics where registered addicts get their daily fixes to the marijuana coffee houses that have menus listing the different types of grass and hash available that day. Those who don't want to smoke might try some Alice B. Toklas brownies or THC-laced chocolate cake with their coffee, carrot juice or milk shakes. Like prostitution, possession of all but a small amount of marijuana is technically illegal, but the police in Amsterdam generally allow the marijuana cafés (there were an estimated 350 in the mid-1980s, but probably less than half that many now) to continue operating as long as they keep out hard drugs and do not serve children.

Many citizens of Amsterdam have mixed feelings about the merits of legalising drugs, but nonetheless defend registration and medical support for heroin addicts. Amsterdammers reluctantly concede their city's status as a world drugs capital, but usually blame the drug-related crime—one of the highest rates in Europe—on non-registered addicts from other countries. They also argue that things would be worse without the controls that registration imposes on perhaps one-quarter of the city's estimated 8,000 addicts—a number that hasn't changed in years, according to officials.

Efforts to clean up the illegal drug trade, in part by deporting the estimated half of Amsterdam's addicts who were not Dutch citizens, have not proved to be a notable success. At the same time, most Amsterdam

Left, transvestite club. Right, wall art, Oude Zijds Voorburgwal.

residents and return visitors would agree that there are still more addicts than there were 20 years ago, but not as many as 10 years ago.

Good intentions: The Netherlands, like Britain, experimented for a time with free heroin for addicts, but finally ended the programme in 1983. In Amsterdam, where registered addicts can get free methadone from clinics or roving drug buses, the city furnished and staffed a houseboat where junkies could shoot up and nod out—off the street and out of trouble, in theory. The houseboat was closed down after the authorities found that it had become a centre for illegal heroin dealing.

prone to using heroin and shared needles.

For many of Amsterdam's upright young citizens, however, the days of free drugs and free love have faded as they face new concerns over their career, home and family. To many of them—call them yuppies if you will—the most visible annoyance that results from living in a *laissez-faire* society is the graffiti that disfigures so many public and private buildings.

New concerns: But even as they redecorate their canal houses or search out the newest and best in Mexican food or sushi, the new middle class of Amsterdam still carries a hefty burden of civic and social concern.

The spread of drug-related AIDS has led to yet another Amsterdam experiment. The Municipal Council is offering a number of heroin addicts free morphine injections to replace the methadone they had been receiving. Many addicts complained that methadone, taken orally, merely dulled the desire for heroin—instead of giving them a "high". Some were still illegally shooting up heroin, often with shared needles, even while registered for the methadone programme. The new programme provides AIDS-proof injections of morphine, which does provide a "high", for those long-term addicts most

Nowhere in Europe, or perhaps anywhere in the world, is public sentiment stronger on issues such as the environment or nuclear weapons. Such is the depth of commitment on environmental issues throughout the political spectrum that the long-popular centre-right coalition government, led by the Christian Democrats, was finally brought down in 1989 for proposing vehicle pollution rules that were not considered tough enough.

A prominent example of the way in which the Dutch deal with current problems is the popularity of euthanasia. Though technically still illegal, many doctors in Amsterdam routinely follow court-specified procedures for assisting terminally ill patients in ending their lives—sometimes with a lethal injection but more often by giving them a potion of fast-acting poison.

Death with dignity: Patients must undergo extensive counselling, including sessions with consultant physicians brought in to advise on each case. The doctor directly involved, typically the long-time family physician, often helps the patient and surviving relatives to plan a brief and simple ceremony for administering the poison. Consequently, doctor-assisted death has become so popular—studies estimate that doctors assist in as many as one in eight deaths in Amsterdam—that public pressure has led the Dutch government to consider legislation that would make it the first, and perhaps the only, country in the world with formally legalised euthanasia.

Another example of how current social concerns have been subject to typically far-sighted and liberally idealistic experimentation is the programme for dealing with reported cases of child sex abuse. As in most other countries, such cases can be dealt with either by the police for criminal prosecution, by social workers in civil procedures, or both. In Amsterdam there is also a third option called the Confidential Doctor Service. Under this programme, teachers, relatives, friends and social workers can refer cases to government-financed centres staffed by doctors who sweep the entire family straight into intensive counselling. Experts believe the system, started in 1972 and now operating throughout the Netherlands, helps to stop the abuse and helps the child recover without necessarily breaking up the family or sending anyone to jail.

Left, Provos launch the White Bike programme. Above, cannabis café.

Exploitation: Despite the reputation for tolerance, the Dutch will sometimes admit that they have let things go too far. A good example is the child pornography that began to be circulated in the 1960s and boomed after Sweden outlawed it in 1980, followed by Denmark in 1982. Pretty soon after the US Customs Service had branded Amsterdam "the 1984 version of Sodom and Gomorrah" and the British news media had made similar accusations, Dutch officials moved in to shut off the trade in books, magazines and videotapes showing children in sexual acts. Legislation was passed outlawing the production and circulation of child pornography, but American officials still complained that it was too lenient: those who break the law receive only a three-month jail sentence, compared with up to 10 years in the US; only pictures of children performing sexual acts were outlawed, instead of all child nudity as in the US.

Tax regime: The libertarian bent sometimes extends from social attitudes into commercial practice, particularly in the tax structure that attracts many foreign individuals and companies to Amsterdam. Residents may pay relatively high taxes, but foreign firms that establish a base in Amsterdam—and there are many of them scattered along the canals in former merchants' homes converted to modern offices—get favoured treatment. Dutch companies, even if only statutorily rather than physically based in the Netherlands, are not taxed on the earnings of foreign subsidiaries. As a result, companies avoid double taxation. These offshore provisions, along with the stable political environment and sound currency, have attracted a number of firms doing business around the world, from the Japanese to the Lebanese, along with high-earning entertainers such as the Rolling Stones.

While the grandest of the big old canal houses have been given over to business, Amsterdam continues to suffer from a severe housing shortage that has plagued the city since World War II. Part of the reason is immigration, much of it from former colonies such as Indonesia and Surinam, and part of it is due to the resettlement, legal or otherwise, of workers from countries such as Turkey and Morocco. Another factor, however, is the remarkably low rent—sustained by government subsidies—paid by many Dutch. For those who can find an apartment, the rent is likely to be the lowest of any northern European capital.

Squats: One ramification of the housing shortage, which affects up to one in 50 Amsterdam families, is that adult children remain at home with their parents much longer than either they or the parents might like. Another effect over the years has been the spread of illegal squatting, sometimes by well-meaning but poor people who try to improve the property, but as often as not by people who devote more of their energy to drugs and crime than to home decoration. In some cases there have been conflicts between junkies and non-addict squatters that have even led one group or the other to plead for assistance from their mutual enemies, the Amsterdam police.

There were, in the late 1980s, a few well-publicised instances in which the government bought squatted buildings, fixed them up and then turned them over to the squatters to live in legally. But more frequently the housing shortage itself has been used as an excuse for simply turning out most of the squatters back on to the streets.

Image problem: Another reason for the crackdown has been the damage the unkempt squats and squatters were doing to the city's image among the 1.6 million tourists—twice the local population—who visit each year. A related factor may be Amsterdam's desire to host the Olympic Games; the city's most recent bids have failed and some people say that this is because members of the International Olympic Committee, a famously conservative group, do not think that Amsterdam is the sort of place to bring wholesome young competitors.

Most of the squatters have indeed been displaced, but at a cost. Their rowdy protests, stink-bombs in tourist areas and graffiti focused even more attention on Amsterdam's problems. When the mayor visited a squat to try to reason with the inhabitants he was spat upon until forced, in front of the cameras, to make a drenched retreat.

In some parts of the city, the crime and vandalism got so bad that area residents formed vigilante groups, something along the lines of the 17th-century civic guards—like the one depicted in Rembrandt's painting *The Night Watch*. Crime has led to occasional strikes by night bus drivers, though they were mollified somewhat when the city authorities installed emergency buttons for calling police.

Left, derelict warehouses transformed into a work of art. Above, teargassed squatters.

As with the drugs situation, many people familiar with Amsterdam would say that crime is still worse than 20 years ago, but has improved in the past decade or so. Certainly the official crime statistics have dropped for much of central Amsterdam, and there is no doubt that the area around the Central Station is now somewhat cleaner and safer than it used to be.

Vanguard: Some of Amsterdam's social liberalism may have dimmed, but the city still prides itself for remaining on the cutting edge in many aspects of art. Since World War II, Amsterdam has become more than a cultural centre with avant-garde aspects. Instead, it is the centre for the avant-garde.

This is equally true of the music that is played in the clubs that open at an hour when most other European capitals are tucked in for the night, and even of the way that Amsterdam clubbers dance. In terms of choreography, Amsterdam has been a hot space for modern and jazz dance developments, whether home-grown or imported by the best of the world's touring troupes.

Questioning: But the avant-garde in the post-war Netherlands is best seen in the paths chosen by popular artists. The Van Gogh-inspired Expressionism of the first half of the 20th century gave way to a more questioning, vivid, witty but sometimes cynical style that was summed up by one artist in this way: "A painting is no longer a construction of colours and lines, but an animal, a night, a cry, a man, or all of these together. Suggestion is boundless, and that is why we can say that, after a period in which art represented nothing, art has now entered a period in which it represents everything."

Instead of expressing something, some local artists—such as Jan Schoonhoven, Armando, Daan van Golden and J.C.J. van der Heyden—avoided expressing anything. They questioned not only the nature of art, but also the nature of how art is created. Other local artists—such as Peter Struycken and Ad Dekkers—suggested that everything and anything could be art. Others again—such as Co Westerik and Reiner Lucassen—created an updated version of the realistic style of the old Dutch School, but combined with the distinct influences of Pop Art, in their witty depictions of everyday objects and images.

Public attitudes: A remarkably high percentage of the Amsterdam citizenry today, as in the Golden Age in the 17th century, seems to have an interest in art and its developments. There is, of course, much good-natured grumbling when the newspapers report that thousands of guilders of government money went into seemingly spurious art-school projects, including one that involved a group of students taking apart an antique ship and then putting it back together again. Despite this, nobody, except for one disappointed foreigner, seemed to mind when the swimming pool was given over to studies in the floating art of life (preservers).

Above, unofficial art. Right, Fabiola, one of Amsterdam's many colourful characters.

THE ARTS

The people of Amsterdam enjoy a huge range of state-funded arts and the visitor does not need to look far to find a feast of cultural options.

The fine arts are encountered as you travel about the city—from the street trams painted by the students of the Rietveld Academy of Art to the numerous sculptures and paintings which often occur in unlikely places. This is often the result of the "1 Percent Rule" under which 1 percent of the total cost of new buildings put up by the state has to go towards art.

At street level the famed Dutch tolerance enables buskers to perform with minimal harassment from the authorities. Performers are almost as common as bicycles in the areas of the city where large groups of people congregate, such as Dam square and the Stationsplein in front of Central Station. Here you will find classical string quartets competing for attention with Japanese puppet theatre, tango dancers, fire-eaters, caricature artists and magicians—not to mention guitar-wielding youths whose low-quality cacophony is pumped out with maximum amplification. In winter Vondelpark is a restful place for meditative walks or brisk jogging. Once the chilling winds give way to balmy summer, the park fills with a sea of visitors and residents, all out for a relaxing time. As well as the profusion of apprentice bongo-players who inflict "Variations on the Thud" upon passers-by, there are professionally organised free concerts from early June to the end of August performed in the open-air auditorium near the 1930s circular tea-room. The range of music embraces everything from classical to punk.

The most traditional form of busking takes the form of ornate barrel-organs which their attendants drive to strategic points all over the city. Their fairground music forms an ever-present sound-track to the daily life of the city. Small oval brass tins are shaken vigorously right under shoppers' noses to demand cash—they are not just here for the benefit of tourists.

The more lofty forms of performance art can be seen at the more established venues. The neo-classical Concertgebouw theatre is home to the world-renowned International Concertgebouw Orchestra. The Stadhuis/Muziektheater, locally known as the "Stopera" due to squatters' protests at the building's construction, houses the National Ballet and the Netherlands Opera. Beurs van Berlage provides the traditional cultural spectacles of classical concerts, ballet and opera. The Beurs, originally built by architect H. P. Berlage as the Amsterdam Stock Exchange, was opened for public performances in mid-1988 and should also be visited as an architectural spectacle in its own right.

The avant-garde and the traditional arts generally remain apart from one another, but a theatre performance in 1986 at the Stadschouwburg, the main theatre, proved that they are not always inseparable. Wim T. Schippers, the well-known Dutch humourist, put on a production whose entire cast consisted of Alsatian dogs. These monosyllabic and temperamental artistes had a full house for three nights and national TV coverage.

The big halls and their high prices have created an open market for the smaller theatres and café back-rooms where more "arty" performances occur. The Ijsbreker, for example, is a café-*cum*-theatre, concert hall and cinema which hosts a wide range of events.

Other venues are excellent in specialist areas: Maloe-Meloe for rhythm and blues, Bimhuis for jazz, the Shaffy for theatre and the once hippyish, now well organised and less interesting, Melkweg (Milkyway) for alternative cinema and world music.

Apart from impromptu events, Amsterdam always has a bewildering choice of performances and exhibitions. Information is available about them all from the Uitbureau at Leidseplein 26. This information centre and booking office publishes a monthly free-sheet called the Uitkrant (which celebrated its 25th anniversary recently by nearly going under). Although turgid in content, as well as being in Dutch, it does offer an overview of the events which feverishly compete for audiences in this city obsessed by art.

BLASIUSSTRAAT
OOST
IBAUT

dag buuf
hee gaat het ermee?
Rembrandt

Working In The City

The working face of Amsterdam has changed dramatically in recent years. The industrial dinosaurs have moved to less cramped quarters or faded away. The monumental city banks and their high-tech camp followers have relocated to the new business parks southeast of the city. The financial market-makers downtown have rebounded strongly to fill the city-centre gaps. Schiphol airport is relocating old tenants to make room for more profitable new ones. And, perhaps most noticeably, the area inside the canals is being colonised by successful, often self-employed, people and multitudes of small commercial enterprises.

This influx has halted a 20-year population slide and fuelled an economic boom that the city should enjoy into the 21st century. But today's employees are not merely yesterday's factory workers in new suits. Education and income levels have risen, resulting in an explosion of upscale shops and restaurants to serve the needs of workers with new affluence and expectations.

Constraints: As industry retooled in the late 1970s, the limitations of a 17th-century city surrounded by water became painfully obvious. Parking and transportation difficulties still head the list of every Amsterdammer's complaints. Canal-side streets are frequently blocked for hours by delivery trucks. The beautiful but problematic historic buildings cannot be safely expanded or legally demolished to create new office space.

As a consequence, the big concerns moved out. Shipbuilding, traditionally centred along the Ij and on the island of north Amsterdam, was the first industry to go. Traces of these old activities lingered on until the early 1980s when KNSM, the last remaining shipping company, moved to Rotterdam. The Mobil Oil refinery and Ford assembly plant left Amsterdam about this time also. By 1985, some 75,000 people, nearly a quarter of the city's workforce, were unemployed. Most were semi-skilled machinists and labourers, unprepared and untrained to participate in the technical revolution that was taking place around them.

Relocation: Adding insult to injury, one of Amsterdam's oldest established businesses—the brewer, Heineken—finally decided to move out to Zoeterwoude in 1986. Long a subject of neighbourhood complaints, the century-old beermaker decided that world-wide transportation of its famous nectar would be much easier once its trucks got out of central Amsterdam. For the sake of thousands of thirsty pilgrims, the old brewery building remains open for tours. Residents rather miss the company now that it has gone but console themselves by saying that at least Heineken is still in the Netherlands; it has not been bought by the Americans or Japanese.

Unemployment in the city is down since the worst days of the mid 1980s and still declining, but many of the former shipyard, refinery and assembly-plant workers remain

Preceding pages: inside-out: three-dimensional mural. Left, Amsterdam's World Trade Centre. Right, composer at work.

on the dole. These men, especially if they are middle-aged and older, are likely to remain jobless until they reach retirement age and disappear from statistical view.

Upheaval: A curious twist, however, is the lack of skilled hands for the local building trades. Most often the people on the scaffolding in Amsterdam are likely to be from the rural province of Freisland or from Ireland or England. But the potentially catastrophic changes in the job market and the migration of people have not weakened the city's economic base. In fact, residents shrug off the upheaval. Historically, they quickly point out, the city has always had a commercial base and not an industrial one.

The municipal government, however, has not taken such a fatalistic view. Faced with a potential collapse in revenue from big businesses, it has aggressively courted American, Japanese and Swiss multinational companies eager to establish European headquarters in time to participate in the single European market. The city is pushing its multi-port advantage combined with the natural Dutch facility for language and the generally high education and production level of the workforce.

Up to 70 companies are expected to answer the siren call in the coming years. Some will undoubtedly take up space in the newly announced docklands regeneration scheme. The whole of the 10-mile (15-km) stretch of waterway that runs behind Central Station to the North Sea is the site of a one-billion guilder project (£330 million/$530 million) that will include conference centres, 20,000 housing units, museums, marinas and parks. Space for smaller harbour, rail and airport-related businesses will also be included.

Distribution hub: The facilities around Schiphol airport southwest of the city have also improved markedly and transportation-related companies are now the second largest private employer in the area. Schiphol is the fastest growing airport in Europe as increasingly more companies from central Holland relocate to be near Amsterdam's major sea, air, and rail terminals.

Greenfield sites: Shrewdly the city also began creating new commercial and residential space in the southeast, an area already well served by public transportation. Neighbouring farmland was annexed and marshes were drained and filled. Cramped companies were so eager to move out of the city that the usual incentives like tax breaks and real estate deals were not needed.

The big banks, such as AMRO and NMB-PostBank, were among the first to move and their computer support services were quick to follow. The country's major teaching hospital, Amsterdam University's Academic Medical Centre, also moved to the area, taking with it a host of other medical research companies.

Exodus: The only representatives of the industrial sector in this same region are the large printers. Even they have taken advantage of the technological revolution—probably more so than anyone. As in London's Fleet Street, most of the city's daily newspapers and major publishers, such as the Netherlands Yellow Pages, have fled central Amsterdam to relocate here. Some downtown cafés and restaurants were hit hard as long-time customers vanished and city old-timers complain that the daytime pace is no longer so exciting.

Commuting: Not everyone who works in Amsterdam lives there. In fact, almost half of the workers in the southeast business parks come from outside the Amsterdam area. About 150,000 people a day come in and out of the city to work. But, despite one of the most efficient public transportation systems in the world, thousands of people insist on clogging the motorways each morning. People continue to drive because public transportation routes and schedule convenience lag behind worker demand and no one likes to cross muddy fields or construction sites to get to a bus or train stop. For older workers, commuting in the company car is a status symbol of privileged suburban living. Most Dutch people also claim that rail travel is too expensive. Driving solo is the same price as the train and two in a car is always cheaper. But this is not likely to continue. The already high cost of driving will probably rise and may eventually be taxed out of the reach of the everyday commuters if government policies succeed.

In the city centre, financial services companies, many of them subsidiaries of large banks, have replaced the traditional industries and come to dominate the economy. Close to 100,000 people work in the financial sector and related fields, making it the largest private employer in the city. Downtown has its own stock, options and insurance exchanges. Naturally, the related administrative services—accountants, audi-

Left, IJ harbour, site of major redevelopment. Above, NMB-PostBank building, Bijlmermeer.

tors, lawyers, notaries and sundry investment consultants—have swarmed in. Small, independent brokerages are also blossoming. Indeed, the banking sector is the only part of the city's economy that is growing.

Public servants: The largest single employer is the government. When staff from two universities and the large social service programmes are included, civil servants total more than 120,000 people, or 30 percent of the workforce. Another constant is tourism. The 1.6 million yearly visitors are the city's cash cow, contributing about 1.4 billion guilders (£470 million/$750 million) to the local economy.

One labour economist estimates that as much as one-third of all business and economic activity in the city comes from the self-employed and their small businesses.

As a result, every canal-side house seems to contain the basement or ground-floor studio of an architect or graphic artist. They obviously enjoy their high profile. Curtains and blinds are never drawn because the brightly lit studio interiors are an advertisement for the values and affinities of the occupants—every item of furniture, every plant and picture, is carefully chosen to make a statement to any passer-by who happens to gaze in. Media-types and assorted advertising industry hangers-on also compete for passing attention.

The liberal and tolerant reputation of the city has also made it a mecca for the country's intellectuals and artists. "Everyone with brains is coming into the city; it's where it's all happening," a business editor for *De Telegraaf* proclaimed.

The same goes for nearly every other branch of creative activity. The influx of highly educated people has created a generally positive boom in what economists call "informal economic activity" and self-employment. Astonishingly, 12,000 Amsterdam residents are freelance researchers, writers, computer programmers and the like.

Artistic hub: Actors, musicians and writers regard Amsterdam as their native habitat. The city has more than 50 theatres and 175 stages; it is home to two orchestras, in addition to the national ballet and dance theatre. Experimental, nouvelle, avant or simply modern: there are 150 art galleries in Amsterdam and this does not include the craftsmen of all flavours whose studios clutter the Jordaan, or the 170 antique shops. For these artists, artisans and dealers, there is nowhere else to live and work—at least not in the

Netherlands. Their influence on the character and spirit of the city is clearly visible and their value immeasurable.

Also inescapable is the aroma of commerce that flavours everything. The increased demand from newly affluent residents and from tourists has fuelled an explosion of shops, and a walk through the city gives the impression that the official figure of 10,000 retail outlets is a conservative estimate. In addition, there are 26 open-air markets, selling everything from marital aids and marijuana pipes to mundane fruit and vegetables.

Chain stores: This bullish period, however, has given some small-store owners cause for concern over the future character of city shops. When the rents go up, it forces out the marginal businesses such as antiquarian bookshops, traditional grocers or specialist retailers trading on slim margins. Those same shops give Amsterdam's side streets their enviable charm. If this continues, one bookshop owner explained, all you are going to get is multinational chain boutiques.

The city's small shops contribute to the quality of life that Amsterdammers universally adore. They may have political disagreements with the city government or contretemps with the climate, but they would never want to live anywhere else. Inner-city residents have a deep affection for their town, unlike residents of some other national capitals where a litany of complaints always seems to precede faint praise.

"Amsterdam has the attitude of a southern European city in terms of atmosphere, street life, entertainment—but combined with northern liberalism. That is very, very unusual. You have to go to Paris, or further south, to Spain, Portugal or Italy to find an attitude like this," one man said proudly.

This attitude is also visible in the workplace. It is hard to find someone to answer the telephone after 5 p.m. as most people have gone home. Holidays are taken very seriously and involve months of preparation. The average office worker gets 35 vacation days a year, an eternity compared with the 10-day average received in the US.

"The quality of life is most important here," a city resident explained. "People don't work as much, or feel they need to stay late to further their careers. Even company presidents leave at five o'clock," he added.

Left, relaxing after work, Westerstraat. Above, fairground organ and attendants.

P3156

Housing in Amsterdam is about more than just the construction or conservation of buildings. Housing policy is one of the city's most visible social engineering tools.

To the relief of residents, the city abandoned the practice of clearing whole neighbourhoods of tenants in order to restore or redevelop the area, a practice that earned it so many enemies in the 1970s. The attitude now is to restore decaying streets house by house, rather than tract by tract, preserving the social fabric of the area intact.

By creating more and better urban housing, the municipal government hopes to keep Amsterdam as a living, residential city, with the well-heeled ensconced cheek by jowl with the ne'er-do-wells. Since 1950, 143,400 new apartment units have been built for low and middle-income tenants. Up to 1970, however, 90 percent of this was built on annexed suburban land. Today, 25 percent is directed toward the city centre.

Renewal: The goal is to boost the inner-city population to 720,000, still 150,000 less than the peak of 1964, but in line with what planners call the "compact city" plan. This way the city escapes becoming the "Venice of the North"—the most dreadful epithet you could attach to Amsterdam, whether you are talking to a city planner or a resident. Both see the Italian city as a slough of stagnant canals whose residents and businesses have fled to higher ground, abandoning the city to the tourist hordes.

Municipal government can exert this kind of social influence because it owns about 70 percent of the land in the city. Amsterdam is unique in that only 7 percent of homes are occupied by their owners. The rest, about 310,000 units, is rental property. The city owns outright about 40 percent of this total. Much of the large residential area beyond the inner canal ring is held in leasing arrangements, under which the city sells long-term rights to land developers, who in turn build or restore the housing and rent out the units.

Shortages: In both these cases, units are set aside for a variety of income levels. Rents, compared with New York, London or Paris, are surprisingly affordable—but bound to rise since developers cannot renovate upmarket apartments fast enough for the monied professionals craving to move back into the city. Amsterdam is probably unique in having an upper-class housing shortage.

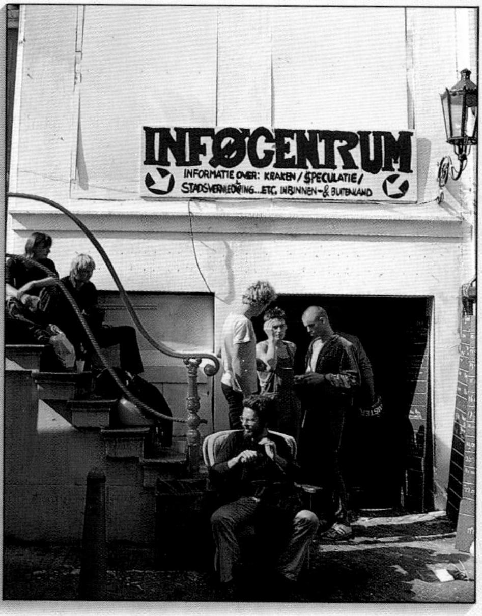

Housing—whether in fashionable Jordaan or in Bijlmermeer tower blocks—is allocated by means of waiting lists. You could get into one of the suburban housing projects tomorrow if you are not fussy about where you live; but if you want to live in the city centre, you could wait at least six years.

The waiting list policy greatly disturbs some residents and contributes to racial friction in the outwardly tranquil city. Newcomers to the city, most visibly foreign immigrants and their families, move to the top of the list. Lifelong Amsterdammers complain of coming out second best.

Preceding pages: floating home. Left, renovated warehouses, Brouwersgracht. Right, Squatter's Information Centre.

If you prefer to rent in the private sector, competition is ruthless. The fact of urban life is that you will never find a good property unless you know someone. When asked how they found their present abode, everyone from squatters to penthouse dwellers will just flash a conspiratorial smile. One honest revelation came from a woman who admitted that her tip-off came from her mother—who happens to work in a hospital for long-stay and terminally ill patients.

Brokers: The less well-connected often sublet or re-rent city apartments from middlemen, or from tenants willing to move out in return for some financial incentive. Demands for "key money"—the fee paid to the resident or "broker" for a technically illegal sublet—are not unusual. The key money for a three-room apartment might be 1,000 guilders, or three months' rent, before they are allowed to move in.

About half of the city's housing and most of the inner canal-side property is owned privately or by quasi-private housing corporations, many of which have benefited from city financing for restoration. In the past 10 years, many stately canal-side homes and old warehouses have been converted into offices and studios to meet demand from the professional and artistic classes. Once renovated, the spacious and airy 17th-century buildings, often with original brick and beams inside, will be on the market for half a million guilders and up (£167,000/US$267,000). Again a bargain compared to almost anywhere else in Europe.

Squatters: Some of the well-to-do residents of these newly restored buildings formerly occupied them as squatters. In the early 1970s squatting was a popular form of existence for young people, who wanted cheap housing in the city centre and were willing to work hard to renovate dilapidated buildings. The exodus of many businesses from the city centre had left scores of buildings dormant and the city without funds to renovate them. It was easy enough to establish a squat. The first thing you had to do was change the locks and take the boards off the windows, replacing them on the floor. Then, provided that the abandoned building was not scheduled for imminent renovation, it took a legal crowbar to dislodge you.

Not to be confused with homeless people or vagrants, the squatters were often students from one of Amsterdam's two universities. They transformed neighbourhoods from ghost towns into lively areas with their own subculture of cafés, shops and cinemas. Enormous banners usually announced the presence of a squat, and a few can still be seen around the city today, urging people to step back from their comfortable bourgeois lives, even for a moment.

Today it is hard to find anyone over 30 who does not claim to have squatted during that heady and romantic period of counter culture and people power. In those days, there were well-organised squatters' advisory offices where you could consult lists of vacant houses and city development plans as well as seek help in carrying out title searches. The squatters have even left an architectural legacy since most city development projects now incorporate large, communal living spaces into their floorplans.

Evictions: In the late 1970s and early 1980s, the city started to erode the substantial public support that existed for the squatters by building more inner-city housing and converting the "illegal" squats into legal rent-paying ones. During the period that the houses were being renovated, squatters were supposed to be relocated at city expense—this was often easier said than done. Violent protests often broke out at eviction time.

Even so, the policy has proved effective. Squatters and city officials estimate that only about 20 large buildings are still occupied and maybe another 50 smaller houses, and most of these are privately owned. Very few city-owned buildings are still squatted and it will not be long before the last wave of eviction proceedings is implemented.

Houseboat living: Many visitors to Amsterdam, seduced by the city's beautiful canals, dream of sailing back one day and mooring alongside Prinsengracht. Forget it. Amsterdam's generous public housing system ends at the shore. The number of canal-side moorings is fixed at 2,600. About 5,000 people live on floating concrete slabs, converted canal barges and the occasional genuine sea-going vessel.

Left, desirable properties: Keizersgracht and Brouwersgracht junction. Above, soulless Bijlmermeer.

Moorings are fixed and sold like conventional building plots, so you cannot sail off at whim for a sunnier pier. A quiet spot behind Westerkerk can cost 30,000 guilders (£10,000 or $16,000), and that does not include the boat. When expenses are totalled, residents estimate that houseboat living is no cheaper than a conventional apartment.

Even so, many people are seduced by the charms of living on the water. "After one week, I knew I would never move back to a flat," was the typical reaction of one convert to life afloat. The attractions of canal-boat living are even greater now that the conditions of the waterways have improved, the result of a 10-year clean-up campaign. Now only the houseboats themselves flush directly into the canals. Ducks, swans and fish have returned as sea water is pumped in nightly through the city locks.

The canal boats, such an integral part of the Amsterdam scene, lack nothing in basic amenities except closet space. Some owners, though, have resolved this problem by installing storage bins below the floor. Usually gas-heated, they are not cold in the winter.

Flexibility: Many people take maximum advantage of their floating domicile. Roofs and decks quickly get converted into porches and balconies as soon as the sunshine appears. Others have sailboats tied up alongside for leisure use. Depending on location, it can take less than an hour to reach the open waters of the IJsselmeer.

Jordaan: Fashionable among bohemian artists and artisans, the Jordaan district is a warren of streets, 1¼ miles (2 km) long and a third of a mile (500 metres) wide, which has its origins in a zig-zag series of polders and ditches dug in the mid-1600s.

In previous centuries the Jordaan was home to thousands of poor, working-class families. In 1890, 85,000 people were crammed into this area, four times the present population. Then, as now, more than 90 percent of the 11,000 apartments had no more than three rooms. In the early 1970s, private developers acted faster and bid higher than the city for many of the area's 700 listed, historic buildings and converted them into attractive, upmarket apartments and studios. As a result, city housing initiatives, designed to keep longtime residents and senior citizens, have scarcely gained a toehold in the area.

New vitality: Traditionally, the Jordaan was home to clothing factories, breweries, distilleries and other small industrial firms. Under the development plan for the area these "nuisance" activities have been relocated and the district has received yet another new lease of life as industrial buildings have been converted to flats, shops, studios and cosy brown cafés to serve the changing needs of the residents.

Even so, many of the old buildings are

considered beyond salvation and are now being rebuilt completely. Residents sigh with resigned frustration at the piecemeal construction that has been clogging their narrow streets for 10 years. It could have been worse, they shrug, referring to the city's ill-fated plan to run a second subway line through the neighbourhood. Faced with that prospect, old timers as well as *arrivistes* are happy that their neighbourhood is now being preserved and consider a few cement trucks a small price to pay in return.

Bijlmermeer: At the other end of the scale, modern Bijlmermeer appears, at least when viewed from the elevated Metro platform, to be a jewel made up of new clean, high-tech business parks. But behind the ultra-modern, corporate facades and plazas, an open-air shopping mall snakes its way back to a honeycomb of concrete high-rises for which Bijlmermeer is infamous. The atmosphere is futuristic, alienating and impersonal.

This 1960s experiment in social planning, designed to provide housing for 50,000 people, was an expensive lesson for the city fathers, and they are still paying. Today it has one of the highest crime rates and concentration of drug problems in the Netherlands. Needless to say, they don't build them like this anymore.

The problem with Bijlmermeer, one city official said bluntly, is that the people for whom it was built never wanted to live there. They preferred to stay in the shabbier parts of the city along with the street life, cafés, markets and cheaper rents.

In the run up to Surinamese independence in 1975, many immigrants moved to Amsterdam and were steered towards the vacant housing units of Bijlmermeer. Now the area's 35,000 Surinamese residents comprise the second largest Surinamese city in the world.

Many Surinamese and Guyanese residents like it there, provided that they live in a building that doesn't have too much crime. Many live with extended families or have relatives living nearby. Moving out is not a priority—as it is for white residents. Unemployment is very high and those residents who are working are embarrassed and sometimes resentful of other more visible immigrants who take conspicuous advantage of generous welfare benefits, giving the community a bad name.

Left, houseboat living. Right, Muslims regard the Dutch as godless.

Connections with their South American home are still strong. The shops, planted under overpasses, sell native staples and one grocery doubles as a Surinamese travel agency-cum-freight office. The thousands of skilled employees and professionals who work in the neighbouring high-tech buildings do not live in the area. They commute out at 5 p.m., glad to be working in a place so

well served by public transportation.

Immigrants: Other concentrations of immigrant communities are found all round the fringes of the old city, and they make up an increasingly visible and fast-growing part of Amsterdam's population—nearly 25 percent in total. Half of the children in Amsterdam schools are from non-Dutch families.

The Dutch-speaking Surinamese make up the largest portion—5 percent—and, as a former colony, they are granted the same rights as Dutch-born citizens. Another 35,000 are Turkish and Moroccan guest workers imported in the 1960s for jobs that

ERDAMSE VIS HANDEL H.LOCHER
Mosselen Kruiden
Zalm Forel 750 PER POND
Verse Wijting 175 PER POND
Kwaliteit Schelvis
CALAMARIS

Dutch people wouldn't do. Government inducements to get them to return to their home—usually a portion of their pension or unemployment benefit—go uncollected. After living for 20 years in the Netherlands, most have no desire to return to lower standards of living at home.

Barriers to integration: Many live in the city housing projects on the eastern and western fringes. The first-generation immigrants, especially those from Muslim countries, remain very closeknit and have not integrated well. Language is the biggest barrier, but so is the highly modern culture. The liberal, often agnostic or atheistic Dutch are seen as frosty and godless.

The children of immigrants have generally mixed much better than their parents. Social activities, like sports, are popular and racially mixed. Dutch boys have even picked up the Arab custom of going around the room with a quick handshake for everyone when they enter. Many of the girls have not been so fortunate. Muslim boys are quick to take advantage of Amsterdam's liberal social life, but their sisters are often trapped at home by traditional parents. When allowed out they must be accompanied by a vigilant younger brother. As a result of vastly unequal opportunities, some teenage girls are driven to attempt suicide.

The Pijp, a highly compact housing area south of Frederiksplein, is a working-class neighbourhood where Turks, Moroccans, Surinamese and Dutch mix better than they do in other areas of the city. Perhaps it is because they are all near the same income level or because they share common interests; most residents are young and just starting families in the squat, brick apartment buildings; most of them like living where they do. The area's colourful grocers, butchers and restaurants cater to all tastes and act as the glue that holds the area together.

Dapperplein, just east of the Zoo, is similar in income and racial make-up to the Pijp. Its market, the city's second largest, is a sprawling and colourful economic magnet for the entire east side of the city.

Multi-ethnic melting pot: Albert Cuypstraat market.

FOOD AND DRINK

Eating and drinking has always been more exciting in Amsterdam than in the rest of the country, though feasts with a wild swan centrepiece are now only to be enjoyed in Golden Age paintings. Compensation has, however, arrived in the shape of culinary expertise from kitchens all over the world. Indonesian food is now as traditional as Dutch, though France and Belgium have had a definite influence.

Recent innovations in home cooking include the greater use of Italian pasta, Chinese noodles and oil as a substitute for butter. Deep-frozen and prepared meals are more popular in the capital than the traditional thick soups and stews and mixed vegetable dishes of the country.

First things: Breakfast, taken from 7 a.m., increasingly begins with the international bowl of cereal or muesli as a prelude to the traditional *boterhammen*—bread and rolls spread with margarine, now, more often than butter, and topped with thinly sliced cheese, smoked ham or cold sliced meats. Plenty of strong coffee is served with thick condensed milk or teas of various flavours from English Earl Grey to mango. Hot chocolate is a favourite winter drink.

The morning break, at home, is taken at 11 a.m. or earlier; it is still customary to set a tray with a cup of coffee, a paper doily on the saucer, a biscuit and often a hand-made chocolate. On special occasions coffee may be accompanied by a *saucijzenbroodje*—a flaky pastry roll with a sausage inside—or a sweet pastry. At work, though, most large companies in Amsterdam have installed vending machines and the coffee break has ceased to be a time-consuming ritual.

Out and about in Amsterdam, especially among the young, food is eaten on the move. The favourite snack is *patat frites*—potato chips or french fries—with mayonnaise (*patatje oorlog*), tomato ketchup or *satésaus* (peanut sauce). Some places serve them in the original pointed paper bag, very hot to handle; others have a moulded plate with space for the chips, eaten with a plastic fork, separate from the sauce.

On the streets: Snack bars, where pizzas, pies and hamburgers are eaten standing up, are ubiquitous. Often food "from the wall" is available at the same places. A portion of breadcrumbed meat, a *kroket* or a sandwich are offered from a coin-operated *automatiek*,

where cooks behind place the food in small compartments with glass doors. A *kroket* is long, round and filled with stew; it tastes better with mustard or eaten in a roll. A *nasibal* is ball-shaped and stuffed with spiced fried rice. A long type of sausage, twice as long as a *kroket* and with very questionable stuffing, is a *frikandel*—nobody knows what they are made from.

Raw herring is eaten freshly cleaned, with chopped onions, at a herring stand, mostly in May and June at the beginning of the fishing season when everyone wants to try the *niewe haring* (new herring, slightly salted). The

Preceding pages: brown café: alternative living room. Left, herring consumption. Right, popular images: cheese and clogs.

very first fish to be caught is presented to the Queen of the Netherlands.

The most popular sweets with adults and children are liquorice drops made of gum and laurel. Available in various tastes and shapes (sweet or salty, animals or coins), they may be bought either in packets or singly. The colours are predominantly black or brown.

Lunch is almost the same meal as breakfast but with a larger choice of meats and cheese plus sausage or fish in a croissant or *broodje* (bread roll) bought from a *broodjeswinkel* (sandwich shops famed for their quality and wide selection of fillings).

the pine-coned roof and fairground horses—opposite the Heineken brewery in Stadhouderskade. Caroussel offers large, thin pancakes, similar to an omelette, with a variety of toppings—cheese, bacon, ham, stewed apples—and smaller ones, including body-warming rum *poffertjes*.

Afternoon tea is taken as early as 2 p.m. It is likely to include yet another cake or biscuit. A favourite is *stroopwafel*, made from two thin pastry wafers with syrup in between, best eaten when warm.

Plain fare: Pastries apart, the Dutch have never been renowned for elaborate cooking. Food is plainly boiled or stewed; grills are

Sweet and savoury: Pancakes are popular as an alternative, especially the *poffertjes* sold from tents set up on the Dam and around Westerkerk or from crystal-chandeliered, mirrored pavilions. *Poffertjes* are small pancakes eaten with large quantities of sugar and dripping with butter. The larger *pannekoeken* is bigger than a dinner plate and filled with savoury or sweet fillings, all served with thick maple syrup or *stroop*—which tastes like Golden Syrup.

More expensive varieties are offered at the Caroussel—a semi-permanent, circular restaurant with gold spiralled poles supporting

virtually non-existent and ovens, where they exist, are only used for cakes. As much food as possible is bought ready-prepared from supermarkets, and vegetables, already cleaned, from street markets. The days when everything was delivered to the door and raised in baskets on long ropes to top-floor apartments has almost disappeared.

Thus a typical evening meal, which is served about 6 p.m., might consist of boiled potatoes, fresh green vegetables, meat, chicken or, less likely, fish, and salad. The meal is often finished with chocolate chips called *hagelslag*, colourful anise-flavoured sweets called *muisjes* (little mice) and spicy biscuits known as *speculaas*. *Vla* too is a popular dessert, similar to custard. Shops and supermarkets sell many different kinds flavoured with vanilla, chocolate or fruit.

Dining out: Eating in restaurants is mostly for tourists, for business people (it is rare to entertain at home) or for special occasions. Tourists are a considerable market, and there are 660 restaurants in Amsterdam where it is said you can eat in any language.

For preference most Amsterdammers will, on a special night out, choose Indonesian cuisine. Although the strong, spicy tastes of East Asian cooking are the precise antitheses of bland Dutch dishes, Indonesian food is nevertheless extremely popular all over the Netherlands and Amsterdam has some of the country's finest restaurants.

Quite a number, though, serve mostly Chinese food. They are ambiguously labelled Indonesian-Chinese and often decorated in heavily velvetted furnishings with wood and paper lanterns in reds and golds.

Authenticity: Usually it is the unsophisticated, plainly furnished restaurants that serve the most interesting and authentic dishes. Restaurants such as these are often family-run, with mother or grandmother presiding over the kitchens and preparing dishes that are unique to a particular village or island in Indonesia. The menu is often extremely simple: some offer *rijstaffel* and nothing else, the choice being between the simple version of 15 dishes, the large at 30, or the deluxe at 50 or more. Good restaurants never serve the same choice twice so each visit is a new experience.

When the *rijstaffel* is served, a hot plate is placed on the table with a large subdivided tray containing the dishes or, more correctly, separate bowls placed around a large bowl of rice. Gone are the days when a multitude of dishes was brought to the table by a procession of white-clad waiters, each bearing a single dish.

The *rijstaffel* is eaten by arranging the rice on your plate then placing a small portion of each dish around the edge, lastly filling in the centre. Typical dishes include vegetables in coconut milk, chicken in peanut sauce, meatballs in saffron, fried bananas and fish and meat prepared in various ways. The dishes themselves are usually spicy rather than hot, but beware of the small saucers of red sambal—they are likely to be too hot to eat and even a hint is likely to destroy your tastebuds for the rest of the meal.

Gin and beer: In Amsterdam nearly everyone drinks beer with their meal, usually the local Heineken lager and Amstel brews, although imported Belgian "white" beer and English dark beer or bitter are becoming increasingly fashionable with the young.

The national drink, however, is *Jenever* or Dutch gin, made from juniper berries. This is drunk at about 5 p.m. when the office day comes to a swift close, and Amsterdammers slip into their favourite local brown café for a reviving *borrel*—a small measure of *Jenever* (pronounced *Yenayver*) served chilled in small, thick-walled liqueur glasses. The *Jonge*, or young *Jenever*, is colourless, less sweet and less creamy than the *Oude*—or old—which has a pale yellow colour and a pronounced juniper flavour. *Jenever* has always been a man's drink and is mostly taken as a ritual in a smoky, comfortable brown café.

Left, french fries. Right, cheese tasting.

Brown Cafés

There are over 500 cafés of one sort or another in the centre of Amsterdam alone and among these the *bruin* (brown) cafés are the friendliest. These traditional drinking haunts derive their collective name from a combination of dark wood interiors, years of studiously unwashed nicotine stains and low-wattage lighting.

They are social centres for the regulars who use brown cafés as an extension to their living rooms: a place to take breakfast, lunch, dinner and nightcaps, open from early in the morning to around 2 a.m. The atmosphere is generally relaxed, and customers are rarely made to feel rushed. You can linger for hours, if you choose, over a beer or coffee, reading a newspaper or book.

As well as their brownness, these cafés distinguish themselves by their spartan decor. A layer of sand is often spread on the bare floor in the morning (by tradition each café used to have its own individual design which was drawn into the sand). The furniture is generally free from upholstery, although in some cafés worn Persian rugs are placed on the table tops to absorb beer spillage, and the walls may be bare except for a yellowing calendar.

Unchanged: Brown cafés are not quaint tourist attractions but rough and ready establishments, truly traditional and thriving. Some are highly successful: the famous Hoppe on Spuistraat, established in 1670, is nowadays renowned for its business-suited clients who spill out on to the pavements in the summer-time. Yet the back bar on the right of the building's facade retains all of its ancient character and exhibits few panderings to modernity—with the exception, perhaps, of the telephone.

Each brown café has its own character and clientele. Ranging from the yuppies of the Hoppe, the jazziness of the tiny Wetering, on Leidsedwaarstraat, or the foreign journalistic babble of Harry's Bar, on Spuistraat, to the loud card games of the Oosterling, on Utrechtstraat, or the rugged talk of beery sailors in the Karperhoek on Martelaarsgracht near the Central Station.

Left, interior of a brown café. Right, traditional Dutch gin.

Spoilt for choice: Behind the bar in a brown café there is often such an extensive range of beverages on offer that knowing where to start can be a baffling business.Three types of beer are normally available on tap. The *pils*, or lager, is usually from the Dutch Amstel or Heineken breweries. The two

other most commonly tapped beers are "blond" and "dark" or "brown" beer, both types nearly always imported from Belgium and stronger than normal *pils*.

Among the blond beers, Hoogaarden and Dentergems are both sweet-tasting brews and can be ordered with a slice of lemon to inject the required tang. The most common brown beer is De Koninck, a smooth, bitter-like lager with a full taste.

Once beyond the realms of the beer on tap, the choice of bottled beers and stronger liquors becomes a minefield of exotic labels. You can choose according to the strength of the beer, country or even region of origin.

Beer tasting: The choice is wider still in cafés like In de Wildeman, at Kolksteeg 3, which is a *proeflokaal* or tasting-place and has 18 different beers on tap alone, or the intimate Gollem, on Raamsteeg 4, which offers a choice of at least five beers from each of the 10 different countries chalked up on the blackboard.

Temptation also comes in the form of beers with evocative names: Thick Neck, Wooden Head, Sudden Death and the extraordinarily named *Grote Lul* (Large Penis) brewed by the small *'T Ei* (The Egg) brewery just outside the city.

Beers to beware: Price is usually a good indication of strength and, for many Belgian beers, the more elaborate the glass the more dangerous the brew. This is certainly the case with Qwak, a beer served in a round-bottomed, narrow-necked glass held upright in a wooden contraption like a test-tube holder. The name stems from the noise of the beer sploshing on to the faces of those who drink this dangerously strong concoction too quickly from these self-regulating vessels.

A more traditional form of drinking is the *borrel*, or short measure, of strong liquor—usually either *Jonge Jenever* (young gin) or ice-cold *Oude Jenever* (old gin) in combination with a glass of *pils*. The short is thrown down the throat followed swiftly by the glass of *pils*. This is called a *kopstoot* or head-banger for obvious reasons.

How to play: It is most common to pay for drinks by running up a bill rather than paying for each individual round. Bar staff juggle rows of small order pads or a large book, in which they keep a record of proceedings.

A mime of the act of writing is usually enough to communicate that you will pay at the end of the evening. Once this has been established it is easy enough to lose track of the amount you have consumed, and that is usually the reason for many an over-enthusiastic tasting. A useful word to learn, therefore, is *afrekenen*, which is the verb for settling-up—and "taxi" is the same word in most languages.

Café society: each bar has its own character and its regular clientele.

Pub
Café - Bar

RESTAU

Amsterdam's New Year is ushered in by the consumption of large quantities of currant-filled doughnuts (*olie bollen* or oil balls) and the throwing of firework parties. There never seems to be much in the way of civic, organised firework displays but the effect of hundreds of small, independent displays is of a fluid crowd flowing from one series of explosions to another.

The Chinese quarter, the Binnenbantammer, is renowned as the centre of attraction for pyromaniacs anonymous. Huge strings of firecrackers are suspended from the upper floors of buildings and ignited from the bottom causing ear-splitting thunderous crescendos followed by loud applause and whistles from the crowds.

Waiting for the freeze: Even during the mildest of winters there is a great deal of talk about weather: whether or not, for instance, it will freeze. When it does, it is a time of national contentment. The nation mobilises, delves into cupboards to dust off seldom-used skates and the city becomes a network of silver thoroughfares packed with woolly hatted skaters aged from two to 92. The last freeze occurred in 1985 and 1986, for an unprecedented two years in a row, and the time before that was 1963.

Further north, if it freezes, the big winter event is the *Elfstedentocht*, a gruelling race on skates between 11 towns in the north of Holland. The entire Amsterdam population, if not competing or spectating by the ice-side, is glued to the television set with hot cocoa permanently ready on the stove.

Miracle remembered: On the night of 17 March the *Stille Omgang*, or silent procession, goes through the town. Thousands of people walking silently in the dark creates a highly individual atmosphere. This primarily Catholic procession dates back to Amsterdam's very own miracle, which took place in 1345, when a communion host thrown into a fire remained undamaged by the flames. Because of its very silent nature the procession is not the liveliest of affairs, yet it is open to anyone willing to participate and has been said to make even the most irreligious feel spiritual.

Koninginnedag, Queen's Day, is on 8 April. Although events in commemoration of the former queen's birthday (the current queen's birthday is seasonally unfavourable) take place throughout the Netherlands, they take a particularly chaotic form in Amsterdam. The day is one of unbridled commercial fever, the result of a decree stating that anyone can sell anything on the streets, within the bounds of legality.

The initial idea was to create a day on which children could sell their handicrafts, but the spirit of enterprise pervades in both old and young nowadays. The entire city becomes a cross between a junk sale and a carnival from around 6 a.m. onwards when early risers begin setting up their pitch on the prize spots. Hundreds of stalls selling old ship's tackle, second-hand bric-a-brac and handmade just about everything, hustlers

Left, Caribbean carnival. Right, the annual Aalsmeer to Amsterdam Flower Parade.

with dice games and people challenging all-comers at chess all form aisles along the pavements for the throngs of slightly perplexed visitors. During the daytime the Vondelpark becomes a prime spot to soak up the atmosphere of the day.

Revelry: As the evening progresses a giant street party develops in the city centre. A solid jam of beer-drinking humans provides the audience for live bands which play on stages erected outside the bars. The late shift of merry-makers witnesses the surreal sight of convoys of water-jetting sweeper lorries which clear the streets of rubbish ready for the dawn of the communal pounding head.

Founded in 1947, the Holland Festival runs throughout June and is the biggest dance, drama and music festival in the Netherlands. This often rather highbrow carnival of the arts is an international crowd-puller and encompasses a series of performances throughout the city all under the umbrella of the given year's specific theme—in 1989 it was the Soviet Union.

The *Uitmarkt*, held at the end of August, is a three-day fair in preparation for the cultural season ahead. Groups of performance artists from across the country flock to the capital to present dress rehearsals, sell season tickets, and generally create an awareness of what there is on offer. The area around Dam square becomes impassable to traffic as pedestrians taking full advantage of these free shows clog the thoroughfares.

Around the second week of September the Jordaan begins 10 days of merriment. This area, with its web of narrow streets, is the heartland of working-class Amsterdam and while yuppies are threatening on the fringes it still thrives as an area of artists and artisans.

The festival involves a good deal of drinking. Accordion groups and vocalists perform traditional folk music characterised by lots of oom-pah and not to everybody's taste. Everyone wears fancy dress. Food stalls and stages are set up around the cafés which serve as social centres. Every sc often, without fail, someone falls into the canal and has to be fished out to the accompaniment of catcalls and laughter. A less raucous affair is the flower parade, held on the last Saturday in September, when imaginatively decorated carnival floats and costumed attendants proceed from the flower market at Aalsmeer to the heart of Amsterdam.

Christmas preparations: Around 17 November Saint Nicolaas arrives "from Spain", proceeding up Prins Hendrikkade to the city centre. Looking rather like Father Christmas, but wearing a bishop's mitre, the saint greets the expectant crowds of children. His blacked-up sidekick, Zwarte Piet, has been the subject of much debate (liberal Amsterdam is wary of implied racism) and reputedly takes away bad children in his sack.

A long parade through the streets heralds the beginning of the build up to St Nicolaas Eve; during this season children put out their shoes for the saint and wake up to find them filled with marzipan cakes, bought from the baker's and shaped into anything from a simple sausage to a computer.

The whole business comes to a head on 5 December when the children receive more substantial presents and when many a staggering Saint Nicolaas, in red costume and mitre, can be seen around the bars and cafés after a heavy day's present-giving.

Left, one-man band. Right, street parties can be spontaneous events.

C&A

HET JUISTE NUMMER
UIT
13

HOLLAND
AMSTERDAM
stationsboekh
MONTAILLOU

10

PLACES

Go to Leidseplein on a chill February evening. A trapeze artist, clad in a scarlet sequined jock-strap, hangs upside down from a pole and performs a muscular aerial ballet to the accompaniment of taped circus music. The crowd applauds and cheers. This is Amsterdam.

Go to a chic café on Herengracht on a wet Sunday afternoon in spring. A tall, blonde woman, dressed in black, carefully tops two glasses of *warme chokolade* with generous dollops of whipped cream. This is Amsterdam.

Go to Brouwersgracht in the fading glow of an autumn sunset. With the trees stripped bare, the view along the wide vista of magnificent houses bordering Herengracht is like a painting of the city's Golden Age. This, too, is Amsterdam.

The city is composed of such memorable scenes, but the list of "musts" is short. The Rijksmuseum, the Museum Van Gogh, the Royal Palace, the Rembrandthuis—every visitor should find time to visit these. But after that, Amsterdam is what you discover it to be.

This city has over 1,000 bridges. The waterways, comprising more than 100 canals, clock up a combined length in excess of 65 miles (100 km). Despite these statistics, Amsterdam's historic centre is very compact and lends itself to easy exploration.

Take a canal boat. There is no better way to see the grand 17th and 18th-century houses of the Grachtengordel. Do plenty of walking: along the canals in the characterful Jordaan; along Staalstraat for the view along Groenburgwal of the Zuiderkerk; even to the warehouses of the Entrepôt Dok, in the east, or Realengracht, in the west, to savour the remnants of Amsterdam's once glorious maritime history. Later, hire a bicycle and venture further afield.

Above all, take time to talk to the people of Amsterdam. Language is rarely a barrier in a town where British TV and radio stations are preferred to the home-grown variety and France, Belgium and Germany are close enough to be regarded as neighbouring counties.

They will share, with frankness and generosity, their views on the city and the world in general. There are few places in Europe where human contact is so easy, and you will end up loving Amsterdam as much for its people as for its scenery.

The trapeze artist in the sequined jock-strap might not be in town at the same time as you. But, without fail, Amsterdam will serve up somebody or something just as memorable.

Preceding pages: rooftops and Oude Kerk; the Magere Brug; taking it easy. Left, Vondelpark sculpture.

WESTERPARK
HAARLEMMERVAART
Haarlemmerweg
Haarlemmerweg
WESTERDOK
Haarlemmer Houttuinen
Haarlemmer Dijk
BROUWERSGRACHT
Groen van Prinststraat
Van Beuningenstraat
De Wittenstraat
Palmstraat
Marnixstraat
KATTENSLOOT
De Kempenaerstr.
WESTELIJK MARKT KANAAL
OOSTELIJK MARKTKANAAL
Centrale Markthallen
Frederik Hendrik Plantsoen
LIJNBAANSGRACHT
Lindengracht
Westerstraat
PRINSEN GRACHT
Prinsenstr.
Herenstr.
KEIZERS GRACHT
HEREN
KOSTVERLORENVAART
Nassaukade
Frederik Hendrikstraat
SINGELGRACHT
EGELANTIERSGRACHT
Admiraal de Ruijter-Weg
Jan van Galenstraat
Westerkerk
BLOEMGRACHT
Raadhuisstraat
Willem de Zwijger Laan
HUGO DE GROOTGRACHT
Rozengracht
Reestr.
Hartenstr.
Lauriersstraat
Bilderdijkstraat
Nassaukade
Admiraal de Ruijter-Weg
ADMIRALEN GRACHT
Van Speijkstraat
Chassestraat
BILDERDIJK GRACHT
DA COSTA GRACHT
PRINSEN GRACHT
KEIZERS GRACHT
HEREN GRACHT
Nieuwezijds Voorburgwal
Elandsgracht
Runstraat
Witte de With Straat
Marnixstraat
Bijbels Museum
KOSTVERLORENVAART
Bellamystraat
Kinkerstraat
LEIDSEGRACHT
LENNEPKANAAL
Lange
Korte
Kerkstraat
Postjesweg
Lootsstraat
Pieter Heijestraat
JACOB VAN
Beetsstraat
Helmersstraat
Stadhouderskade
American Hotel
Leidsedwarsstraat
Leidsedwarsstraat
Nwe. Spiegelstraat
PRINS
Staringstraat
Overtoom
Vondelstraat
Paradiso
Wetering Schans
Filmmuseum
Vondelstraat
Helmersstraat
Rijksmuseum
Overtoom
Van Baerlestraat
Hobbemakade
Van Gogh Museum
Stedelijk Museum
Van Eeghenstraat
VONDELPARK
Quellijnstraat
Van Breestraat
Concertgebouw

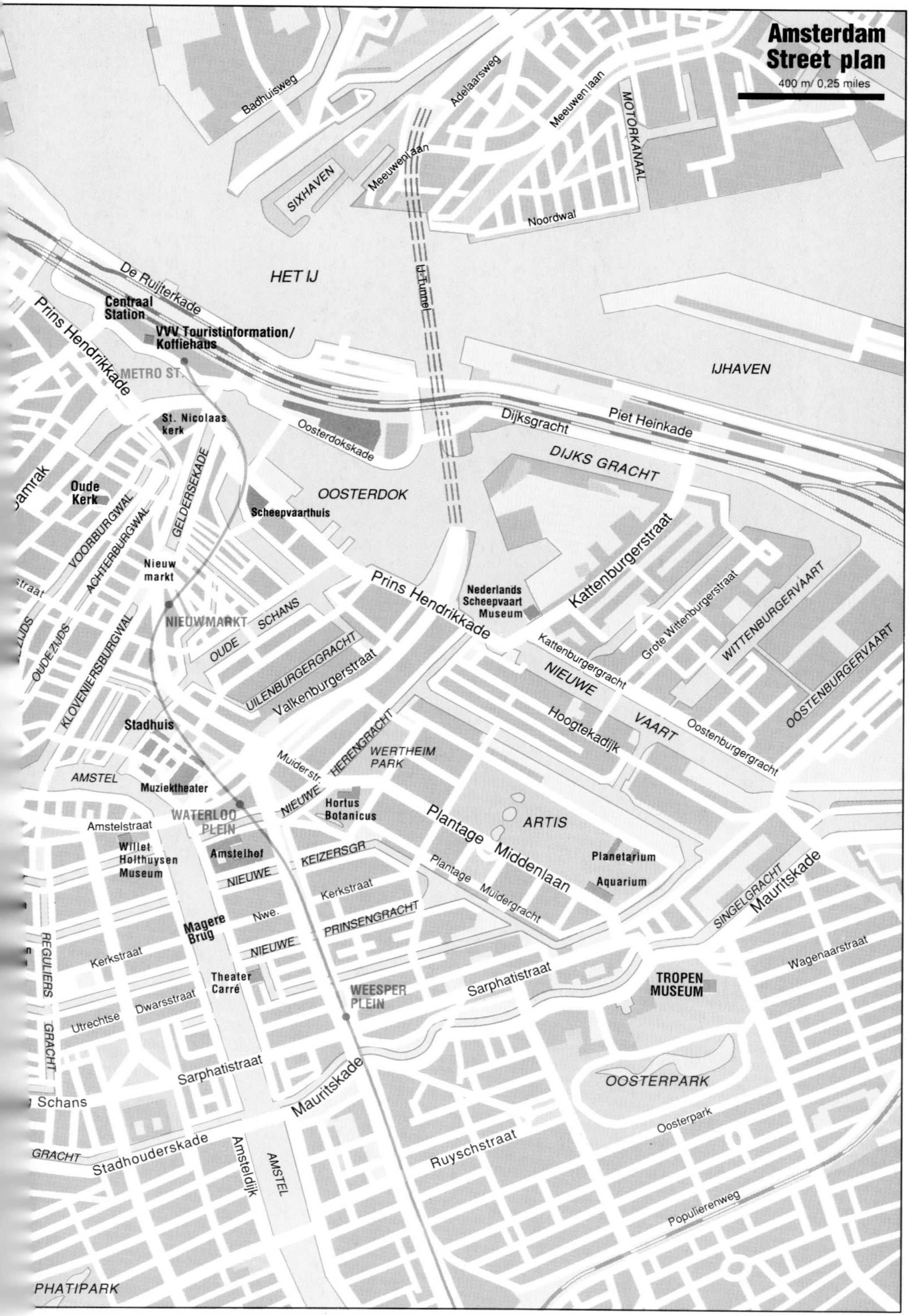
Amsterdam
Street plan
400 m/ 0,25 miles
Badhuisweg
Adelaarsweg
Meeuwenlaan
MOTORKANAAL
SIXHAVEN
Meeuwenlaan
Noordwal
HET IJ
IJ-Tunnel
De Ruijterkade
Centraal
Station
VVV Touristinformation/
Koffiehaus
Prins Hendrikkade
METRO ST.
IJHAVEN
Dijksgracht
Piet Heinkade
St. Nicolaas
kerk
Oosterdokskade
DIJKS GRACHT
GELDERSEKADE
OOSTERDOK
Oude
Kerk
VOORBURGWAL
ACHTERBURGWAL
Scheepvaarthuis
Kattenburgerstraat
Nieuw
markt
Prins Hendrikkade
Nederlands
Scheepvaart
Museum
Grote Wittenburgerstraat
WITTENBURGERVAART
NIEUWMARKT
OUDE
SCHANS
OUDEZIJDS
KLOVENIERSBURGWAL
UILENBURGERGRACHT
Valkenburgerstraat
Kattenburgergracht
NIEUWE
VAART
Hoogtekadijk
Oostenburgergracht
OOSTENBURGERVAART
Stadhuis
Muiderstr.
HERENGRACHT
WERTHEIM
PARK
AMSTEL
Muziektheater
WATERLOO
PLEIN
NIEUWE
Hortus
Botanicus
Plantage Middenlaan
ARTIS
Amstelstraat
Willet
Holthuysen
Museum
Amstelhof
KEIZERSGR
NIEUWE
Planetarium
Plantage Muidergracht
Aquarium
Kerkstraat
SINGELGRACHT
Mauritskade
Magere
Brug
Nwe.
PRINSENGRACHT
NIEUWE
REGULIERS
GRACHT
Kerkstraat
Wagenaarstraat
Theater
Carré
WEESPER
PLEIN
Sarphatistraat
TROPEN
MUSEUM
Utrechtse
Dwarsstraat
Sarphatistraat
OOSTERPARK
Schans
Mauritskade
GRACHT
Stadhouderskade
Amsteldijk
AMSTEL
Ruyschstraat
Oosterpark
Populierenweg
PHATIPARK

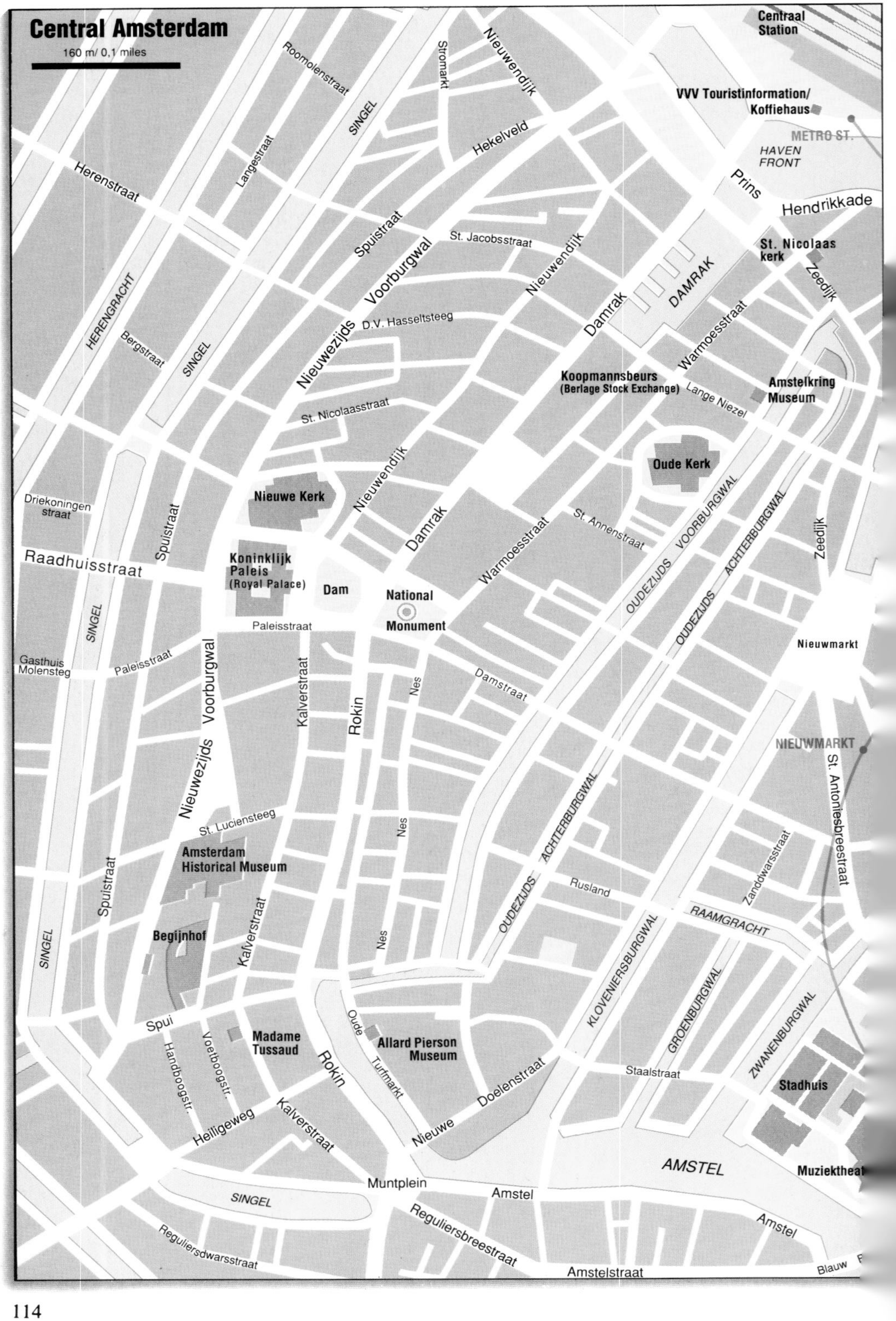
Central Amsterdam
160 m/ 0,1 miles
Centraal Station
VVV Touristinformation/ Koffiehaus
METRO ST.
HAVEN FRONT
Prins Hendrikkade
St. Nicolaas kerk
Zeedijk
Roomolenstraat
Stromarkt
Nieuwendijk
SINGEL
Hekelveld
Langestraat
Herenstraat
Spuistraat
Nieuwezijds Voorburgwal
St. Jacobsstraat
DAMRAK
Damrak
Warmoesstraat
HERENGRACHT
Bergstraat
D.V. Hasseltsteeg
Koopmannsbeurs (Berlage Stock Exchange)
Lange Niezel
Amstelkring Museum
St. Nicolaasstraat
Oude Kerk
Driekoningen straat
Nieuwe Kerk
St. Annenstraat
OUDEZIJDS VOORBURGWAL
OUDEZIJDS ACHTERBURGWAL
Raadhuisstraat
Koninklijk Paleis (Royal Palace)
Dam
National Monument
Paleisstraat
Gasthuis Molensteg
Kalverstraat
Rokin
Nes
Damstraat
Nieuwmarkt
NIEUWMARKT
St. Antoniesbreestraat
St. Luciensteeg
Amsterdam Historical Museum
Rusland
Zanddwarsstraat
RAAMGRACHT
Begijnhof
KLOVENIERSBURGWAL
GROENBURGWAL
ZWANENBURGWAL
Spui
Madame Tussaud
Oude Turfmarkt
Allard Pierson Museum
Handboogstr.
Voetboogstr.
Heiligeweg
Nieuwe Doelenstraat
Staalstraat
Stadhuis
AMSTEL
Muziektheat
Muntplein
Amstel
Reguliersbreestraat
Reguliersdwarsstraat
Amstelstraat
Blauw

Central Amsterdam

Standing in Dam square today, it is tempting to try and block out the trams, cars and pedestrians for a moment and conjure up a romantic mental image of a medieval settlement built around a dam set back from the shoreline of the Zuider Zee. That ancient dam, of course, lives on in name only. But the very idea of it begs a few moments of mental reconstruction on the part of every visitor. Was it ever easier to imagine the way a modern European city looked right at the beginning?

The first dam: The dam of old was built across the Amstel river sometime in the 13th century and proved to be the catalyst for rapid growth. By 1546 Amsterdam was a town of 14,000 people, an important transit point for Baltic grain and a place where tolls were paid on beer from Germany. One of the first clear pictures we have of Amsterdam is a town plan, dating from 1544 and drawn by the cartographer Cornelis Anthoniszoon (see illustration, page 29). This "three-dimensional" view of the city shows the Amstel river flowing freely through the heart of Amsterdam, emerging beyond Dam square as the Damrak. This final stretch of water extended all the way to the harbour, each bank crowded with small boats.

oninklijk Royal) alace, Dam uare.

Much of that central waterway has since been built over and the Dam—Amsterdam's heart—is now landlocked. All that is left on the harbour side of the Dam today is a small cul-de-sac of water opposite the Central Railway Station. It still shares the same name as the street beside it, Damrak. But the cargo boats of old have been replaced by motorised canal boats which take tourists on nostalgic trips through Amsterdam's past. In the other direction, beyond the Dam to the south, the Amstel comes to a halt opposite the eastern end of Spui.

Historic centre: The Dam has always been the heart of what was destined to become a mighty city and at different times much of Amsterdam's public life took place here. One of the original medieval buildings is the Nieuwe Kerk, first mentioned in 1400 and still dominating Dam square today. Two other historic buildings—the old Town Hall and the Weigh House—have disappeared but are depicted in many surviving paintings and are familiar elements in the historic townscape.

The medieval Town Hall, with its squat tower, was a symbol of municipal independence and a busy administrative centre. This was where burgomasters made decisions affecting the city and the Republic. The meeting place of sheriffs and aldermen, it also housed the Exchange Bank, one of the most powerful financial organisations (at the time) in the world.

Ships and lighters: The Weigh House was constructed in 1565 and was the city's first large Renaissance-style building. Because navigation by small boats was possible from the seaward side as far as the Dam, this area was a busy trading centre. Goods arrived by sea but the river mouth was blocked off by a long line of stakes stretching across the shallow bay in the IJ. This meant that ships reaching Amsterdam dropped anchor just outside and their cargo was transferred in lighters which offloaded near the Dam.

During Amsterdam's heyday, all goods weighing more than 50 lbs (23 kg) had to be recorded at the Weigh House. In the Amsterdam Historical Museum are some of the many contemporary pictures showing scenes of busy activity with porters pushing wheelbarrows across Dam square.

Another of Amsterdam's important early buildings was the 17th-century exchange building constructed across the river. The Rokin was the name given to the stretch of the River Amstel which stood behind it. Barges departed with goods along the Amstel to the other major towns in Holland. Merchants came from all over the world to do business at the exchange. Depicted in many paintings of the time, the building was erected between 1608 and 1611 but demolished in 1838.

New Town Hall: The scene at the Dam changed with the construction of the new Town Hall, the great building flanking the west side of the Dam today, which has since come to serve as the Royal Palace. This new edifice was completed in 1655 and expressed the glory of what was by then one of the world's most powerful cities. Work began in 1648 with 13,659 piles being driven into the ground to provide foundations. While it was under construction, the old Town Hall burnt down. Rembrandt provided a record of the scene when, curiously, he drew the old building in ruins, rather than the new one rising beside it.

The Dam was now an even more imposing hub. Executions were usually carried out on a scaffold in front of the new Town Hall. On such occasions the

Dam square festivities.

"staff of justice" was publicly displayed in one of the Town Hall windows. The corpses were taken to the gallows across the water of the IJ where they were hung as a warning to those who entered Amsterdam by ship.

The Dam continued to provide a busy focus for the city well into the 19th century and countless paintings and engravings show how it looked at various times. For a long time it was a fish market. A painting in the Amsterdam Historical Museum, for example, entitled *Dancing Round the Tree of Freedom at the Dam Square, 19 June 1795*, shows a long line of boats drawn right up to the edge of the 16th-century Weigh House.

The Weigh House itself, however, suffered an ignoble fate when in 1808 it was demolished at the order of King Louis Napoleon who, having made his headquarters in the new Town Hall, found that the building obstructed his view. Only the weather vane and a wooden statue have survived—they too are on display in the Amsterdam Historical Museum.

Organs and buskers: The Dam is still a hive of activity. On Saturdays especially it provides an impromptu stage for buskers, barrel-organs or street performers. In the summer, this large open space has even played host to noisy and colourful funfairs. And it does, after all, hold two of the city's major buildings—the former Town Hall, now the **Royal Palace**, and the **Nieuwe Kerk**.

With such a grand name as "the Royal Palace" you would expect this to be one of Amsterdam's top attractions. But it's not. The Royal Palace hides its light under a bushel. The problem is one of highly restricted opening hours—outside the tourist season it sometimes opens only two or three times a month. And access is from the rear, opposite the Post Office. First-time visitors to Amsterdam, happening upon what appears to be a disused building, can be forgiven for not including it on their itineraries.

The exterior is hardly palatial in any

Fairground organ, Damrak.

case. It was constructed with imported stone, a Dutch application of the classical style then recently revived in Italy. The splendid, ornate interior, however, is a different matter, redolent of the power that Amsterdam enjoyed during its Golden Age. When Louis Napoleon quit his residence at the Royal Palace he left behind a rich collection of Empire furniture, clocks and chandeliers. All this makes a visit highly worthwhile. Out of season, it is even worth planning a trip to Amsterdam to coincide with the few times the Royal Palace is open.

The New Church: More rewarding, and more accessible, is the **Nieuwe Kerk**, which dubs itself "an indoor extension of the Dam square". In terms of its historical importance and new role as an arts centre, the claim is easily justified.

By 1400 the construction of the Nieuwe Kerk had already begun; at that time the building was dedicated to the Virgin and St Catherine. Around 1500 the church was enlarged to its present size and decorated with paintings, sacred images and altars. After the Great Fire of 1645 the Nieuwe Kerk, by then in Protestant hands, was refurnished with elegant pews for the gentry, a copper gate in front of the choir and a highly decorative pulpit. Jacob van Campen, the architect of the Royal Palace on Dam square, designed the housing for the enormous organ.

Through its many tombs and monuments to maritime heroes and poets, the church acquired national importance. Among the numerous famous Amsterdammers buried here are the naval hero Admiral Michiel Adriaensz de Ruyter (died 1676) and the 17th-century poet Joost van den Vondel (died 1679).

The investiture of Dutch monarchs has taken place here since 1841. On these occasions the States General (the joint houses of Parliament) convenes in Amsterdam instead of The Hague. The last time this took place was in 1980 when Queen Beatrix took the constitutional oath. Since a recent restoration the church has been run by a foundation with a policy of putting the building to the widest possible use. Concerts, discussions and exhibitions have brought a new lease of life to this ancient ecclesiastical building and transformed the Nieuwe Kirk into a meeting place, where people can gather together to talk, to look and to listen.

History lessons: The city gives its best history lesson at the **Amsterdam Historical Museum**, a short walk south of the Dam. The museum's quiet courtyard location off Kalverstraat is reason enough to go—the museum occupies 17th-century buildings that were once home to the Civic Orphanage. More to the point, it puts Amsterdam's colourful history into quick perspective, making subsequent walks around town more informative and enjoyable.

Don't be put off by the fact that most of the captions are in Dutch. The museum provides useful booklets in other languages that will help you make sense of the exhibits and there are some explanatory panels in English. Many ex-

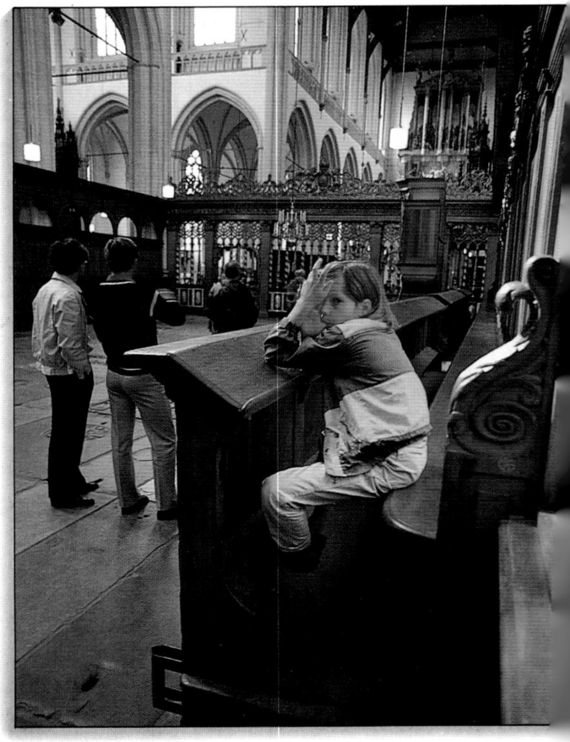
Nieuwe Kerk.

hibits need little explanation anyway. One of the best is an illuminated flat plan of Amsterdam that shows clearly how the city grew. Starting in the year 1050, a light picks out each 25-year period down through the centuries and simultaneously illuminates the relevant phase of the city's growth.

The museum offers an excellent survey of the history of Amsterdam from the mid-13th century to the present. Given that the richest source of archives has come from the 17th and 18th centuries, the collection naturally concentrates on those periods. It is particularly strong on the era of Dutch maritime exploration. A wide selection of paintings depicts all of the city's historic landmarks as they appeared in their contemporary cityscapes.

Civic dignitaries: The passageway from the Amsterdam Historical Museum to the Begijnhof is a modest history lesson in itself and a sudden unexpected art gallery as well. Hung along the walls are the oversized canvases of the Amsterdam civic guard, posing in attitudes of grandiose self-importance.

The civic guard originated at the end of the 14th century, when Amsterdam marksmen began joining together for civic defence and to help maintain public order. They founded three guilds: St George's for the crossbowmen; St Sebastian's for the archers, and the Guild of Harquebusiers, armed with early firearms. Each had its own meeting place, with rooms for social and business gatherings and a shooting range in the garden.

Around 1530, the civic guard companies began to commission group portraits to hang in their guildhouses. The annual banquet was a favourite occasion for such paintings. The portraits grew larger and livelier over the years and culminated in the enormous canvases of the 17th century.

The guilds were merged in 1580 with other groups of militiamen drafted from Amsterdam's 11 municipal districts. In 1672, the old guilds were dissolved and

Amsterdam Historical Museum.

the civic guard was re-organised. After 1650, no more group portraits were commissioned. Of all those painted in Amsterdam, some 50 have been preserved—the largest collection of paintings in this genre in existence.

The passageway serves as a link to the second part of the museum, where the displays bring the history of Amsterdam up to date; paintings and photographs reveal the reasons why the city developed progressive welfare programmes from the mid-19th century and coped with the problems of unemployment during the 1930s depression. The permanent exhibits are supplemented by temporary displays used to illustrate themes as diverse as homosexuality and the diamond industry.

Ancient courtyards: Next door to the museum is the **Begijnhof**, a magnificent diamond-shaped cobblestone courtyard of 17th-century buildings, and easily the most picturesque place you can visit in Amsterdam's centre. The freshly painted houses with their bright window boxes, the cast-iron lamp posts, and an unexpected air of solitude and tranquillity, make it difficult to believe that the city's busiest shopping street, Kalverstraat, is just a minute away.

There are many *hofjes* (little courtyards) in Amsterdam and this is not only the best known but the easiest to reach. The Begijnhof was founded in 1346 as a cloister-like home for Catholic lay sisters. In 1578, with the Reformation sweeping over Holland, all the Catholic churches became Protestant, including the one standing within the Begijnhof and now known as the English Reformed Church. This is not the only church here for the courtyard is also home to the concealed Begijnhof Catholic church. Most of the houses date from the 17th century and are built of stone. One of the last two wooden houses remaining in Amsterdam, dating from around 1550, has been moved to within the walls of the Begijnhof (the other is at Zeedijk 1).

The Begijnhof.

You might have a little trouble finding the Begijnhof (you can also gain access from Spui) but you'll know soon enough when you are in **Kalverstraat**, one of Amsterdam's busiest shopping streets. On Saturdays any month of the year this pedestrian-only boulevard is impossibly crowded.

The fact that Kalverstraat is home to Madame Tussaud's waxworks is proof of just how commercial this mall is. Whether or not you take this opportunity to be "face to face with fame" or join "the millions of people who have visited Madame Tussaud in Amsterdam since it opened in 1970" is up to you.

Archaeology: If you are in a serious frame of mind you might head instead for the **Allard Pierson Museum**, just a two-minute walk away on Oude Turfmarkt. You will gain no specific insights about Amsterdam here. This museum contains the archaeological collection from the University of Amsterdam. Finds from Egypt, the Near East, Iran, Greece, Tuscany and the Roman Empire make for an academic but nevertheless captivating display that occupies two floors.

If you exit from Kalverstraat, in the direction of the Central Station, you will find yourself in **Nieuwendijk**, another pedestrianised shopping street but with a distinctly downmarket feel. The denim here is more faded than in Kalverstraat. The fast food is faster. And sex is creeping into the shopscape here as elsewhere in Amsterdam. Venture along Nieuwendijk only if you are in need of a live peep show or a direct route to the Central Station.

Nearby, parallel to Nieuwendijk, **Damrak** doesn't do much better. Souvenir stores, amusement arcades, cheap restaurants and cheap hotels catch the eye. Across the road, however, the long profile of the **Beurs** is a different story.

Monumental architecture: This was one of the few large building projects undertaken in the last half of the 19th century and it replaced the Exchange Building that dated from 1611. The Beurs sprang

Berlage Stock Exchange.

in 1896 from the brain of one of Holland's most famous architects, Hendrik Petrus Berlage. For many years the Beurs, also known as the Berlage Stock Exchange, was considered the most important Dutch architectural monument of the *fin de siècle* period. The stockbrokers have since moved away and the building is now used for concerts and exhibitions.

The three sections of this long building give you ample opportunity to peep inside. The southern section of the building—the old Produce Exchange Hall—is administered by Stichting de Beurs van Berlage (the Berlage Stock Exchange Foundation), which puts on a variety of exhibitions, cultural events, conferences and dinners. Since 1987, more than 20 Dutch companies have exhibited works from their modern art collections in this building.

The northern part of the building has been occupied by the Netherlands Philharmonic Orchestra since 1988. The one-time Shipping Exchange was thus transformed into a magnificent concert hall. At the front of the building, the Berlage Hall—formerly the meeting place of the Chamber of Commerce—has retained its elaborate murals and today serves as a chic café.

The best time to view the southern section is during an exhibition—and if you have any kind of interest in architecture or design the Beurs is definitely worth visiting. Its cavernous and echoing interior is an impressive mix of pastel-coloured decorative brickwork, wooden flooring, stone pillars and steel roof girders from which hang long pendular globe-shaped lights. Around the periphery of the hall, small wooden cubicles, where deals were made, are a reminder of the building's original function as an exchange.

Around the station: The **Central Station**, north of the Beurs, dominates the Damrak in a different way—it blocks off the view over the harbour (something which stirred up controversy during its construction at the end of the 19th

Central Station and the Koffiehuis.

century). The terminus was built along the original line marked by the palisade of stakes that once stopped larger ships trying to enter Damrak. Back-packing tourists and Amsterdam commuters crowd the Stationsplein daily. Tram stops, snack bars, litter, bicycles and buskers set the scene here and, for anybody arriving by train, Stationsplein is unfortunately an untidy introduction to the historic heart of Amsterdam.

Apart from the monumental sculptures that adorn the station building, the only other reason for anybody to come this way is for the VVV tourist office, situated in the **Noord-Zuid Hollands Koffiehuis**, opposite the station. The ornate wooden coffee house, with its terrace overlooking the water, was built in 1911. It is what you could call a born-again meeting place, for the terrace was demolished to make way for the metro in the 1970s but the pretty Koffiehuis building was reinstated in 1981 following popular demand.

Patron of seafarers: Not far from Stationsplein, however, there are several places that are worth visiting. All of these lie in the direction of **St Nicolaaskerk**, across the road to the east (left) as you emerge from the station. St Nicholas is the patron saint of sailors and the proximity of this church to the harbour easily explains the dedication. Built in 1887 in neo-baroque style, the interior is a striking mix of black marble pillars and wooden barrel vaulting. Other than that, the church has little to offer and restricted opening hours do little to attract visitors.

Past St Nicolaaskerk and left along **Zeedijk** is one of only two remaining timber houses in Amsterdam. This house, with its gabled roof, dates from around 1550. Originally the house was clad with vertical oak boarding but oak became so scarce that, when the house was renovated, the facade was covered with horizontal pine boarding.

Not far away is another example of a well-preserved historic building. **D'Leeuwenburgh House**, on Oude Zijds Voorburgwal, is a fine example of early 17th-century architecture: a steep-gabled house dating from 1605 with a basement projecting out on to the street. The gable shows the arms of Riga, which points to trade relations with this Baltic port.

Hidden church: Another place in the centre of Amsterdam you should certainly visit is the **Museum Amstelkring**, just a few yards further along from D'Leeuwenburgh House. This is one of many clandestine churches that flourished in Amsterdam in the 17th century. Its discreet entrance right next door to the Red Light District means that, even today, it has managed to hide itself from view and it attracts nothing like the stream of visitors that justifiably flood to "sights" such as the Anne Frank Huis.

From the time of the Alteration in 1578 (the changeover from a Catholic to a Protestant city council in Amsterdam), Catholics were compelled to hold their religious gatherings secretly, in

striking
hurch: St
icolaaskerk.

domestic rooms, an attic or a barn. Around 1650 Catholic worshippers began to build clandestine churches, which in time were enlarged and heightened by the addition of galleries resting on pillars.

There used to be scores of clandestine churches in Amsterdam. Wealthy merchants such as Jacob van Loon and Aernout van der Mye, who in 1662 were immortalised in Rembrandt's painting called *The Syndics*, were among the owners of these houses of worship hidden behind simple domestic exteriors.

Best-preserved: In 1661 a gentleman by the name of Jan Hartman started building a residence on the Oude Zijds Voorburgwal, together with two adjoining houses in the Heintje Hoecksteeg. He furnished the combined attics of these three houses as a church. Although recent investigations have brought to light the remains of former attic churches in various Amsterdam houses, nowhere else in the Netherlands has so well preserved a clandestine church as the Amstelkring been found.

Over the years Hartman's buildings underwent various alterations but the **Sael** (living room) is still preserved in all its 17th-century sobriety and beauty: the combined coat of arms of Jan Hartman and his wife stands forth proudly above the imposing fireplace.

The church was separate from the house proper, with its entrance in the side alley, and for more than two centuries this served as a parish church. In the beginning, when the church was smaller, the officiating priest lived in a room in Hartman's family house. Around 1740 the church was enlarged and a new altar was built, while the priest moved into the house itself.

This situation continued until St Nikolaaskerk, near the Central Station, was completed. From 1888, when the house was opened as a museum, this building has been known as *Ons Lieve Heer op Solder* (Our Lord in the Attic).

Open secret: It is difficult to imagine

Amstelkring Museum.

how anybody could have carried on clandestine services here. With 60 seats spreading back from the altar and additional seats in a further two storeys of galleries above, more than 150 people would have been easily accommodated. Neither does the church organ compromise on size. A full congregation singing the praises of the Lord would have been as discreet as a claustrophobic bull locked in a barn. The arrival and departure of 150 people would have been equally difficult to conceal. The truth is that the existence of these churches was often an open secret, though they had to be unobtrusive enough for the city to be able to turn a blind eye.

Fine statuary, ecclesiastical paintings, a Roman Catholic liturgical collection and 17th and 18th-century furniture make this church all the more worth visiting. Do not let the sombre "museum" sign outside on the street deter you from investigating. The Museum Amstelkring is one of central Amsterdam's best-kept secrets.

On the other hand the **Oude Kerk**, just south by two blocks in Oude Kerksplein, can be one of the most difficult buildings in Amsterdam to enter. Do go in, if you are lucky enough to find it open when you are passing. This is the city's oldest church, begun in 1200, though the present Gothic structure dates to a rebuilding of the 14th century.

Beautiful paintings survive on the wooden roof vaults, including pictures of ships, reminding us that the church is dedicated to St Nicholas, patron saint of sailors. The stained glass in the north choir, showing scenes from the life of the Virgin, dates from 1555 and the misericords of the choir stalls are carved with lively scenes from fable.

The graceful spire was built in 1565 and you can usually climb to the top in summer (open Mon and Thurs 2–5 p.m., Tues and Weds 11 a.m.–2 p.m.). If you happen to be here on a Saturday, listen out for the beautiful 17th-century carillon of bells, which is played between 4 and 5 p.m.

Left, ***Ons Lieve Heer op Solder*** **(Our Lord in the Attic). Right, Oude Kerk.**

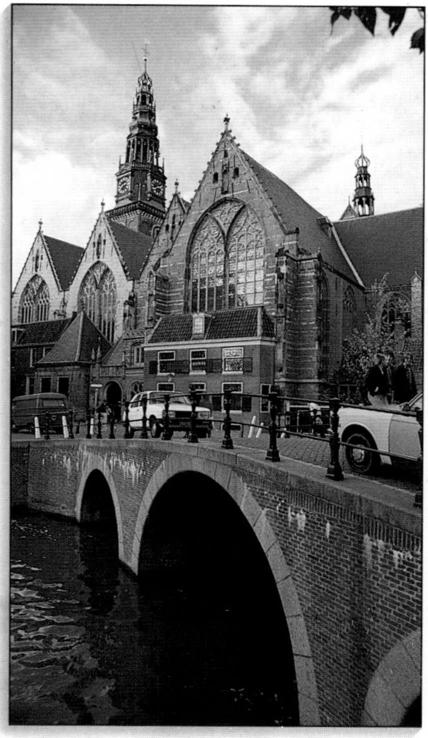

CANTHAR
PRODUKT
THEAT

WALBURGA ABDIJ

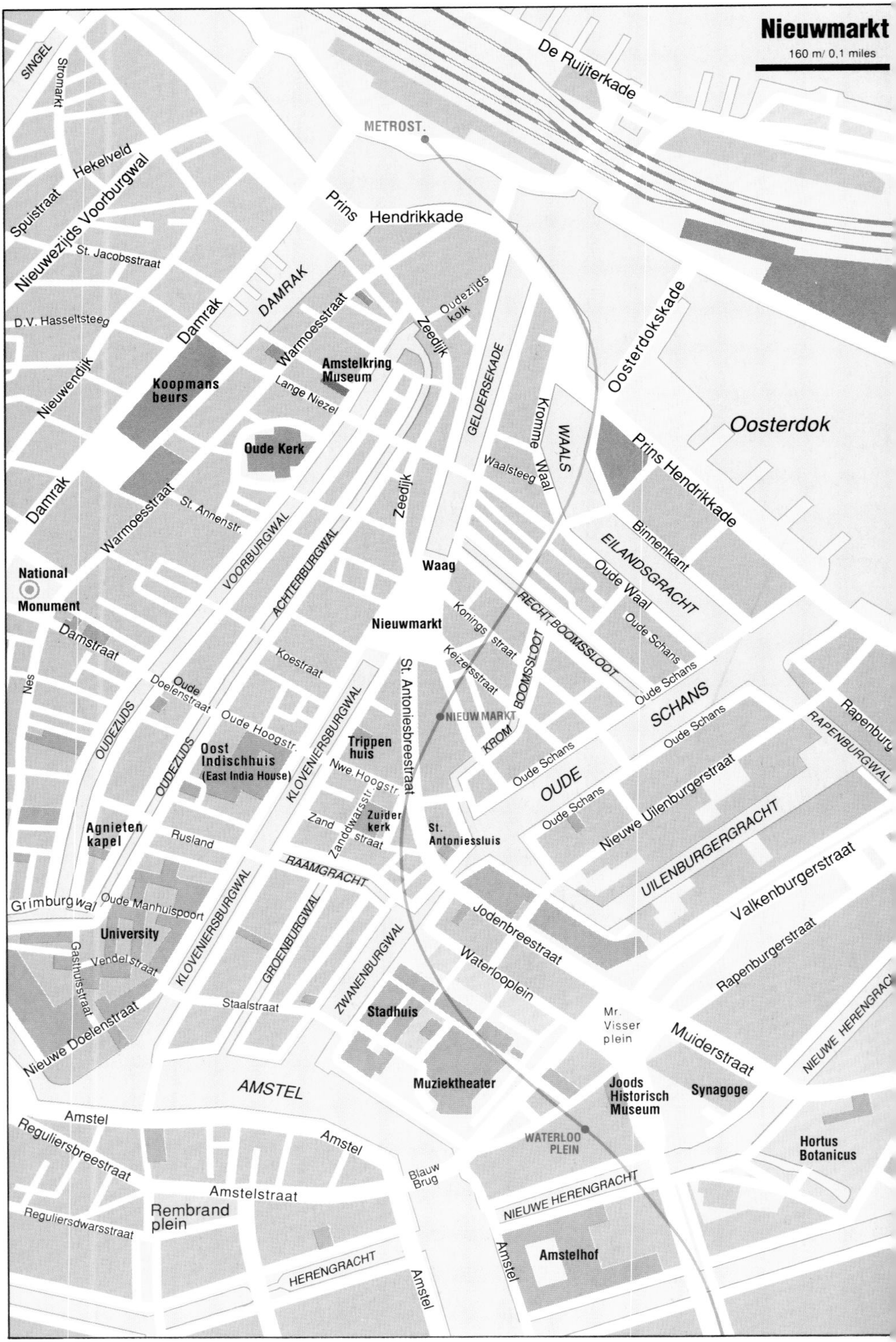
Nieuwmarkt
160 m/ 0,1 miles
De Ruijterkade
METROST.
Singel
Stromarkt
Hekelveld
Spuistraat
Nieuwezijds Voorburgwal
Prins Hendrikkade
St. Jacobsstraat
DAMRAK
Damrak
D.V. Hasseltsteeg
Warmoesstraat
Amstelkring Museum
Oudezijds kolk
Zeedijk
GELDERSEKADE
Oosterdokskade
Oosterdok
Koopmans beurs
Lange Niezel
Nieuwendijk
Oude Kerk
Kromme Waal
WAALS
Waalsteeg
Prins Hendrikkade
St. Annenstr.
VOORBURGWAL
ACHTERBURGWAL
Binnenkant
EILANDSGRACHT
Oude Waal
Waag
National Monument
Nieuwmarkt
Konings straat
RECHT BOOMSSLOOT
Oude Schans
Damstraat
Koestraat
Keizersstraat
BOOMSSLOOT
Oude Schans
SCHANS
Rapenburg
RAPENBURGWAL
Nes
Oude Doelenstraat
Oude Hoogstr.
KLOVENIERSBURGWAL
St. Antoniesbreestraat
NIEUW MARKT
KROM
OUDEZIJDS
Oost Indischhuis (East India House)
Trippen huis
Oude Schans
OUDE
Oude Schans
Nieuwe Uilenburgerstraat
Nwe. Hoogstr.
Zand straat
Zanddwarsstr.
Zuider kerk
St. Antoniessluis
UILENBURGERGRACHT
Agnieten kapel
Rusland
RAAMGRACHT
Valkenburgerstraat
Grimburgwal
Oude Manhuispoort
University
GROENBURGWAL
Jodenbreestraat
Gasthuisstraat
Vendelstraat
KLOVENIERSBURGWAL
ZWANENBURGWAL
Waterlooplein
Rapenburgerstraat
Staalstraat
Stadhuis
Mr. Visser plein
NIEUWE HERENGRACHT
Nieuwe Doelenstraat
Muiderstraat
AMSTEL
Muziektheater
Joods Historisch Museum
Synagoge
Amstel
Reguliersbreestraat
Amstel
WATERLOO PLEIN
Hortus Botanicus
Blauw Brug
Amstelstraat
NIEUWE HERENGRACHT
Rembrand plein
Reguliersdwarsstraat
Amstel
Amstelhof
HERENGRACHT
Amstel

NIEUWMARKT

Sex and drugs, noise and neon, antiques and old books, first-class Thai food and a mini Chinatown, one of Amsterdam's oldest medieval buildings and the brave new face of 1970s re-development, photogenic Staalstraat and the seedy alleys of Zeedijk; Nieuwmarkt presents an eclectic menu.

Nieuwmarkt proper is a small market place that sits between the two canals of Kloveniersburgwal and Geldersekade. But walk a few minutes in any direction into the surrounding neighbourhood and you'll see that Nieuwmarkt is much more than this. Head to the northwest for the Red Light District. Make your way down Oude Zijds Achterburgwal and you are in one of Amsterdam's centres of learning, made busy by books and bicycles. Go southeast and you are in St Antoniesbreestraat, a redeveloped street that leads into Amsterdam's historic Jewish quarter. Walk northeast to the tree-lined canals of Kromboomsloot and Rechtboomsloot and you will find a discreet and tranquil neighbourhood that seems a long way removed from the modernism of St Antoniesbreestraat and the brash and illicit hedonism of the Red Light District.

eceding ages: Le oudoir, ude Zijds chterburg-al. Below, ea market Nieuw-arkt.

Centre of protest: Start out at the wide square of **Nieuwmarkt**. This was at one time a fish market, supplied by boats that would tie up at the southern end of Geldersekade. Today, Nieuwmarkt looks run-down and uninteresting, enlivened only briefly by an antique market held in front of the Waag on Sundays.

The neighbourhood around Nieuwmarkt suffered severely with the construction of Amsterdam's metro system, which runs from the Central Station out into the southeastern suburbs. In protest against the large number of houses around Nieuwmarkt that had to be demolished, squatters moved in. It took attacks by riot police to clear the way for the bulldozers. The city-wide protest movement against the metro was loudest around Nieuwmarkt; the station itself (on J.B. Siebbeleshof) recalls these events with depictions of the demolition work and the wider history of this area.

Chequered history: The bulky form of the **Waag**, Amsterdam's largest medieval building, has experienced its own share of redevelopment. The Waag started life as a turreted gateway, originally known as St Anthoniespoort and built in 1488 as part of the city walls. By the end of the 16th century, the city was expanding rapidly and the gate was redundant so it was rebuilt around 1619, as a weigh house for checking the weight of ships' anchors and ordnance.

The octagonal tower at the centre wasn't added until around 1690; it served as the dissecting room (Theatrum Anatomicum) where the Surgeons' Guild gave anatomy lessons. The guild commissioned Rembrandt's famous painting *The Anatomy Lesson of Dr Nicolaas Tulp* (now in the Mauritshaus Gallery in The Hague) and other pictures on similar subjects. In more modern times the Waag housed the Amsterdam Historical Museum, then the Jewish Historical Museum and it is now being refurbished yet again.

Many of the buildings on **St Antoniesbreestraat**, one of the few modern streets of central Amsterdam, were designed by architects Theo Bos and Aldo van Eyck. This area, too, has seen city planners do battle with conservationists. The Jewish quarter, which really begins with Jodenbreestraat, was dramatically changed by construction work in the 1970s. Plans to develop St Antoniesbreestraat to match the newly widened Weesperstraat and Jodenbreestraat placed the much-prized 17th-century **De Pinto House** (at No. 69) under threat of demolition.

Isaac de Pinto, a Portuguese Jew who fled first to Antwerp and then to Holland to escape the Inquisition, was one of Amsterdam's wealthiest bankers. He bought this building in 1651. Subsequent alterations nearly 30 years later gave it a number of painted panels and ceilings as well as an ornate exterior in the style of the Italian Renaissance.

Victory: Public opinion against the initial redevelopment won the day. The De Pinto House was saved and plans to make this road suitable for heavy traffic were shelved. This building is now a branch of the public library and visitors are allowed inside. Fittingly, the De Pinto House is home to a special section dealing with the protection of ancient monuments and city-centre restoration.

Less than a minute's walk further south from the De Pinto House is **St Antoniessluis**, which provides a clear view all the way down to the Montelbaanstoren. St Antoniessluis was once a market place with a good share of street traders from the flourishing Jewish community east of Oude Schans and south of Jodenbreestraat. The presence of the market did not signify tolerance of Jewish neighbours. A petition by the non-Jewish inhabitants of St Antoniesbreestraat in 1750 asked that the city should find a separate living space for Jews, saying that "their shabbiness put the Christians who live in that district to the greatest inconvenience".

From St Antoniessluis, Zandstraat leads to **Zuiderkerk**, the first Protestant church to be built in Amsterdam. It was completed in 1611 and its architect, Hendrick de Keyser, lies buried within. The church itself is not open to the public but you can climb the tower between June and September for views over the whole Nieuwmarkt district.

City mansions: Along Kloveniersburgwal, the canal south of Nieuwmarkt, are four historic buildings that date from Amsterdam's Golden Age. At Nos. 10–12 Koestraat is the **Wijnkopersgildehuis** (House of the Winebuyers' Guild)—actually three 17th-century buildings converted into one residence. A more substantial landmark, on the eastern side of Kloveniersburgwal, at No. 29, is the grand facade of the **Trippenhuis**, designed in

Zuiderkerk spire.

1660 by Justus Vingboons for Louis and Hendrick Trip. The Trip family owned large iron and copper mines and cannon foundries in Sweden. In acknowledgment of the owners' trade, the two chimneys on the roof were made to resemble mortars.

Even though the Trippenhuis has a single facade it once concealed two separate dwellings, one for each of the Trip brothers. The effect to the outside world was of a single grand household. Two main doorways at street level, however, provided separate access. The Trippenhuis was converted into one unit in 1815 to accommodate the forerunner to the Rijksmuseum.

Servants' quarters: On the other side of the canal, at No. 26 Kloveniersburgwal, is the **Kleine Trippenhuis**, also known as the "House of Mr Trip's Coachman". The story that Mr Trip's coachman said he would be content with a home no wider than the front door of the Trippenhuis is probably apocryphal. Another version says the little house was built with stone left over from the Trippenhuis. In any event, at just over 3 ft (1 metre) across, the Kleine Trippenhuis is modesty itself.

If you go a little further south along Kloveniersburgwal and turn right into Oude Hoogstraat you can enter the courtyard of the **Oostindische Huis** (East India House). The house was built in the 16th century and rented to the Dutch East India Company in 1603. Today part of it is used by the University of Amsterdam. On the same street, Kok Boeken is a large antiquarian bookshop on two floors selling a wide selection of old prints and maps.

Fine prospect: At the very southern end of Kloveniersburgwal you reach **Staalstraat**. A photogenic view of Zuiderkerk is to be had from the bridge that links the two sides of this street across Groenburgwal.

Staalstraat itself is one of Amsterdam's many picturesque "film-set" streets, a stark contrast to the modern architecture that looms into view at the

ast India ouse, Oude oogstraat.

Zwanenburgwal end. A smart Thai restaurant, a cosy bookshop, and a chic coffee shop make Staalstraat even more attractive. The linen trade once flourished here and at No. 7b Staalstraat sergeworkers met in the 17th-century Saaihal (Serge Hall). The stained-glass windows decorated with laboratory motifs originate from the 19th century when the Saaihal was occupied by the chemical laboratory of the Athenaeum Illustre, a forerunner to the University of Amsterdam.

Academic centre: Back on Kloveniersburgwal, a passageway leads off to the left on to Oude Zijds Achterburgwal. This is **Oudemannhuispoort** (Old Men's Home Gate), a covered arcade of antiquarian bookstalls—you'll find some of these open everyday but Saturday is busiest. Halfway along is a courtyard of late 18th-century buildings, originally used as almshouses for accommodating elderly men. (This was unusual because almshouses had hitherto been exclusively for women.) The University of Amsterdam has occupied these buildings since 1877.

The surrounding streets form one of the centres of Amsterdam's university life. Weekdays on Grimburgwal, a narrow street which cuts across the southern end of Oude Zijds Voorburgwal and Oude Zijds Achterburgwal, there is always a tangle of bicycles attached to the canal-side railings left by students attending lectures. Behind the Binnengasthuis (the building with the small white tower bearing the date 1875), and around Gasthuisstraat and Vendelstraat, there are a number of other university buildings.

Old schools: Amsterdam is the only city in Holland that has two universities: the University of Amsterdam and the Free University. The former has its roots in the Athenaeum Illustre, which was founded in 1632 in the **Agnietenkapel** (Agnieten Chapel) at No. 231 Oude Zijds Voorburgwal. Originally a chapel attached to the convent of St Agnes, dating back to 1470, today it houses the Historical Collection of the University of Amsterdam.

The Athenaeum originally existed to prepare students for higher schooling elsewhere but, ever since the French occupation of the Netherlands in the early 19th century, it has provided full tertiary education. The University of Amsterdam officially came into being in 1877 and today comprises a number of buildings located throughout the city centre. (The Free University is based in the southern suburbs.)

The names of the two main canals here, Voorburgwal and Achterburgwal (before and behind the city wall), refer to historic city boundaries. This southern tip of Oude Zijds Voorburgwal was nicknamed the "velvet canal", in reference to the wealthy merchants who came to live in this neighbourhood.

Another building that serves the university today is the **Huis aan de Drie Grachten** (House on the Three Canals). Built in 1609, it takes its name from the fact that it is situated at the junction of

Bargain hunting in Nieuwmarkt

Oude Zijds Achterburgwal, Oude Zijds Voorburgwal and Grimburgwal. Today it is a bookshop selling academic books on art and literature.

Red Lights: At this end of Oude Zijds Achterburgwal everybody is busy pursuing academic knowledge. Follow this canal north past a point marked by Oude Doelen Straat and Oude Hoogstraat and suddenly the pursuit of carnal knowledge is the name of the game.

Amsterdam's celebrated Red Light District is concentrated on Oude Zijds Achterburgwal but also occupies parts of Oude Zijds Voorburgwal and the alleys connecting and branching off from them. Just take six words—sex, porn, live, cabin, shop and video—and mix 'n' match; you can account in this way for most of the places of interest. There are sex shops, porn shops, live sex, video porn and video cabins everywhere. A sex museum, offering "erotic art and specialities", is another way of delivering the same product.

All of these are lit pink, purple, magenta, violet—and the canals themselves are hung with a canopy of a thousand red fairy lights reflected in the dark water below. Prostitutes in lacy underwear tempt from within their neon-lit glass-fronted cubicles. Some of the girls stand smiling, apparently full of enthusiasm, and give a sharp beckoning tap on the window if you stop for just a second. Others look shell-shocked, expressionless, stultified.

Ironies: With so much to catch your eye on these streets you could be excused for missing a couple of incongruities. Above the main entrance to the **Erotic Museum**, at Oude Zijds Achterburgwal No. 52, is a historic stone decorated with maritime motifs; it proclaims boldly *God is myn burgh* (God is my stronghold). On Oude Zijds Voorburgwal, on the other side of the canal to the Oude Kerk, is the **Amsterdam Chinese Church**, situated right next to a coffee shop with a brightly lit sex cinema below. A figure of Christ peers through the window on one side, a scantily clad prostitute touts for business on the other.

The **Hash Information Museum**, at No. 148 Oude Zijds Voorburgwal (open Fridays and Saturdays only), is a showcase of this area's other preoccupation. In the Red Light District, perhaps more than elsewhere in the city, the smell of marijuana is accompanied by the sure knowledge that harder drugs are there for the asking. This is the centre of street drug-dealing in Amsterdam.

There is a faint hint of Chinatown on the northern edge of Nieuwmarkt, around Zeedijk. Zeedijk itself traces the line of a sea-dyke which once protected Amsterdam from the sea. Even today, Zeedijk still seems to be on the edge of things—transient, seedy and furtive. Along the northern end of Warmoesstraat, on the fringe of the Red Light District, touts drum up business for cramped low-budget hostels, and there is the ubiquitous promise of hard and soft drugs. This is a downbeat way to finish your explorations.

**udemann-
uispoort
cade.**

RED LIGHT DISTRICT

It is 10 p.m. in the Bananen Bar at No. 37 Oude Zijds Achterburgwal, in the heart of Amsterdam's Red Light District. Your money buys you just 30, 45 or 60 minutes of the Bananen Bar's pleasures—and these are strictly timed. On a shelf in the foyer, your name is written on a till receipt and placed under one of around two dozen alarm clocks. Arranged in a fussy, straight line, they stand ticking under the warm glow of the neon strip light.

You step through a gap between a pair of heavy red curtains. On the other side, on a raised bar upholstered with crimson-coloured fake leather, naked girls sit cross-legged, or lie defensively on their stomachs. They serve glass after glass of free beer (as much as you can drink in the time you have purchased) and willingly negotiate additional "trick-or-treat" entertainments. Upstairs, there is a room with a mini dance floor. Chairs line the walls. The revellers—most, though not all of them, are male—eagerly await the next "show".

There are places like the Bananen Bar in many of the world's major cities and Amsterdam's Red Light District has its full quota. Its famous "windows" are more innovative. Worked on a shift basis the majority of the windows are occupied most of the day. A girl can expect to pay upwards of 100 guilders (£35/$56) for an eight-hour tenancy.

There are some houses in the Red Light District where all the floors above the ground floor are empty—the owners can make so much money from renting the ground floor for prostitution that they are prepared to give up the rest of the house. Other houses have two entrances; one leads to the upper rooms where the owners live private domestic lives, the other is controlled by the girl who rents the ground floor and plys her trade in the rooms below.

Sex is big business in Amsterdam and the Red Light District is the showcase of the city's sex emporium. When there is a big conference or exhibition at the Amsterdam RAI, there is a virtually guaranteed overspill at night into this neighbourhood. Tour groups, too, are often brought here, to attend the live sex shows and enjoying attractive group discounts into the bargain. But the Red Light District is not just for tourists—customers include many local men.

What you see is not the only sex you can get. One of Amsterdam's sex-shop chains has its mail-order headquarters on Oude Zijds Achterburgwal and exports pornography around the world. Not so widely advertised is the fact that Amsterdam is also one of Europe's biggest centres for child pornography.

Amsterdam has always prided itself on its *laissez-faire* outlook. Historically it has been tolerant of minority groups and has provided sanctuary for victims of persecution. From that perspective, its tolerance has been a strength. Maybe that tolerance has, in the Red Light District at least, been taken to such an extreme that it has become a weakness.

The neighbourhood has had its setbacks. In 1986, when AIDS had finally become a recognised fact of life in Europe, the district went into a lower gear. With fewer girls in the windows and on the streets, there was a noticeable drop-off in the number of people visiting. Some of the girls gravitated to the city's clubs and stayed there. But new girls have taken their place and, so far as sex is concerned, the Red Light District is looking forward to a rosy future again.

The story for drugs is different. There is now a strong police presence in the area. Local people protested more than once that the drug scene was too intrusive. They asked for more surveillance and since 1986 drug dealing has become more discrete. There were also economic reasons for this. Many buildings have been renovated in recent years in an attempt to make this a more desirable area. Prostitution has kept its foothold (it is colourful, it attracts tourists, and so benefits the local economy). Drugs are being chased out and the fear of AIDS has helped ease the way.

In addition, there is a strong support structure of government and religious agencies available to anyone who comes to see their lifestyle as a problem. Many of the girls have chosen their particular lifestyle because of the money it offers but, with help, some do manage to break free.

CASA ROSSO
PRESENTS
films
real fucking
live show
baiser sur scène
chiavare veramente
おまんこショー
תיאטרון זיונים
50-
75-

CANAL CIRCLE: NORTH

Amsterdam's horseshoe-shaped network of canals is, in one sense, like a fingerprint. There is only one city in the world with a street plan like this and it is instantly recognisable. The long semicircle of three parallel canals—called the Grachtengordel (literally: "canal girdle")—was part of the most ambitious piece of town planning the city has ever seen. Those three canals are probably the first of Amsterdam's place names that tourists learn. From inside moving outwards they are: Herengracht (Gentlemen's canal), Keizersgracht (Emperor's canal) and Prinsengracht (Princes' canal).

By 1600 Amsterdam was one of the most powerful trading nations in the world. For a long time the old city, with its walls and turrets, had been little more than a small horseshoe clinging to the Amstel river. Now, at the beginning of the 17th century, the medieval town that had grown up around Dam square was spilling out beyond its walled and turreted boundary. Three canals on either side of the river had already been dug to drain land for expansion. But in 1609 city planners decided to build another three large canals that would encircle the existing nucleus. Hendrick de Keyser was appointed city architect and by 1613 the plan was underway.

Starting point: It is appropriate to begin exploring these canals from the northwestern side, beyond Central Station, because construction actually started near here. This section of the canal circle is the least visited by tourists, even those who stay in the many low-budget hotels at the port end. Yet the area contained within a boundary marked by Brouwersgracht to the north and Raadhuisstraat to the south is manageable and worthwhile. It contains the Anne Frank Huis, one of the most visited places in Amsterdam, and next door, so to speak, is the Jordaan, a lively network of much narrower streets with second-hand shops, ethnic restaurants, boutiques and bookshops.

The first phase of digging took the new canals from near the port down to the bottom of the horseshoe as far as Leidsegracht. The second phase began in 1665 and the canals were extended to the Amstel. Parks were built on the opposite shore of the Amstel (the so-called Plantage) and the entire project was completed at the end of the 17th century. It was a mark of distinction to build a house on the new canals. The elegant Herengracht was the most sought after, followed in exclusiveness by the Keizersgracht. Prinsengracht and Singel had many of the warehouses and workshops. Today, in the summer, whichever part of the Grachtengordel you visit, the canals seem to form one long, leafy and peaceful suburb.

Touring by boat: You should also make a point of joining one of the canal-boat tours of the circle, so as to see the buildings from a different perspective.

'receding ages: under ed lights; on e march: e Salvation rmy; well-annered chitecture. **eft,** iderkerk. **ight,** water urs.

Some boats offer bland taped commentaries but others are hosted by knowledgeable guides who help to bring alive the history of the Grachtengordel. Walk or cycle along the canals as well, so that you can get to know the many interconnecting side alleys, which still serve their intended purpose as shopping streets, positioned at regular intervals between unbroken rows of warehouses and residences.

Preservation policy: Most of the canal-house facades which can be seen today date from the 17th and 18th centuries although the houses behind them are often older. Those buildings of significant historical and aesthetic value to Amsterdam (Stadsmonumenten) are the responsibility of a variety of institutions. Between them they spend many millions of guilders annually on repair and restoration.

An easy landmark to start your exploration from is the great baroque dome of the **Ronde Luthersekerk**, overlooking the Singel canal. Built between 1668 and 1671, this church was extensively restored in the early part of the 19th century after a disastrous fire. It has since been deconsecrated and now serves as an annex to the Sonesta Hotel; it is not open to the general public but the exterior alone is very pleasing and forms a fine focal point to the views down the surrounding streets.

Nearby, at Nos. 4–6 Kattengat, are two attractive 17th-century gabled houses. Dating from 1614, and therefore among the first to be built after the canals were dug, they carry the fetching names of **De Gouden Spiegel** and **De Silveren Spiegel** (the Golden Mirror and the Silver Mirror).

Narrow house: You will see grander houses than these, of course. But first take a look at one of Amsterdam's most curious dwellings. In the 17th century, taxes were levied on property owners according to the width of their house frontage. The original owner of **No. 7 Singel** (next to the Liberty Hotel) was perhaps determined to pay as little as

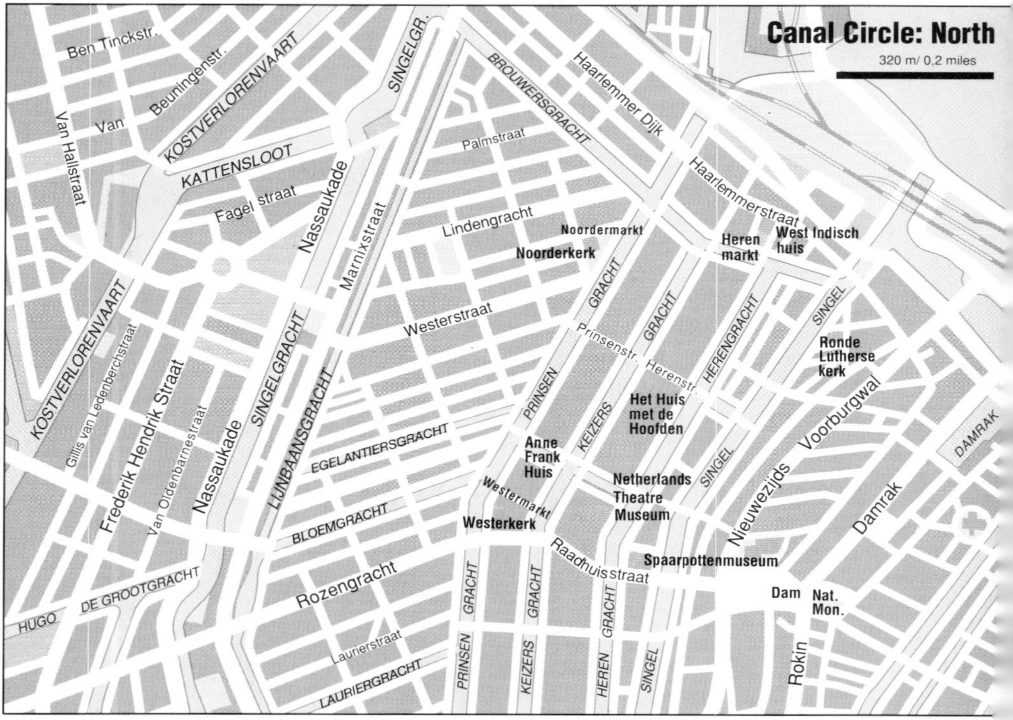

possible and so he built the narrowest house in Amsterdam.

On the opposite side of the canal is another curious household, the "**cat boat**". The owner provides board and lodging for around 150 cats and these floating felines have become one of the most popular, if unconventional, sights of Amsterdam. It is worth continuing a short distance southward along the Singel to the first bridge past the cat boat. In the stonework of the bridge itself is a 17th-century prison called the **Tower Sluis**. The unfortunate souls who were incarcerated here would frequently have found themselves up to their waists in water as the level of the canal changed with the incoming tides.

Canal vistas: If you go back up along the Singel to **Brouwersgracht** you will find yourself in one of the best places in Amsterdam to enjoy wide vistas down each of the three main canals. The picture is perhaps best in autumn and winter, preferably at dusk, when the trees bordering the waterways have been stripped of their leaves, allowing uninterrupted views southwards to the point where the canals make a bend just before Radhuisstraat.

Overseas trade: These canals were made possible by the wealth of the new Dutch empire. The East Indies (Indonesia) produced the greatest riches but the Netherlands had a foothold in the west as well. The **West Indisch Huis** (West India House) faces on to Haarlemmerstraat but backs on to Herenmarkt—a tidy little square off Brouwersgracht—and is closely associated with those days of empire. Constructed in 1617, it owes its current name to the period when it was let to the Dutch West India Company, beginning in 1623. When the naval hero Admiral Piet Heyn captured the Spanish "silver fleet" off Cuba in 1628, the booty (a prodigious prize of silver) was stored here.

On Saturdays, **Noordermarkt** (a short distance south along Prinsengracht) is just as its name suggests—a market place. In the middle is the oc-

ft, Ronde thersekerk. ght, esterkerk.

JORDAAN

The name Jordaan is said to be a corruption of the French word *jardin*. It is a feasible explanation. Many of the streets—Palmgracht, Bloemgracht, Rozengracht and Laurierstraat—are named after trees and flowers.

The Jordaan grew up at the same time as the major phase of canal construction in the 17th century. It was the ambition of designer Hendrik Staets to create a self-contained community of artisans. The dense grid of streets and narrow canals was cut east to west along the course of existing polders (drainage ditches). At the beginning of this century the Jordaan was nothing less than a slum. After World War II the area was refurbished and today the Jordaan has its own distinct charm. More than 800 buildings here are listed as being of architectural or historical interest. Seven of the original 11 canals have been filled in but the area still retains its shopkeepers and artisans—there are more than 900 small businesses registered here.

The buildings in the Jordaan are on a different scale to the grand households of Prinsengracht, Keizersgracht and Herengracht. The streets are narrower, the houses are more compact and there are bookshops, second-hand stores, ethnic restaurants, boutiques, bakeries, cafés and bars that help to make this neighbourhood feel friendly and full of interest. There are a number of concealed *hofjes* in the area. One of these, the small cobble-stoned courtyard of Raep Hofje, is right at the "top" of the Jordaan at Nos. 28–38 Palmgracht.

A rather romantic picture has been painted of Jordaan. If these descriptions are to be believed, each street corner is crowded with artists, students, musicians and sundry other bohemians. In reality it has a full quota of thoroughly conventional citizens quietly going about their business. That is a plus because, above all, the Jordaan offers an escape from the crowds of tourists that are an inevitable part of the daily scene in Leidseplein or Museumplein. Things can be livelier in the evenings. There are two good jazz clubs in the Jordaan: the Café Alto, at Korte Leidsedwarsstraat No. 115, and the Bamboo Bar, at Lange Leidsedwarsstraat No. 66.

One famous resident was Jan van Riebeek, the founder of Cape Town, who lived on Egelantiersgracht between 1649 and 1651. Another was Rembrandt, who was forced by poverty to move to the Jordaan towards the end of his life. In 1656 Rembrandt had been declared insolvent and in the following two years his house and many of his personal possessions were sold to pay off his debts. Normally bankruptcy would have seen Rembrandt put in prison but he escaped this by gaining legal cession of his estate. But the glamour of his former lifestyle on Jodenbreestraat was over. In 1660 Rembrandt, along with his mistress Hendrickje and his son Titus, went to live in Rozengracht. Rembrandt died nine years later.

The Rozengracht no longer has its canal; a tram line has taken its place. Bloemgracht, one of the most popular streets in the Jordaan, has fared better. With its numerous gabled houses, this street became known as the Gentleman's Canal of the Jordaan. The step gables at Nos. 87–91 are the most noticeable. This building dates from 1642 and belongs to the Vereniging Hendrick de Keyser, a foundation established to preserve this architect's works.

Egelantiersgracht (named after the eglantine or honeysuckle) has also retained its canal and for this reason is another of the Jordaan's photogenic streets. At Nos. 201–03 and 213–15 are four houses built in exactly the same style and all bearing the same family coat of arms. Between Nos. 107 and 114 is the entrance to the Sint Andrieshofje, which dates from 1616. Nearby, at the end of Egelantierstraat, is Café 't Smalle, the site of a distillery established at the end of the 18th century by a man called Peter Hoppe. He produced a Dutch gin called Hoppe Jenever that became famous around the country.

Wider exploration of the Jordaan is well rewarded, and at No. 109 Elandsgracht and No. 38 Looiersgracht there are two indoor antique markets (open daily except Sunday) which make for excellent browsing and might be a source of some unusual souvenirs of old Amsterdam.

tagonal shape of the **Noorderkerk**, the first landmark you see as you go down Prinsengracht. Construction of this church began in 1620. It is only open for services but the plain and unremarkable interior hardly merits a special visit.

On the other side of Prinsengracht, however, are two *hofjes* that you should definitely look for. **Van Brienenhofje**, at Nos. 89–133 Prinsengracht, is an impressive square of almshouses overlooking a wide peaceful courtyard. The story goes that Jan van Brienen, who once locked himself inside his own safe and who was rescued from suffocating only just in time, showed his gratitude by founding these almshouses.

Tranquil spot: A little further along Prinsengracht, at Nos. 159–71, is **Zon's Hofje**. The Frisian Mennonite community in Amsterdam bought a building here called "De Kleine Zon" (The Little Sun) in 1720. It was used as a church and renamed "De Arke Noach" (Noah's Ark). This community merged with another and so in 1765 the church was converted into almshouses for widows. Be careful not to disturb the residents if you come here but sit quietly on the bench opposite the tree in the courtyard and enjoy what is surely the ultimate in secluded, tranquil living.

If you next turn left along Prinsenstrasse you will come quickly to Keizersgracht. Turn right to follow the eastern bank of the canal until you reach No. 123, known as "**Het Huis met de Hoofden**," (House with the Heads). Built by Hendrick de Keyser for a wealthy merchant in 1624, the name of this building refers to the six classical busts on either side of the entrance depicting the deities Apollo, Ceres, Mars, Athene, Bacchus and Diana.

No. 123 Keizersgracht houses the offices of the main organisation involved with the conservation of Amsterdam's architectural heritage, the city's Bureau Monumentenzorg (Municipal Office for Historic Buildings' Preservation), established in 1953.

Legal protection: Soon after its forma-

ft, Jordaan utique. low, canal-de ntem-ation.

tion, the Bureau made an inventory of buildings considered irreplaceable. In 1961, the buildings on this list found protection under the law, so that Amsterdam now has 6,826 historic buildings in its old centre—more by far than in any other city in the Netherlands.

These monuments, as they are called, are protected by law and, without a permit from the Bureau, may not be modified or demolished. The Bureau has its own architectural office, a warehouse for storing valuable remnants of buildings which had to be torn down, and occasionally does some restoration work itself. It also assists private organisations and individuals who are actively involved in restoration work.

New homes: In keeping with Amsterdam's entrepreneurial traditions, the private sector has also helped with Amsterdam's mammoth conservation task. One company active in this field is the Amsteramse Maatschappij tot Stadherstel N.V. (The Amsterdam Company for City Restoration). Formed in 1956, it aims to restore as many inner-city houses as possible while providing housing to help alleviate the city's critical housing shortage.

Herenstraat, the side street that links Keizersgracht to Herengracht, owes much to the work of Stadherstel and is just one small example of what can be done. The company owns nine premises here and has helped to revive what was once a run-down street badly in need of refurbishment.

Right at the north end of Herengracht, a short walk from Brouwersgracht, is "**Het Huis met Pilastergevel**" (the House with the Pilaster Gable) at Nos. 70–72. This house dates from 1642 and, as its name indicates, has a gable ornamented with pilasters, which are the slightly protruding flat stone columns.

A more attractive exterior is the **Bartolotti Huis** (Bartolotti House) at Nos. 170–72 Herengracht, just before you reach Raadhuisstraat. This bright and ornate four-storey building was renovated as recently as 1971. The

Gables, Prinsengrac

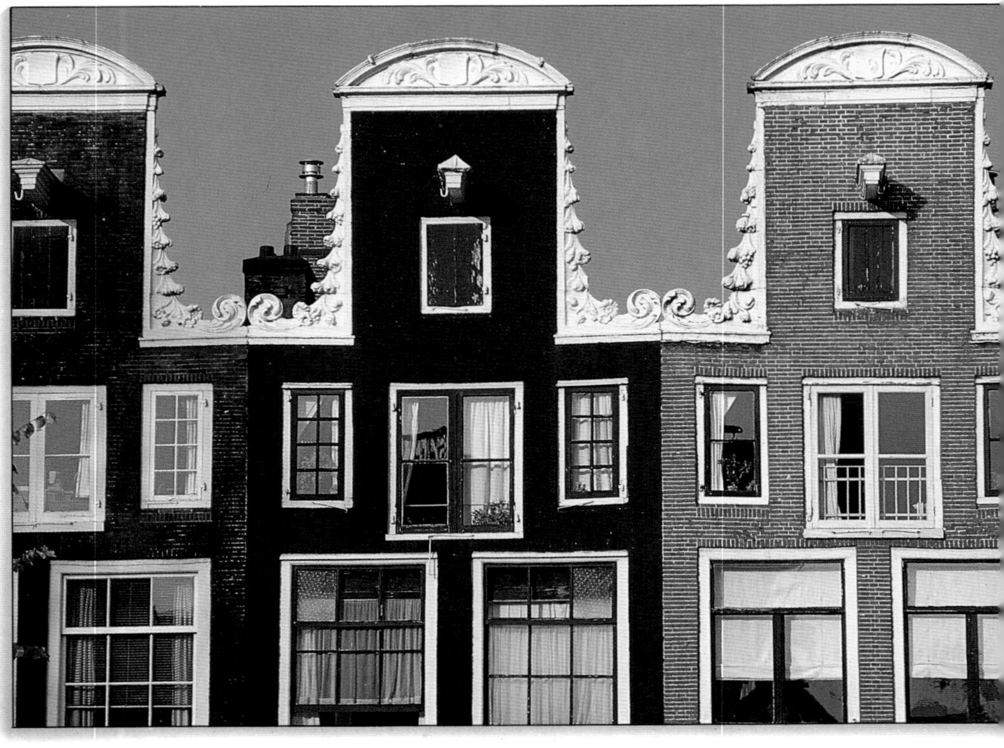

house was designed by Hendrick de Keyser in 1621 for Guillielmo Bartolotti, who made his fortune as a brewer and later became a rich banker.

Histrionics: Opportunities to see inside the grand buildings that border these canals are restricted to a handful of excellent museums that help preserve a sense of 17th-century opulence. One of these, the **Netherlands Theatre Institute**, is right next door to the Bartolotti House, at No. 168 Herengracht.

Owned by the Dutch Reformed Church, this building became home to the Theatre Museum in 1959. No. 168 Herengracht started life as a confectionery shop but in 1637 a city magistrate by the name of Michael de Pauw bought the building and commissioned architect Philip Vingboons to build a new facade. The bottle-neck gable he designed was later widely imitated by other buildings along the canals.

Painted walls: It is worth making a visit to this building to look at the two reception rooms on the ground floor. The grand murals and painted ceilings were part of an extensive redecoration scheme undertaken between 1728 and 1733 in the style of Louis XIV. Isaac de Moucheron and Jacob de Wit, two fashionable artists, were commissioned to paint the murals in oils on canvas. De Moucheron painted the landscape and de Wit was responsible for the figures and the ceiling.

The Theatre Institute is really a resource centre that happens to double up as a museum. Its main role is to provide a meeting place for actors, actresses, directors and writers. But an elaborate miniature theatre dating from 1781, along with models depicting the development of scenery and stage management in 18th-century Dutch theatre, merit a visit. The Institute also stages occasional exhibitions.

If you enjoy eccentric museums, or have children to entertain, you should also pay a visit to the **Spaarpottenmuseum** (Money Box Museum), at No. 20 Raadhuisstraat. Here you will find

ft, useboat ing. Right, nging loose Wester- aat.

over 12,000 examples from all over the world; some are skilful creations and others are in entertaining bad taste.

Landmark: Heading west from here, along busy Raadhuisstraat, you reach Westermarkt, the best-known corner of this section of Amsterdam's Grachtengordel. The **Westerkerk**, considered to be the masterpiece of architect Hendrick de Keyser, was built between 1620 and 1638. Rembrandt's grave has recently been rediscovered here and Princess Beatrix and Prince Claus of the Netherlands were married here in 1966. The Westerkerk tower is topped by the Imperial Crown of Maximilian of Austria and commemorates the fact that in 1489 Amsterdam was granted the right to bear the emperor's crown on its coat of arms. The tower is open to visitors in the summer months and provides excellent views over the city.

Visiting the **Anne Frank Huis**, nearby on Prinsengracht, has become something of a tourist pilgrimage. As a symbol of Jewish suffering during World War II, this building certainly deserves such a strong measure of respect. But the sheer volume of visitors has its downside. What should be a sobering and contemplative tour of rooms made world famous by a gifted adolescent diarist is, during the peak summer months at least, a crowded and sometimes frustrating procession through constricted passageways.

An exhibition in the Anne Frank House itself ties together three important themes—the Diary, the House and the Anne Frank Foundation. With its account of pre-war history, of World War II itself, and of subsequent conflict around the world, it makes visitors aware of the wider significance of this building and how the Foundation is promoting the ideals of Anne Frank. Half a million people from the Netherlands and abroad visit the Anne Frank House every year. Wherever else you go in this part of the Grachtengordel, you should, despite the queues, make every effort to join them.

Below, floating flowers. Right, Anne Frank.

ANNE FRANK

On Monday 6 July 1942, Anne Frank accompanied her family into the *achterhuis* (the back annexe) of Prinsengracht 263; she was not escaping from Nazi persecution for the first time in her life. Born in Frankfurt in 1929, her family had already fled their native town in the summer of 1933. Escape from Frankfurt to Amsterdam brought a respite that lasted just six years. After the Germans had invaded Holland in 1940, the country was subjected to the same anti-Jewish measures as other occupied nations. In February 1941, the Nazis began their first round-up of Jews in Amsterdam. Otto Frank was already planning a second escape. Though he had been forced by the Germans to leave his prosperous business, he was still able to prepare several rooms on the top floors and back of Prinsengracht 263, a combined warehouse and office for his company, as a secret hiding place. The safety of his family and four other Jews was to hinge on a swinging cupboard concealing the stairs to the back portion of the building.

Otto Frank had planned to disappear on 16 July but on 5 July a deportation order for his daughter Margot arrived. The plan was brought forward and at 7.30 a.m. on the following day the Frank family made their way to Prinsengracht 263. Another family—Mr Van Daan, his wife and their son Peter—joined them. In November another refugee, Albert Dussel, became the eighth member of this clandestine household.

Anne Frank's record of life in their secret refuge is remarkable not just as a diary of a Jewish family in hiding. The real fascination of her book comes from witnessing the intellectual growth of a young girl already blessed with obvious literary talents as she passes through her formative adolescent years under fearful circumstances. As you turn the pages her steadily maturing mind is the real source of interest behind her narrative.

The second entry of her diary is as naive as could be expected from any 13-year-old. Three days after her birthday she writes: "I had my birthday on Sunday afternoon. We showed a film *The Lighthouse Keeper* with Rin-Tin-Tin, which my school friends thoroughly enjoyed. We had a lovely time."

In July 1944 the same diarist, now 15 years old, wrote: "It is a great wonder that I have not given up all my expectations because they seem absurd and unfeasible. But I still cling to them, despite everything, because I still believe in the inner goodness of humanity. It's absolutely impossible for me to base everything on death, suffering and confusion."

Just 20 days later the refugees in the annexe at Prinsengracht 263 were discovered and taken away. On 4 August, following a tip-off thought to have been provided by a Dutch informer, the Gestapo discovered the hiding place. The Franks, the Van Daans and Mr Dussel were sent to Westerbork, the Dutch staging post to concentration camps further east. On 3 September, the day the Allies captured Brussels, those eight were among the last shipment of around 1,000 Jews to leave the Netherlands.

Of all the occupants of the "Secret Annexe", Anne's father alone returned. Anne Frank died in the concentration camp at Bergen-Belsen in March 1945 at the age of 15, only three weeks before a British battalion liberated it.

Anne Frank's diary had been left behind among old books, magazines and newspapers lying on the floor. Of the many mature and perceptive passages written in her last weeks of hiding, the most famous quotes come from the final paragraphs of her entry for 15 July. Ironically, three months previously, on 4 April, she had written: "I want to live on after my death."

Anne Frank's spirit, and her wish to "live on", provide the key to the real significance of Prinsengracht 263. The Anne Frank House is more than the place in which a world-famous diary was penned. It should also be more than a voyeuristic opportunity to see the very premises in which she and her co-refugees lived. It is both a living monument to all those who were victims of racism, fascism and anti-Semitism in World War II and a warning to the modern world that intolerance and racial violence is still with us.

CANAL CIRCLE: CENTRAL

Amsterdam's greatest asset, the magnificent buildings lining Herengracht, Keizersgracht and Prinsengracht, often feel as if they are off limits. Your natural instinct is to want to stop and look inside. But the only houses you can visit as you walk along Amsterdam's three main canals are now museums. Some of these show you just how grand and opulent these canal-side buildings were in the 17th century when they belonged to the city's *nouveaux riches*. Others are specialised and, for many visitors, have only limited appeal.

Many of the buildings of the central stretch of the canal circle belong to banks and embassies, others serve as the Dutch headquarters of large multinational companies. Most of the time you can do little more than admire ornate facades, though you should take a walk along the canals at dusk to catch fleeting glimpses of the lit-up interiors through uncurtained windows.

Left, canal-side cycle lane.

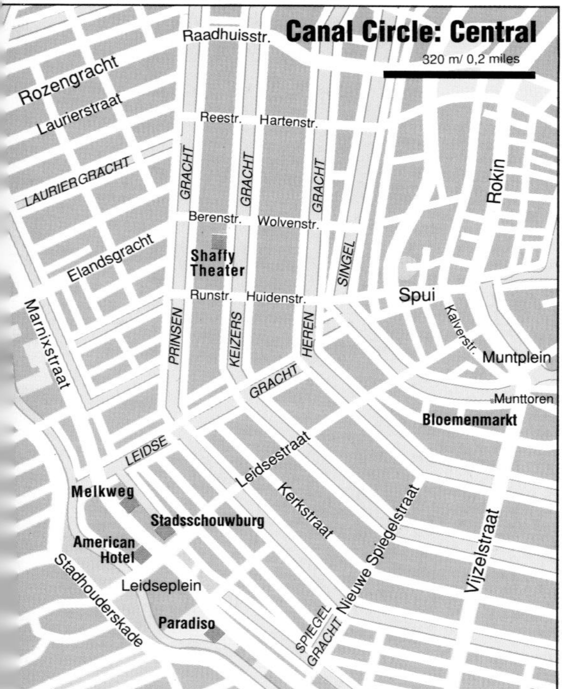

When the city expanded during the 17th century, Herengracht was undoubtedly the most sought-after of the three new canals. Where the Herengracht turns towards the southeast at Leidsegracht, and again towards the east just before Vijzelstraat, the richest and most splendid houses were built. This stretch was dubbed "the Golden Bend". You can get an idea of how superior these buildings were by comparing property prices. In 1820, for example, a house on the Herengracht would have sold for 30,000 guilders while a house in the nearby Jordaan would have fetched only 3,000.

Best stretch: From a visual point of view, the stretch of canals between Raadhuisstraat and Vijzelstraat are the most rewarding. If you don't want to do too much walking, or you have limited time, restrict yourself to exploring the Golden Bend.

Take a canal-boat ride and the first features that will be pointed out to you are the different styles of gable that the buildings possess. A typical "Dutch" gable is the ornate upper part of the facade used as an ornament to disguise the shape and appearance of the roof behind. This feature is not unique to Amsterdam. However, the fact that taxes based on the width of the frontage were once levied here means that many of the houses were deliberately built to be narrow but deep—they were built "end-on" to the canals.

Gable types: Ornamented gables are ubiquitous and a range of styles developed throughout Amsterdam; the most common types are the step gable the spout gable, the neck gable, and the bell gable. You don't have to be too interested in architecture to spot the four main types but a little guidance will make a walk along any of Amsterdam's canals more enjoyable.

The step gable—a Gothic style—ascends geometrically like a small stairway up to the pinnacle; builders often used the pale colour of sandstone to offset the darker colour of red brickwork. This type of gable is very much associated with Hendrick de Keyser, who died in 1621. Step gables are a good indication that the building is from the late 16th or early 17th century (though there are later step gables).

Also a product of the late 16th and early 17th centuries, the spout gable, a simple inverted V-shape reflecting the slope of the roof, characterises many of Amsterdam's warehouses. The neck gable is very much part of the 17th century and is often attributed to a famous Amsterdam architect, Philip Vingboons, who died in 1675. This type of gable takes the form of an elevated centrepiece culminating in a triangular pediment, often in association with heraldic statuary. The bell gable, which developed in the 18th century, is easily recognisable because it has a rounded top with concave sides just like a large church bell.

French influence: Gables do not account for all of the canal-side facades, of course. When the Golden Age had passed, Dutch architects imported much from France, especially the baroque style of Louis XIV. During the late 17th century and throughout the 18th century, gable-fronted houses gave way to buildings with squarer facades and flat cornices.

Given a choice between the three main canals as they run between Raadhuisstraat and Vijzelstraat, Prinsengracht definitely comes last. There are few places worth taking the time to visit so you should concentrate on Herengracht and Keizersgracht. First walk southwards along **Herengracht** from Raadhuisstraat down to Huidenstraat. Many of the finest town houses were built to the east of Leidsegracht and Herengracht was envisaged as a mainly residential area from which many industries were banned. These included sugar refining because of the fire hazard, brewing because of the smell, and barrel-making because of the noise.

On the way south to Huidenstraat there is a confusing jumble of styles though there are several 18th-century gables on the western side of the canal. One good example is "**De Witte Lelie**" (The White Lily) at No. 274, with an ornate Louis XIV-style balustrade rising to a crested top.

Gables galore: Still going south, take the short stretch from Huidenstraat to Leidsestraat slowly and walk along the east side. No. 386, with its classical pilastered facade, is one of the many houses on this bend that were designed by Philip Vingboons.

Another Vingboons building is the four-gabled **Cromhouthuizen** at Nos. 364–70, dating from 1662. The name derives from the crooked piece of wood that was the trademark of a builder called Jacob Cromhout, who lived at No. 366. Today, his house is used as the **Bijbelsmuseum**. This is a highly specialised collection that illustrates the history of the Bible and Jerusalem. The themes are non-denominational and

Step gables.

give as much attention to Judaism as Christianity. Include this in your itinerary only if you are a real enthusiast for religious history. Most of the collection is captioned in Dutch, though notes for guidance are available in other languages. You can arrange for a guided tour but need to book at least one month in advance.

New York import: The ornate decoration at Nos. 380–82 may not be to everybody's taste. It was built in 1889 for a client who wanted to emulate the chic mansions of New York's Fifth Avenue. Further along are good examples of twin houses, so called because they are double the width of most canal-side plots. The gables of Nos. 390–92, are adorned with a carving of a man and a woman stretching a rope between them and date to the mid-17th century like Nos. 396–98 and 409–11.

The Golden Bend runs from Leidsestraat to Vijzelstraat, though you might think that buildings on other sections of this canal are more attractive. A highlight of this stretch is No. 475, dating from the 1730s and built in an ornate Louis XIV style.

Flower market: A short walk from the Golden Bend, the **Muntplein** marks the junction of Kalverstraat with Rokin and Vijzelstraat. The **Munttoren** was built in 1490, though the steeple was added in 1620 by Hendrick de Keyser. For a short time in 1672 money was minted in the building adjoining the tower, hence the name. This area is always crowded—one of the attractions is the **Bloemenmarkt**, a flower market which has been held here since at least the 18th century.

On **Keizersgracht**, heading south from Raadhuisstraat, there are a number of stylish exteriors on either side of the canal. At No. 209 is a statue of Hope holding a basket of fruit. A short distance along, at No. 220, a Syrian Orthodox church breaks up the skyline.

Thus far down Keizersgracht there is not a single building that you can actually enter. The rule is broken by the Pulitzer Bar at No. 234, an expensive

Bell gables.

restaurant with a large patio at the back. The style changes again with the dark walls of Nos. 244–46, a matching pair of powerful-looking houses with Louis XIV-style cornices.

High culture: Without doubt, the most notable building on this stretch of Keizersgracht is the **Shaffy Theatre**, also known as the Felix Meritis Building, at No. 324. It is instantly recognisable because of the four thick pillars that make up this classical facade. It was built in 1788 for the Felix Meritis (Latin for "deservedly happy") Society, whose aim was to broaden knowledge of the arts and sciences. At one time Haydn and Grieg conducted in the building's concert hall.

From 1946, the building was used as the headquarters of the Dutch Communist Party. Then, in the 1960s, the Shaffy Theatre Company, named after the actor Ramses Shaffy, took rooms here and this became one of Amsterdam's first experimental theatres. The Communists later moved out and the Shaffy Theatre subsequently took over the whole building.

Today it has four performance rooms (three theatres and one cinema) and specialises in progressive European drama, accompanying this with film performances when appropriate. Even if you are not planning to see a play or film here, step inside anyway and ask whoever is at the ticket desk to see their latest copy of *Pravda*. The Communists moved out long ago yet Moscow still has this building on its mailing list.

If you still haven't seen a good example of a neck gable, look across to the other side of Keizersgracht. No. 319 Keizersgracht, designed by Vingboons, has one that dates from 1639.

Former theatre: Back on the western side of Keizersgracht, you'll see a gateway at No. 384. This was the entrance to the former **Stadsschouwburg** (city theatre), destroyed by fire in 1722. Look across the canal and see if you can spot the Gilded Star at No. 387 Keizersgracht, an excellent example of the

Majolica and Delftware in the Spiegelkwartier.

elevated neck-gable style, dating from 1668, near the end of the Golden Age.

The style of building changes here so rapidly that it is difficult to take in all the detail. Just look at the buildings between No. 440 Keizersgracht and No. 454, near the junction with Leidsegracht. With its enormous great windows and a decorative mixture of sandstone and red brick, No. 440 is a stark contrast to No. 446, a Louis XIV-style dwelling from the 1720s. The latter was at one time the home of a well-known art collector by the name of Adriaan van der Hoop. Both of these buildings back on to and form part of the Openbare Bibliothek. Another contrast is provided between the pillars and balconies of the bank occupying No. 452 and the stylish example, at No. 454, of how Amsterdam's warehouses can be converted into comfortable apartments.

Refreshment interlude: If all this street level facade-gazing is proving tiresome, head for the furniture store of **Metz & Co**, situated on the corner of Keizersgracht and Leidsestraat. A large clock tower makes it easy to spot; at night the roof of this building is elaborately illuminated. Go up to the top-floor café and enjoy excellent views over Amsterdam. The food is not only good up here, it is also inexpensive—you can just drink coffee if you don't want to eat. Come here early on in the day, when it's quieter, and you can choose a table with a good view.

After refreshment it is time to explore some of the cross-streets connecting Herengracht with Singel to the east and Keizersgracht to the west. **Hartenstraat**, an upmarket shopping street (below Raadhuisstraat and joining Herengracht with Keizersgracht), is one of the most interesting, but it is the charming old shops of the **Spiegelkwartier** which attracts most visitors.

Street of galleries: Antique dealers have been doing business here for over a century, attracted to the area because of its proximity to the Rijksmuseum, which opened in 1885. The first dealers opened their shops in **Nieuwe Spiegelstraat**. Later they were joined by art dealers who opened galleries along the canals leading into Nieuwe Spiegelstraat, helping to create what has since become a renowned centre for fine art and antiques. The area grew quickly in the 1960s when antiques became more popular and some provincial antique dealers, who saw their trade disappearing to the capital, moved out of necessity to Amsterdam, swelling the number of shops in the Spiegelkwartier.

Best choice: While Rokin is still the main centre for upmarket antiques—there is a branch of Sotheby's there—the Spiegelkwartier has a much more welcoming atmosphere. In a street only 100 ft (300 metres) long there are no less than 80 antique dealers and 15 galleries. Many of the stores have specialists who can advise prospective buyers, though you should still ask for a signed certificate of authenticity from a dealer when making a purchase.

At **Nieuwe Spiegelstraat 34**, a num-

intner's gn.

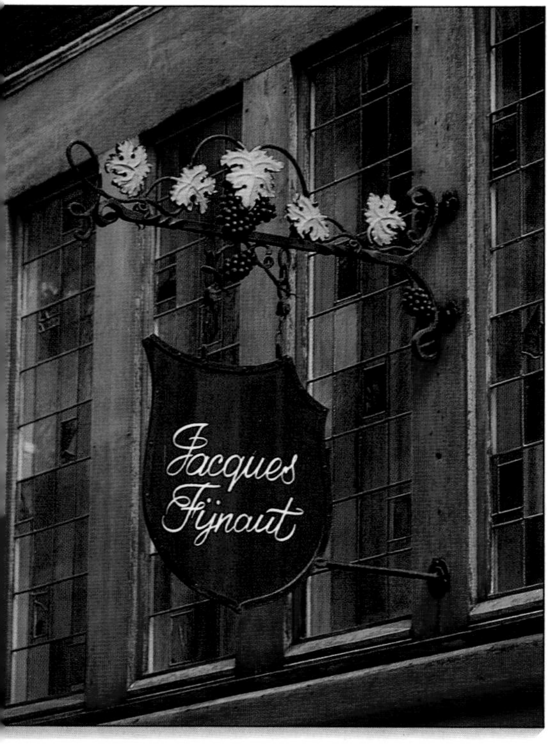

ber of dealers have gathered together under one roof to create the Amsterdam Antiques Gallery, which offers icons, dolls and 19th-century paintings. At No. 58 a shop specialises in Art Nouveau and Art Deco pieces. Altogether the choice is very wide and antiques available in the Spiegelkwartier include earthenware, furniture, porcelain, engraved glass, Asiatic art, sculptures, jewellery, gold, silver, tin, bronze, clocks, nautical instruments, drawings, books and engravings.

Buskers and nightlife: From here it is a short walk along Leidsestraat into one of the centres of Amsterdam nightlife: **Leidseplein**. There are cinemas, bars, restaurants and clubs aplenty here. Proof of its pedigree is the fact that this is the place to gather on New Year's Eve. It is almost as much fun on any other night of the year. Street performers of every shade are invariably at the centre of attention; jugglers, mime artists, magicians and musicians take their turn at entertaining the crowds.

There are two unmistakable buildings on Leidseplein, each making its own contribution to an evening's entertainment. The red-brick building with its wide verandah and mini turrets is the **Stadsschouwburg**. This venerable theatre has been entertaining Amsterdam with performances since 1894.

There is a different kind of ambience at the American Hotel. Built in 1904 by W. Kromhout, it is an architectural gem. On the right of the main entrance, the **Café Americain** overlooks most of Leidseplein and has long been a fashionable meeting place, especially for theatre goers in the evening.

Something for everyone: Leidseplein caters to all tastes in entertainment—the conservative and the progressive. A shrine to the latter is Amsterdam's famous **Melkweg** (Milky Way) on Lijnbaansgracht. Rock, jazz, Latin and reggae, fringe theatre productions, art exhibitions, video and puppet shows all make for a lively and alternative "multimedia" arts centre that stays open into the small hours. The Melkweg first became the centre of alternative arts in Amsterdam when the former dairy building was converted in the 1960s and even today it is still going strong.

A kindred spirit to the Melkweg, albeit on a much more serious level, is **De Balie**, a two-minute walk away on Gartmanplantsoen. De Balie is, in its own words, a centre for "culture and politics", which stages a variety of events including theatre, exhibitions, political debates and conferences. Anybody is entitled to attend. A little further along, on Weteringschans, is the **Paradiso**, another night-spot which emerged in the 1960s and which still provides a lively venue for rock and jazz bands from all over Europe.

When you have finished with a morning or afternoon of tramping around the canals and you are in need of refreshment and entertainment, don't fail to spend at least one evening on Leidseplein. But don't expect to make an early start the next day!

Left, escape disco. Right Café Americain.

American Hotel

Despite the noisy antagonism of the late 20th century, or perhaps because of it, the American Hotel seems more firmly moored on the Leidesplein than any of the modern buildings around it. Amid a sea of neon and traffic, this unique hotel has anchored the western corner of the busy square on the Singelgracht canal since 1902. Today, the 188-room Art Nouveau hotel and the stunning Art Deco Café Americain are both classified as protected monuments in Amsterdam.

As captivating as the exterior of the hotel may be, it is the authentic museum-quality furnishings from the 1930s and Gatsby-society atmosphere which continually fills the café seats. The pieces were all collected by one of the early owners. The hotel is popular with power-lunching bankers, *au courant* late-night diners and curious tourists, all anxious to soak up that romanticised period with the help of the Café's vintage decor.

In the 19th century, the Leidesplein crossroads was just beginning to grow into the entertainment and restaurant mecca it is now. The small stage near the old city gates had developed into the major theatre it is to this day, along with a supporting cast of dozens of coffee houses, bars and restaurants. In 1879, a Dutchman named Steinigeweg returned to Amsterdam after many years of living in the United States. He judged the location ideal for a hotel, which opened in neo-Gothic splendour in 1882.

Steinigeweg named it the American Hotel and imported the decor to match. Over the doorway hung a 12-ft (4-metre) bronze eagle, cigar-store wooden Indians stood in the lobby along with murals of North American landscapes, including the Niagara Falls. The hotel soon became a popular meeting place for the theatre community, the critics and art world gossip-mongers.

But 20 years later the neo-Gothic design was judged *passé*. With a new century approaching and a swarm of new artistic styles emerging, a decision was made to raze the old hotel.

The new American Hotel was designed by Dutch architect Willem Kromhout, incorporating some of the old hotel's features with his own brand of Art Nouveau architecture. Art Nouveau was a design movement which took its name from a trendy Paris shop which opened in 1895. Its followers rejected the stiff, ordered forms of classical and Gothic design and took their inspiration from natural, organic shapes. The new movement lasted about 10 years, less in the Netherlands, and was an important bridge from the neo-classical designs of the 19th century into Bauhaus and modern building design.

Manfred Bock, a professor of architecture at Amsterdam University, regards Kromhout's building as noteworthy because it introduced Art Nouveau to the Netherlands and yet remains outside of the mainstream Art Nouveau style. The brick facade is unique, and almost completely ambiguous in style and inspiration because of its lack of hard lines. In The Hague, there are more "typical" Art Nouveau-style buildings influenced by the Hotel Tassel in Brussels, the Art Nouveau masterpiece of the Belgian architect, Victor Horta. The only other Kromhout building of significance in the city is near Muntplein on Regulierbreestraat, somewhat compromised now because of the huge McDonald's take-away on the ground floor.

But Kromhout, for all his originality, was forever overshadowed by H.P. Berlage, the brilliant Dutch architect of the time. Among the experts in the field, like Bock and Amsterdam Historical Museum Curator Hwuub Glerum, the American Hotel is doomed to be called forever the "second most important modern building in Amsterdam" after Berlage's Beurs building on the Damrak, which was completed in 1903, the year before the new American Hotel opened its doors.

As for the hotel itself, modernisation in the mid 1980s resulted in the loss of much of its internal character. In the Rijksmuseum basement you will find some of the decorative glass, porcelain, cutlery and furnishings that once made the American the city's most splendid hotel.The hotel's elegant Café Americain, by contrast, has survived untouched, with its colourful stained glass, murals and Tiffany-style chandeliers.

50 tulpen 45,=
50 tulpen
100 div bollen 45,=
25 tulpen 15,=
40 div bollen 15,=

50 FO
25 FO

447

SUPER CROWN #991

06/03/96 18:08 6 22 8022
REFUNDS WITHIN 30 DAYS WITH RECEIPT ONLY
MAGAZINE SALES FINAL

PUBLISHER PRICE	CROWN SAVINGS		CROWN PRICE
REMAINDER			
1@ 5.99 X599	0%		5.99
TIME OUT LONDON			
1@ 14.95 0140248730	10%		13.46
INSIGHT GD AMSTERDAM			
1@ 21.95 0395661862	10%		19.76
SUBTOTAL		$	39.21
SALES TAX @ 7.75%		$	3.04
TOTAL		$	42.25
TENDERED Check		$	42.25

YOUR SAVINGS AT CROWN... $ 3.68

SUPER CROWN #991

06/03/96 18:08 6 22 8022
REFUNDS WITHIN 30 DAYS WITH RECEIPT ONLY
MAGAZINE SALES FINAL

PUBLISHER PRICE		CROWN SAVINGS	CROWN PRICE
REMAINDER			
1@ 5.99 X599		0%	5.99
TIME OUT LONDON			
1@ 14.95 01402487730		10%	13.46
INSIGHT GD AMSTERDAM			
1@ 21.95 0395661862		10%	19.76
SUBTOTAL	$		39.21
SALES TAX @ 7.75%	$		3.04
TOTAL	$		42.25
TENDERED Check	$		42.25

YOUR SAVINGS AT CROWN... $ 3.68

Canal Circle: East

The final stretch of the Grachtengordel, going east from Vijzelstraat, comes to a bold full stop at the Amstel. This stretch is part of the second stage of canal construction that took place after 1665. Commentaries on the canal-boat tours often dry up on this south-easternmost stretch of the canals and, if your stay in Amsterdam is governed by priorities, a thorough exploration of the canals between Vijzelstraat and the Amstel can be put low on your list.

But don't, for one moment, write this neighbourhood off altogether. Four of Amsterdam's best museums are tucked away here. A stone's throw north of Herengracht is Rembrandtsplein, at night always bright and busy. And just to the south, overlooking Singelgracht, is the Heineken Brewery, one of Amsterdam's most popular and convivial tourist attractions.

'receding ages: loemen-narkt. Left, oorcase, ingel.

If Leidseplein is Amsterdam's most popular haunt at night, then **Rembrantsplein** comes a close second. The square was originally part of the 16th-century city ramparts. Later it was a butter market. It took its name in 1876 from the statue of Rembrandt that stands at the centre of the square. Topless bars, music bars, small bars, expensive bars—Rembrandtsplein has them all. Unfailingly lively any night of the year, it has inevitably become very commercialised.

The cobblestoned and shaded square of **Thorbeckeplein**, which leads on to Herengracht, is a tidy and deliberately quaint extension to Rembrandtsplein that extends the nightlife repertoire. Ringed by cafés, hotels and restaurants, the pavement terraces are usually crammed full in summer and in winter the Thorbeckeplein seldom lacks custom. You can stagger from bar to bar here—and people do!

Constitutional pioneer: Standing in the middle of the square is a statue of **J.R. Thorbecke**, a significant figure in the history of the Netherlands. In 1814, after a brief interlude under the rule of Napoleon Bonaparte, the former Dutch Republic had become a monarchy. Belgium was then part of this new nation. By 1830, however, Belgium had seceded and 18 years later the Netherlands had a new constitution, for which J.R. Thorbecke was responsible.

It is ironic that the statue celebrating a man who played such an important role in the development of his country should stand amid all this carefree merriment. But perhaps not; Mr Thorbecke was above all a liberal, part of a political tradition that ultimately accounts for much of this country's pragmatic outlook.

If you have already been on one of the canal-boat tours by the time you get to Thorbeckeplein, you'll probably recognise the six-arched bridges of **Reguliersgracht** just south of the square. The view down Reguliersgracht cuts across all three of the main canals almost as far as the Singel; this particular perspective is a favourite with photographers.

Silver screen: Heading northwest out of Rembrandtsplein, you enter the crowded Regulierbreestraat where, among the fast-food stalls, you will find the **Tuschinski cinema**. Go to see a film here just to enjoy the interior. The man behind this beautiful Art Deco building was a Polish Jew, Abram Tuschinski. He first came to the Netherlands by way of Rotterdam, where he started a theatre company. When World War I ended, he came to Amsterdam with the ambition to build a unique theatre. Tuschinski purchased a piece of land in Reguliersbreestraat occupied by slum buildings and known as Duivelshoek (Devil's Corner). He was closely involved in the design of the building, a lavish Art Deco creation that is perfectly in tune with the era during which cinema was emerging as a popular entertainment form.

The cinema opened in 1921. Tuschinski himself died at Auschwitz in 1942, though the cinema—one of the most beautiful interiors in Amsterdam—ensures that his name lives on. The general public can enter the foyer for free, where a plaque behind the bar commemorates Tuschinski and his two co-founders. You need a cinema ticket to go further inside. Fortunately, the current owners of this building have preserved all the fixtures and furnishings intact so that the original style is just about unblemished. Amsterdam has a rich collection of Art Deco buildings and the Tuschinski is the proudest of them all.

Lives of the gentry: You need walk only a short distance to the east of Rembrandtsplein to enjoy a lavish interior from an earlier era. One of the most stunning insights into life in the grand canal houses of the 17th century is provided by the **Willet-Holthuysen Museum** at No. 605 Herengracht.

This three-storey building with a street-level basement was built in 1689 for Jacob Hop, a prominent burgher of Amsterdam, and his wife Isabella

Statue of Rembrandt, Rembrantsplein.

Hooft. The house changed hands many times and eventually, in 1855, came into the possession of Pieter Gerard Holthuysen. When he died three years later his daughter continued to live there. In 1861 she married Abraham Willet and together they built up a valuable collection of glass, ceramics, silver and paintings. Willet, who had a keen interest in art, was a friend of many of the artists of his time. The couple had no children and so, when Mrs Willet died in 1895, the house and its contents were left to the city of Amsterdam.

Ridiculed: One condition of the legacy was that the premises were to be opened to the public under the name "Museum Willet-Holthuysen". The museum opened its doors on 1 May 1896—but the public showed no interest. A standing joke ridiculed this museum for being one of only two places in Amsterdam where a gentleman could meet his mistress unobserved (the other was Kalverstraat on a Sunday morning).

Extensive restoration has subsequently widened the scope of this museum so that it now contains a number of period rooms, including a fine 18th-century kitchen and a late 19th-century bedroom. Oriental lacquered cabinets, antique clocks, carpets, chandeliers, fireplaces, a grand stairway with gilded cast-iron bannisters, painted ceilings, wall tapestries, silver, porcelain, pottery and glass are part of a valuable collection housed in an authentic and stately interior.

Not to be missed: Today the Willet-Holthuysen Museum is no longer ridiculed, nor does it lack visitors. At the back of the building is an ugly seven-storey office block of metal and glass that serves only to enhance the nostalgia of the rich mansion in which you are standing. Constructed three years after the final stage of the Grachtengordel was complete, and almost the last building on this the most elegant of the three main canals, the Willet-Holthuysen Museum is a grandiose endpiece to the Herengracht. Don't miss it.

schinski ema.

There is more furniture, porcelain and silverware in the **Six Collection** at No. 218 Amstel, between Herengracht and Keizersgracht. But the real reason for coming here is to view the small collection of 17th-century Dutch painting. Dating from 1700, No. 218 Amstel still belongs to the family of Jan Six, a wealthy and well-connected 17th-century art collector. Six was burgomaster of Amsterdam in 1691 and a friend, patron and, later, creditor of Rembrandt. The house is a private residence—a direct descendant of Jan Six still lives here—and for this reason visitors are only admitted by a note of introduction, which is obtainable from the Rijksmuseum on presentation of your passport.

Select masterpieces: The small collection is spread between just five rooms but brings together works by some of the most important Dutch artists. Best known of the works is probably Rembrandt's *Portrait of Jan Six*, which was painted in 1654 and is considered by many to be his finest portrait. Dr Nicolaas Tulp (the same man depicted in Rembrandt's early work, *The Anatomy Lesson of Dr Nicolaas Tulp*) is the subject of a portrait by Frans Hals. Dr Tulp was an important patron of the arts as well as Jan Six's brother-in-law. Other important artists represented include Albert Cuyp, Govert Flinck and Jacob van Ruisdael.

The Amstel was at one time the city's main artery. Amsterdam itself was named after this river, which in the 16th century flowed freely to the Ij. Once you've adjusted to the scale of the city's canals, the breadth of the Amstel seems out of place, but it nevertheless makes for a popular Sunday afternoon walk.

The Amstel used to be an invisible border line that marked the beginnings of the Jewish quarter. The Nieuwe Keizersgracht and the Nieuwe Prinsengracht, because of their position on the east side of the Amstel, were not popular among Amsterdam's wealthier citizens and this allowed some of the richer

The Mager Brug.

members of the city's Jewish community to move in. The effect has survived down the centuries and there is still a strong contrast between the canal-side streets on either side of the river.

Postcard view: One of the most prominent landmarks on this stretch of the river is the **Magere Brug**, which means "skinny bridge". This restored wooden drawbridge, more than 300 years old, gets its name from an even narrower bridge that once stood here. Featured on canal-boat tours, postcards and tourist brochures, it has become one of the clichés of scenic Amsterdam. A more remarkable landmark, on the eastern bank and opposite the Six Collection, is the **Amstelhof**, an old people's home dating from 1681.

The museum theme continues back on Keizersgracht near the junction with Vijzelstraat, with two contrasting collections staring at each other across either side of the canal. The Van Loon Museum, providing another of those tantalising glimpses into old Amsterdam, is complemented by a quizzical, spacious and modern gallery on the opposite bank.

The **Van Loon Museum** is worth visiting on a Monday if you are in a museum frame of mind. Most of Amsterdam's museums are closed on that day; the Van Loon makes Monday its sole opening day. Run by the Van Loon Foundation, the centrepiece of this collection is a sequence of family portraits which provide a unique record of one of the most respectable families of the period. It is a giant family album that includes paintings from the 17th century all the way through to this century as well as photographs.

Graffiti: Architect Adriaen Dortsman built this house in 1672 and the first tenant was the painter Ferdinand Bol, one of Rembrandt's pupils. Among subsequent owners were Abraham van Hagen and his wife Catharina Trip who lived here in the mid-18th century (they left a discreet note to posterity by initialling the staircase balustrade).

Gardens: The Van Loon family arrived on the scene when the building was purchased by Hendrik van Loon in 1884. The Van Loon Foundation started working on it in 1964, with the aim of restoring its late 18th and early 19th-century appearance. The efforts the Foundation put into this venture have paid off handsomely. In contrast to the glitz of the Willet-Holthuysen Museum, the fixtures and furnishings here have been worn by time. It makes a morning or afternoon spent here all the more atmospheric. Uniquely among historic houses in Amsterdam, it also has a well-preserved formal garden.

The **Fodor Museum**, on the other side of Keizersgracht, specialises in exhibitions of work by contemporary Amsterdam artists. Its roomy interior is uncompromisingly modern and its exhibitions have a reputation for being uncompromising too. Representational art is generally absent. Instead exhibits, at the Fodor Museum usually combine a striking mixture of wry humour and

illet-
olthuysen
useum.

radical inventiveness that says much about the city's young artists today. The sober and fine collection of Dutch paintings housed in the Rijksmuseum seems much more than just a 10-minute walk away. If you want to see what Amsterdam's young artists are producing, you should include the Fodor Museum on your itinerary.

Timber church: Tucked away between Keizersgracht and Prinsengracht, **Kerkstraat** is a thoroughfare with no canal. Go to the junction of Kerkstraat and Reguliersgracht and you will find the wooden **Amstelkerk** sitting in the open space of the Amstelveld. The church was built in 1670 as a temporary place of worship for Protestants but the plan to replace it with a more permanent structure of brick was shelved. Nevertheless, the wooden church survived. It is best seen on Mondays, when a plant market is held in the square alongside.

One place you should visit just for fun is the **Heineken Brewery**, on Stadhouderskade, overlooking Singel. Trams coming from the centre of town navigate a large roundabout at the southern end of Vijzelgracht (a road built on a filled-in canal). At night, the neon Heineken sign is clearly visible.

Popular tour: You can no longer take a full tour of the brewery proper because Heineken has transferred its operations to two provincial plants at Zoeterwoude and Den Bosch. But no matter; if you like guided tours to be short, and your beer to be free, then pay your respects. Conducted tours take place each morning and afternoon. They always sell out so go early to be sure of a ticket. You should also check with the VVV tourist information centre on the current status, since Heineken is in the process of turning the oldest part of the premises into a museum (the remainder of the complex is to be demolished).

Beer has been brewed on this site for around 400 years. The original brewery, called De Hooiberg (The Haystack), was established in 1592. Gerard Adriaan Heineken, founder of the pres-

The River Amstel.

ent firm, acquired it in 1864. His company prospered; today it is an international operation with outlets in 150 countries. One ingredient in this success has been Heineken "A" yeast, developed by a pupil of Louis Pasteur. The formula has been closely guarded and passed down from generation to generation, thereby ensuring that the brew has remained a winner. Its popularity, however, has been its undoing in that demand has forced Heineken out of Amsterdam. Disruption of traffic by Heineken delivery trucks, along with the relatively small capacity of the Amsterdam plant, contributed to its closure. The Amsterdam operation was able to produce only 80,000 bottles of lager an hour. That sounds like a lot but Amsterdam itself consumes beer at the same rate. The Heineken plant at Den Bosch has a capacity of 350,000 bottles per hour and the one at Zoeterwoude manages a hefty 700,000 (when demand requires, production can be boosted to 1 million bottles).

Already the former brewery has the makings of an excellent museum. Visitors are told about the invention of beer by the ancient Sumerians, of how whole medieval villages in Europe were burnt down by careless brewing operations, and of how the Teutons introduced public brewing houses where the product could happily be consumed at the point of origin. Stories such as these are all part of a brisk tour around vast, though now unused, copper vessels and through a clutter of antique brewing paraphernalia.

Alcoholic climax: The best part comes at the end when the separate tour groups reconvene in the Heineken beer hall. The ice is quickly broken by as many glasses of frothy beer as you can manage, free snacks, and a nostalgic film made on the day the last horse-drawn cart laden with lager ventured out along Stadhouderskade. This is fun for fun's sake, Amsterdam at its most convivial. As the company's advertising slogan says, "Only Heineken can do this"!

Van Loon Museum.

KG-12-KX

NL
JP-18-SK

Museum Quarter

Amsterdam's three major art galleries are all focused on Museumplein, south of the canal circle but only a short stroll from Leidseplein. The dominant building is the palatial **Rijksmuseum**, built by P. J. C. Cuypers towards the end of the 19th century to house the national art collection of the Netherlands. The facade, which looks more like that of a medieval French château than a Dutch national museum, reflects Cuypers' strong penchant for the Gothic style (he also designed the Central Station and you can see the similarities in the towers and brick overlay).

The highlights of this great collection are indisputably the paintings of the Golden Age, top priority going to the *Night Watch* and 20 or so other works by Rembrandt. This section alone merits several visits but constitutes only about a quarter of the museum. The rest is devoted to the decorative arts, Asiatic and foreign art, Dutch history, prints and Dutch paintings from 1800–1900.

The proportions of the place are forbidding and it pays to be selective. Useful references are the floor plans at the entrance, the reasonably priced *Guide to the Rijksmuseum* and the *Viewfinder* leaflets, which pick on specific themes (such as "Landscape Paintings from the 17th to the 19th Centuries" or "How Paintings Tell Stories") and take you round the relevant sections of the museum, pointing out about 15 of the most pertinent works of art.

Medieval paintings: The earliest works in the Rijksmuseum date to the 15th century when art was still predominantly involved with religious life. The most important painter of the time was Geertgen tot Sint Jans, whose *Adoration of the Magi* (Room 201) is acutely observed and finely executed, yet primitive in comparison to what was already going on in Renaissance Italy in the 1480s.

Mannerism: The works of the 16th-century artists in Rooms 203–206 introduce large-scale narrative figure pieces or biblical stories in real landscapes—shifting away from scenes where a religious subject inevitably took priority. In Room 204 Lucas van Leyden's *Adoration of the Golden Calf,* painted *circa* 1530, is a brilliant and lively piece of pictorial mannerism. The figures are realistically grouped, the narrative detail is lovingly observed and the colour is sparkling. Completely different in feel are the bold compositions of the Haarlem High Mannerists in Room 206. Worth singling out is Cornelisz van Haarlem's *Bathsheba in Her Bath,* depicting three elegantly posed nudes in a mysterious landscape.

The Golden Age: The prosperity of the 17th century led to a prodigious output of painting. Art was not only judged on its aesthetic merits but was also seen as an investment and people of all walks of life were buying paintings to hang in their homes. Most artists restricted themselves to a specific type of art—landscape, genre, portraiture or history—often depending on the subjects they found most marketable. For the first time in the history of Western art painters were no longer dependent entirely on wealthy and powerful patrons.

Portraits: Frans Hals is now one of the most admired artists of the Golden Age, and his paintings make a radical departure from the typical portraiture of the early 17th century. Compare the stiff, formal portraits of the regents and regentesses of the Leper Asylum by Werner van der Valckert (Room 208) with the far more lively and realistic portrayal of his subjects in the works by Frans Hals in Rooms 209 and 210.

In the *Portrait of Isaac Massa and his Wife* (Room 209), Hals has introduced symbolic allusions, such as the winding ivy clinging to the tree—symbolising steadfast love and dependence—and the peacocks, which refer to Juno, goddess and protectress of marriage. *The Merry Drinker* (Room 210), painted in

Preceding pages: the palatial Rijksmuseu[m]; B. van der Helst, ***The Banquet of the Civic Guard.*** **Below**, Fran[s] Hals, ***Isaac Massa and his Wife.***

swift impressionistic brush strokes, shows Hals' remarkable capacity to depict a fleeting gesture. This portrait is typical of Frans Hals' style at its most lively, and the sitter appeals to us through his smile and gestures.

Early Rembrandts: Room 211 contains some of the finest examples of Rembrandt's early period in Leiden, including an outstanding self-portrait. Works such as *The Prophet Jeremiah Lamenting the Destruction of Jerusalem* and *The Prophetess Hannah* (the model was generally believed to be Rembrandt's mother) already show Rembrandt's mastery of observation and skilful use of chiaroscuro, the dramatic contrast of highlights set in relief by areas of deep shade.

Landscapes: The realistic country scenes in Room 214 show how landscapists had abandoned the Flemish mannerist and schematised approach and instead had begun to paint what they actually saw. One of the finest examples is Van Goyen's *Landscape with Two Oaks*, which monumentalises the two old oak trees and dwarfs the human beings below. His limited range of colours, verging on the monochromatic, is typical of his later works.

Another master of atmospheric perspective was Jacob van Ruisdael whose *Windmill at Wijk bij Duurstede* (Room 17) is one of the great landscapes of the 17th century. Again a single element—this time a great stone mill tower—is monumentalised and set against a sky which is full of tension and atmosphere. Rooms 220 and 221 show the very different works of Italianate landscapists whose scenes are bathed in golden light.

Genre and hidden meaning: The merry genre scenes in Rooms 216–19, typified by the bawdy tavern interiors of Jan Steen, are not just intended as realistic and witty portrayals of everyday life. Like the still lives of the 17th century, these works are frequently filled with symbolism and allegorical allusions which were evident to most literate 17th-century Dutchmen.

an Steen,
lerry Family.

Jan Steen's *Merry Family* (Room 216), in which children are following the example of their parents by smoking, drinking and disporting themselves with great abandon, warns against loose morals and bad upbringing. In his painting of *The Toilet* (Room 219) the allusions are erotic—red stockings symbolised a whore; a dog on the pillow, candlestick on the chair and chamberpot on the floor were all indications of lust.

Domestic scenes: There are only 30 known works by the Delft master Vermeer (1632–75), and four of the most famous are in Room 222. They may well be familiar through reproductions but no copy can do justice to these superb works of art.

Perhaps the loveliest of all is *The Kitchen Maid*, a silent and serene domestic interior depicting a simple scene of a woman pouring milk into a bowl. Here the beauty of the colour and the play of sunlight, falling in little dots of paint, transforms an everyday chore into poetry. In the same room are some of the best works of Pieter de Hooch, another master of peaceful domestic scenes, who was equally fascinated by and sensitive to the play of light.

The *Night Watch*: The most dazzling of Rembrandt's masterpieces occupies a whole wall to one end of the Gallery of Honour. The painting is a militia piece, an official portrait of the civic guard that defended the city. The subject matter is *The Company of Captain Frans Banning Cocq* and the Captain is giving his company orders to march. Unlike the militia pieces that had gone before, in which the figures, seated or standing, looked stiff and lifeless, Rembrandt's painting portrays a group in action, each figure moving or about to move, and the overall activity is enhanced by the play of light. To appreciate how far portraiture has come, compare the *Night Watch* with Bartholomeus van der Helst's lifeless regents (celebrating the signing of the Treaty of Münster in 1648), which hangs in the same room.

The layers of varnish and grime which had accumulated on the *Night Watch* led 19th-century experts to believe this was a night scene—hence the mistaken title. Details of the painstaking process of restoration and cleaning of the painting can be seen in a film shown twice a day in the auditorium.

To the left of the *Night Watch* stairs lead up to Room 225 with paintings by a variety of non-Dutch painters. Highlights are works by Piero di Cosimo, Carlo Crivelli, Goya, Fra Angelico, Rubens and Tiepolo. But the logical follow-on from the *Night Watch* is the Gallery of Art where the late Rembrandts are hung, along with the works of some of his eminent pupils.

Late works: Contrary to what people believed for many years, Rembrandt received some important commissions in his last years, among them *The Anatomy Lesson of Dr Deyman* and the *Sampling Officials of the Drapers Guild*. The *Jewish Bride* (whose subject matter still remains a mystery) is one of the great late works. The paint itself—

Jan Steen, *The Toilet*.

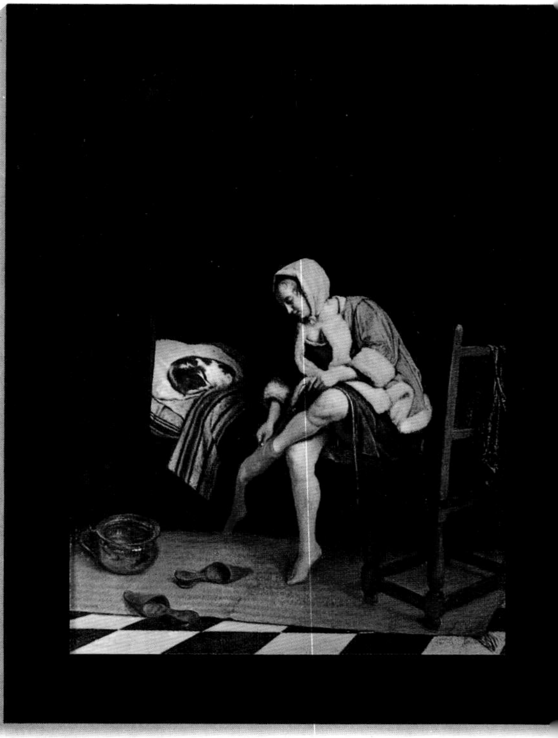

particularly the heavily impasted glowing golds and reds—evokes a mood of warmth and tenderness. Van Gogh was so enamoured by the painting that he once said he would give 10 years of his life to be able to sit in front of it with a loaf of bread.

Dutch School paintings: Paintings from the later schools of Dutch art are set out in Rooms 134–149 in the somewhat neglected Drucker Extension at the back of the museum. They form an inevitable anticlimax after the gems of the 17th century. The 18th century was a time of prosperity and contentment and nothing very dynamic was happening in Dutch art. Cornelis Troost's pretty conversation pieces and portraits show comfortable lifestyles and the influence of his French contemporaries, Watteau and Boucher.

Adjoining the works by Troost in Room 139 are the charming pastels of his Swiss contemporary, Jean-Etienne Liotard. Of the late 18th-century works, the most striking is the little painting of *A Man Writing at his Desk* (Room 142), by Jan Ekels the Younger. Rooms 144 and 145 show the quiet mood and sober realism of the Dutch Romantics, far removed from the ardent spirit of the French Romantics.

The last rooms are devoted to landscapes and beach scenes painted around The Hague and to Amsterdam Impressionists. Worth singling out are the bold canvases by Georg Hendrik Breitner, including *Paleisstraat, Amsterdam* and *Horse Artillery*.

Sculpture and applied art: This huge and variable collection is somewhat confusingly laid out on three floors—you start at Room 238 on the first floor, with medieval sculpture, and end in the basement, in Room 35 with works from the Art Nouveau period.

Labels are unfortunately only in Dutch. The medieval sculpture alone makes a visit worthwhile, particularly the lively oak carvings by Adriaen van Wesel in Rooms 238–242. Room 248 features bronze sculptures, majolica

Rembrandt, the *Night Watch*.

and furniture from the Italian Renaissance, the influence of which can be seen in the following rooms. Fine furnishings and sumptuous silver and glass portray the prosperity and comfortable lifestyles of the 17th century.

Doll's house: Rooms 255–57 are devoted to a beautiful collection of Delftware, with delightful pieces, such as a polychrome pair of pointed, high-heeled shoes and a violin, among the more familiar jugs and plates. The next highlight is in Room 162 (access down the staircase from Room 261) where you will find exquisite and fantastically detailed dolls' houses, complete with tiny Delft plates, paintings and copper pots, most of which were made in the 18th century. A series of rooms with French-influenced 17th and 18th-century furnishings then leads you to the superb collection of Chinese-inspired Meissen porcelain.

The remaining rooms on this floor contain mainly Dutch and French furniture of the 18th century. For the Louis XVI, Empire and Art Nouveau pieces, follow the signs down to the neglected basement section.

Dutch history: For all its potential, this tends to be the least inspiring section of the museum and the least frequented. Paintings, weapons, costumes, documents, models of ships and memorabilia relating to the seafaring history of the Netherlands are all laid out on the ground floor.

The tour starts with the great 16th-century clock from the tower of St Nicholas' Church in Utrecht, but the main emphasis is on 17th and 18th-century history: The Revolt of the Netherlands against Spain (Room 101) and The Seventeenth Century (Room 102), the latter a large open room covering colonial history, the Eighty Years' War and sea battles, mainly against England. Rooms 105–9 cover the period of the Stadholders (1672–1702).

The dominant feature in the section on the French period (Rooms 110–12) is the monumental canvas of *The Battle*

Rembrandt, the *Jewish Bride*...

of Waterloo by Jan Willem Pieneman. The mounted Duke of Wellington is the focus of attention, while the Dutch Prince William lies on a stretcher, looking surprisingly unruffled by the fact that a bullet has just gone through his left shoulder.

Asiatic art: The basement collection of *objets d'art* from Asia is unjustifiably deserted. Rare exhibits are clearly displayed, explanations given in English (unlike other departments) and the size of this section (12 rooms only) is far from daunting. Start in Room 12 with the fascinating and somewhat forbidding stone sculptures from Indonesia, such as the pot-bellied, bearded Hindu god *Agastya,* complete with trident, rosary, water bottle and fly whisk.

Several rooms are devoted to Japanese and Chinese fine and applied art. The *Bodhisattva Akalokiteshivara*, relaxing in Room 15, is an impressive example of late Sung wooden sculpture, skilfully rendering various textures such as metal, silk, skin and hair. From the same period is the lively bronze south Indian statue of *Shiva* (Room 17), dancing amid a halo of flames.

The last rooms show the development of Chinese pottery, from prehistoric pots through to Ming and later porcelain. The exhibition ends with Japanese textiles and earthenware from the 18th and 19th centuries.

The Print Room: Temporary exhibitions are held in the Rijksprentenkabinet (Print Room) but the vast majority of works, including an unrivalled collection of drawings and etchings by Rembrandt, are kept in storage. Most of these can be made available for viewing in the Study Room.

Vincent van Gogh: A short stroll down Paulus Potterstraat brings you to the newest of the city's three great art museums: the Van Gogh Museum. Designed by the de Stijl movement architect Gerrit Rietveld, the museum stands in stark modern contrast to the neighbouring Stedelijk. It was built in the early 1970s as a permanent home for

and detail.

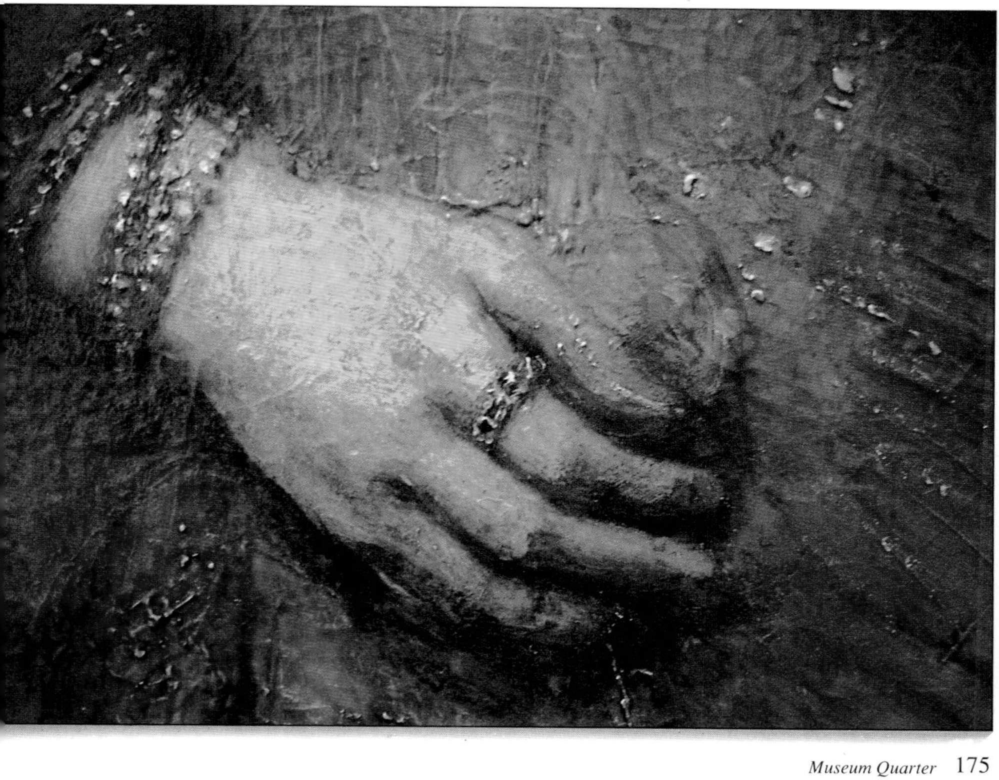

some 200 paintings and 500 drawings by Van Gogh, together with a collection of works by friends and contemporaries—all bequeathed by Van Gogh's nephew, who was also called Vincent.

The interior, which was given a complete facelift for the centenary exhibition, is suitably light and spacious with whitewashed walls and open-plan floors. Space allows for only part of the collection to be on permanent display; other works are brought out from time to time as part of thematic exhibitions, either on the ground or top floors. The museum also has an active workshop where you can try your hand at painting and a café/restaurant, overlooking gardens, which provides a welcome respite from crowds and a surfeit of swirling forms.

Earliest works: The permanent collection of Van Gogh paintings are hung in chronological order on the first floor. The early works, typified by scenes from the daily lives of peasants, show Van Gogh's preference for heavy forms and dark, sombre colours. The numerous studies of peasants in the Brabant culminates in the *Potato Eaters*, a painting which Van Gogh regarded as one of his finest works but whose uncompromising ugliness did not impress friends or critics.

Van Gogh's intent was not to idealise or sentimentalise, but to portray peasant life as he observed it. "I have tried to make it clear," he wrote, "that those people, eating their potatoes in the lamplight, have dug the earth with those very hands they put in the dish, and so it speaks of *manual labour*, and how they have honestly earned their food."

New vision: The move to Paris in 1886 shows his vision transformed. Exposed to the rainbow colours and broad brush strokes of Impressionism and other new painting styles, he began to paint with a brighter and lighter palette. The passionate intensity of his period in Brabant gradually disappears and gives way to lively scenes of Parisian streets, café interiors, windswept landscapes and vivid portraits of friends.

Woman Sitting in the Café du Tambourin has the subject matter, the swift brush strokes of pure colour and the vivid effect of the Impressionists. It was a café he knew well; he took meals there, swopped canvases for food, was friendly with the Italian woman who owned it (this may be her) and used it as a venue to exhibit his collection of Japanese prints. Tired of city life and passionate for "a full effect of colour", Van Gogh had moved to Arles. Enthused by the intense light and warm colours of the Midi, he produced some of his most vivid landscapes and portraits, all created with great speed and intensity.

The famous *Sunflowers*, one of a series of five pictures of this subject, shows his love of warm colour, light and simplicity. The predominant colours of this period are blazing yellows, ochres and oranges, as in *The Yellow House* (where Van Gogh lived), *The Harvest at La Crau*, *Self-Portrait with Straw Hat* and *Van Gogh's Bedroom, Arles*. Of the

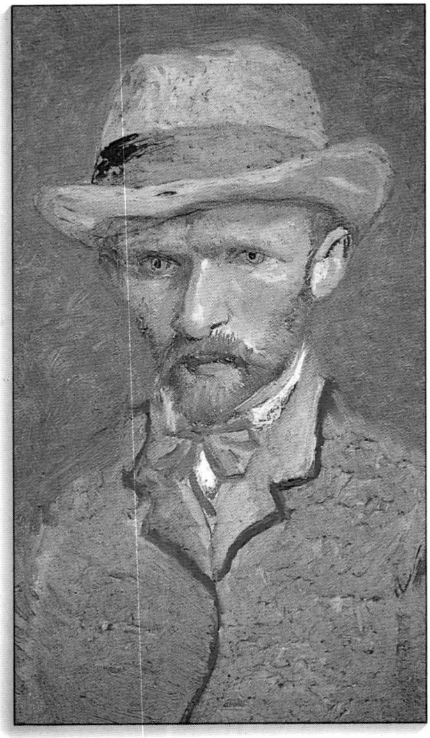

Van Gogh self-portrait

latter picture, he wrote that the colour was "to be suggestive of rest or sleep in general. In a word, to look at the picture ought to rest the brain or rather the imagination."

Following the incident in which Van Gogh quarrelled with Gauguin, and then cut off his own ear, Vincent admitted himself to the asylum at St Remy. His paintings of the landscapes around the asylum become bolder and more visionary, the canvases less colourful and heavily impasted. Of the *Olive Trees with Pink Sky* he writes: "What I have done is rather hard and coarse reality… but it will give a sense of the country and will smell of the soil."

Foreboding: In *Cypresses, St Remy*, he shows the trees as swirling dark flames, reflecting his growing anguish and tormented sensibility. In the final period at Auvers, the landscapes are similar but fiercer, painted in a frenzy of creation between fits of insanity. *Wheatfields and Crows* is the most ominous and desolate of the last works. "They are vast fields of wheat under troubled skies and I do not need to go out of my way to try and express sadness and extreme loneliness." Only a few weeks later, Van Gogh shot himself.

The second floor of the museum is devoted to Van Gogh's drawings. These brilliant evocative sketches from his early period are often overlooked in favour of the more familiar paintings. Also on this floor is Van Gogh's collection of Japanese woodcuts (exhibited on a rotating basis) whose exotic subject matter, fresh colour tones and clear outline had a strong effect on his work.

Works by Van Gogh's friends and contemporaries are hung on the top floor of the museum, many of them brought out only for temporary exhibitions. Among these are works by Toulouse Lautrec, Gauguin and Emile Bernard, all of whom had an influence on Van Gogh's own work.

Stedelijk Museum: The eccentric Dowager of Jonkheer, Lopez Suasso, whose heterogeneous collection of an-

n Gogh's
ats.

tique furniture, coins, jewellery, watches and trinkets filled the rooms of the Stedelijk when it first opened, would be indignant if she could see the museum today. Her whole collection was cast out in order to accommodate a large collection of paintings, sculpture, applied art and industrial design, for the most part uncompromisingly modern. Today the collection comprises a smattering of the "classics" of modern art (Manet, Monet, Van Gogh, Cézanne, Picasso, Matisse and Chagall are all represented in Room 221a) but the main emphasis is on provocative post-war movements.

Transformation: The neo-Renaissance Dutch facade, embellished with gables and turrets, gives no hint of the strikingly modern interior where walls were ripped down to create large open spaces, ceilings partially glassed and rooms whitewashed to offset large, colourful canvases.

The museum's main problem today is one of space. The collection consists of over 25,000 works of art, excluding the collection of applied art and industrial design. Of these, a mere fraction are on permanent display and most of the museum (particularly during the winter months) is devoted to temporary exhibitions. Works are not chronologically arranged and even with a plan (which you can pick up in the main hall) the place is rather confusing.

Developments: Under the dynamic Willem Sandberg, director from 1945 to 1963, the museum was drastically modernised. The aim now is to concentrate on the evolution of art trends or of a specific artist. An example of this approach is the collection of paintings by Kasimir Malevitch. Room 221 is devoted entirely to his work, enabling you to trace the transition from the early, severely simplified scenes from peasant life painted around 1912 (e.g. *The Woodcutter*), through the Cubist phase (*An Englishman in Moscow*) to the "suprematist" abstract works.

"Suprematism", a term coined by

Barnett Newman study, Stedelijk Museum.

Malevitch himself, was a form of analytical Cubism where the purely painterly elements—form, colour, technique—were paramount. The ultimate was a white square on a white ground (Museum of Modern Art, New York).

Similar in style, though more balanced and tranquil, are the works of Mondrian (Room 212), another pioneer of abstract art. His *Composition with Two Lines* (1931) is one of the most radical expressions of "neo-plasticism", defined by Mondrian as a means of reducing natural forms and colours to pure geometrical proportions, using determinate primary colours. Mondrian's neo-plasticism and Gerrit Rietveld's simplistic furniture are together the best examples of the Dutch de Stijl movement—a group which based itself on bringing art back to its essence.

New Europeans: The museum has many works of the COBRA movement, founded in defiance of the artistic complacency of post-war Europe and named after the members' native cities: Copenhagen, Brussels and Amsterdam. The emphasis was on vitality and colour, as in Karel Appel's childlike murals commissioned for the coffee bar of the museum (in the corner of Room 15).

Loosely linked to the COBRA movement, but whose crude and childlike works defy categorisation, is the idiosyncratic French artist, Jean Dubuffet. Abstract Expressionism, the first leading American school of art, has extensive coverage, including the severely simplistic *Cathedra* by Newman (Room 211) and the more energetic *Rosy Fingered Dawn at Louse Point* (currently in the upstairs gallery).

Perhaps the most provocative exhibit of the whole collection is Keinholz's *The Beanery* (Room 12), a reconstruction of a down-at-heel Los Angeles bar, where grime-coated drinkers have clocks for faces. Just along the corridor and far more inviting is the café/restaurant serving excellent lunches, which you can eat while looking out of the windows over the sculpture garden.

edelijk useum and aircase.

THE VAN GOGH PHENOMENON

"He has painted one or two portraits which have turned out well, but he will work for nothing. It is a pity that he shows no desire to earn some money because he could easily do so here."

—*Theo van Gogh* (*brother of Vincent*)

During his lifetime Vincent van Gogh sold only one painting. Today he is arguably the most popular and most reproduced modern artist and his paintings fetch world-record prices. Despite his knowledge of the art markets and influential contacts in the art world—three of his uncles were successful art dealers—Van Gogh never showed any desire to prostitute his style and pander to bourgeois tastes. His letters express disappointment at the failure of his work to sell yet there was never any real effort on his part to become commercial.

He lived entirely on the generosity of his ever-supportive brother Theo (also an art dealer), and any worldly goods he acquired he gave away. For much of his adult life he was severely undernourished, subsisting on paltry quantities of protein and a constant supply of caffeine and alcohol. By the time he had reached his early 30s, his teeth were breaking off.

The characterisation of Van Gogh the misfit has always tended to shadow Van Gogh the painter. There is an inevitable fascination with the eccentric who, in a stormy exchange, threatens Gauguin with a knife, slashes off his own ear with a razor, wraps it in newspaper and takes it to a prostitute; the *isolé* who preferred to share the hardship of the coalminers than live in middle-class comfort; the idiosyncratic who befriended and slept with an ugly, pregnant, alcoholic prostitute, who was deeply religious and spent hours of his life translating the Bible into French, German and English, who painted all night out of doors with candles stuck in his hat.

From an early age Van Gogh had shown signs of eccentricity and his attempts to make friends met with hostility. His rejection by the first girl he fell for (his landlady's daughter in London) was the first of several disastrous efforts to bestow love or receive it. "One may have a blazing hearth in one's soul and yet no one ever comes to sit by it. Passers by see only a wisp of smoke rising from the chimney and continue their way."

Face to face with Van Gogh.

Art therefore became the only means of expressing his passion and avenging the failures that he had suffered in his lifetime. His art was personal and unsophisticated. The sunny scenes of Arles with their vivid lights, fresh colours and bold, loose brushwork convey his own excitement and passion: "the emotions are sometimes so strong that one works without being aware of working… and the strokes come like words in a speech or a letter."

Van Gogh's artistic output was torrential. His career spanned only 10 years (he died at the age of 37), yet he produced close on 2,000 works. The paintings of the period in Arles—200 in 15 months—were produced in a frenzy of haste, almost as though he knew the end was near. Some of his most famous canvases were dashed off between fits of depression, isolation and insanity.

Despite this, neither his paintings nor his correspondence show signs of insanity. In his letters to Theo, he writes with great insight about his own illness and describes his paintings in graphic detail. His art is certainly impetuous and the frenzy of creation is always evident in the swirling, flame-like forms that cover his canvases; yet equally there is always an over-riding concern for balance and order.

Although Van Gogh's art was rarely praised during his lifetime, it was not long after his death that the paintings were causing a stir. In 1891 a critic for the *Echo de Paris*, previewing the exhibition at the Salon des Artistes Indépendants, wrote of his works: "When one stands before these canvases, whose black mourning ribbon draws the attention of the indifferent mass of passers-by, one grieves to think that this brilliantly gifted painter, this most sensitive, instinctive, visionary artist, is no more." During the 1890s his works were exhibited at least once a year.

To mark the artist's centenary in 1990 the Van Gogh Museum in Amsterdam and the Rijksmuseum in Kroller-Muller, Otterloo (60 miles/100 km from Amsterdam), combined to hold the largest-ever retrospective. For the first time the various versions of familiar paintings such as *The Bedroom in Arles* and *The Reaper* were shown together, and 250 drawings, many of which had seldom seen daylight, were put on display. This, together with numerous special events including a film festival and opera, was a fitting celebration for the artist who was seen as a failure and misfit in his own lifetime but whose works now command the highest auction prices in the world.

…e Van Gogh …dustry.

ANJA

JODENBUURT AND PLANTAGE

The Jewish quarter of Amsterdam (Jodenbuurt) was once a lively, colourful, distinct and proud neighbourhood. Though many parts were poor, it was invariably hardworking. Those days have gone forever. During World War II, the Jewish community in Amsterdam, which had numbered 80,000, was reduced to only 5,000. The Jodenbuurt, the most populous part of Jewish Amsterdam, became a virtual ghost town. Jewish street life disappeared.

Since then it has been a victim again, this time of property development and road-building. Stand at the broad junction of Mr Visserplein and look at the dull concrete embankments flanking Jodenbreestraat to the north, the gaping underpass which leads traffic from Weesperstraat north towards the IJ Tunnel, and the great square hulk of the Town Hall overlooking Waterlooplein, and you can't help feeling that Amsterdam is just another modern, ugly city.

Yet the Jodenbuurt, and neighbouring Plantage, has a strong story to tell. There are enough places to visit to occupy a full day and, if you are interested in Amsterdam's Jewish past, more careful exploration is amply rewarded.

Ironically, the thoroughly modern setting of **Waterlooplein** is an appropriate place to start exploring the Jodenbuurt. At Nos. 33–39 Waterlooplein, Amsterdam's first public synagogue was completed in 1639 (it was demolished in 1931). This area was known as the Vlooyenburg, a stretch of marshy ground regularly flooded by the Amstel, and was the site of the original Jewish quarter, accommodating the first Jews who came to Amsterdam.

Origins: The name Vlooyenburg comes from the old Dutch word for "flood". Two canals, Houtgracht and Leprozengracht, ringed Vlooyenburg to the north and east, creating an island. Here the Jews lived in poverty. In the 19th century, when Jews were allowed to practise trades and crafts for the first time, many small businesses were established in houses that were already too small and so conditions worsened. In 1882, the canals of Houtgracht and Leprozengracht were filled in to create Waterlooplein. Markets on Sint Antoniesbreestraat and Jodenbreestraat were transferred there and the market place became the focal point of Jewish life in the area.

Jodenbreestraat (The Broad Street of the Jews) was once the lively business centre of the Jewish quarter. Today you can do little more than imagine all that colour and life—redevelopment has left its scar. The long concrete block that runs down the northern side of Jodenbreestraat today is just one of the many insensitive modern buildings that have torn the heart out of Amsterdam's Jewish quarter.

The construction of the subway, which runs right under Waterlooplein, and extensive redevelopment at the

receding ages: **luziek-eater and tadhuis omplex.** **eft,** **ortuguese-raelite ynagogue iterior.** **ight,** **aterlooplein usker.**

southern end of Sint Antoniesbreestraat have further contributed to the changes that have completely destroyed the character of this area. In 1977 the flea market on Waterlooplein was moved to Rapenburgerstraat and did not return until the Stopera project (the combined Muziektheater and Town Hall) was completed. That market (open between 10 a.m. and 5 p.m. daily except Sunday) is worth visiting as the last vestige of the once-vital community life of the area.

The Mozes en Aaronkerk (Moses and Aaron Church) is proof that Waterlooplein was not exclusively Jewish. It was completed in 1841 but stands on the site of an earlier clandestine church. The philosopher Spinoza is thought to have been born (in 1632) in one of the houses demolished to make way for the building you see today.

Controversial: If you enjoy opera and ballet you would do better to make your visit here in the evening, having bought tickets for a performance at the Muziektheater. The centrepiece of redevelopment on Waterlooplein, the **Muziektheater and Town Hall** complex was one of the most controversial pieces of property development that Amsterdam has ever seen. Opposition to the plan was widespread; many felt that the area should be residential and squatters rioted here in the late 1970s. Attempts to stop the building failed and the complex was completed in 1986. Ironically, the nickname *Stopera*, given by protesters to the complex, has stuck and passed into common parlance.

Cultural centre: From a tour boat on the Amstel you will need little persuasion that the architecture of the complex is totally out of keeping with the scale and style of buildings nearby. But the Muziektheater (if not the Town Hall) has at least brought a measure of charisma to this area. Two resident companies perform here: the Netherlands Opera and the National Ballet accompanied respectively by the Netherlands Philharmonic Orchestra and the Netherlands Ballet Orchestra. Together they quickly

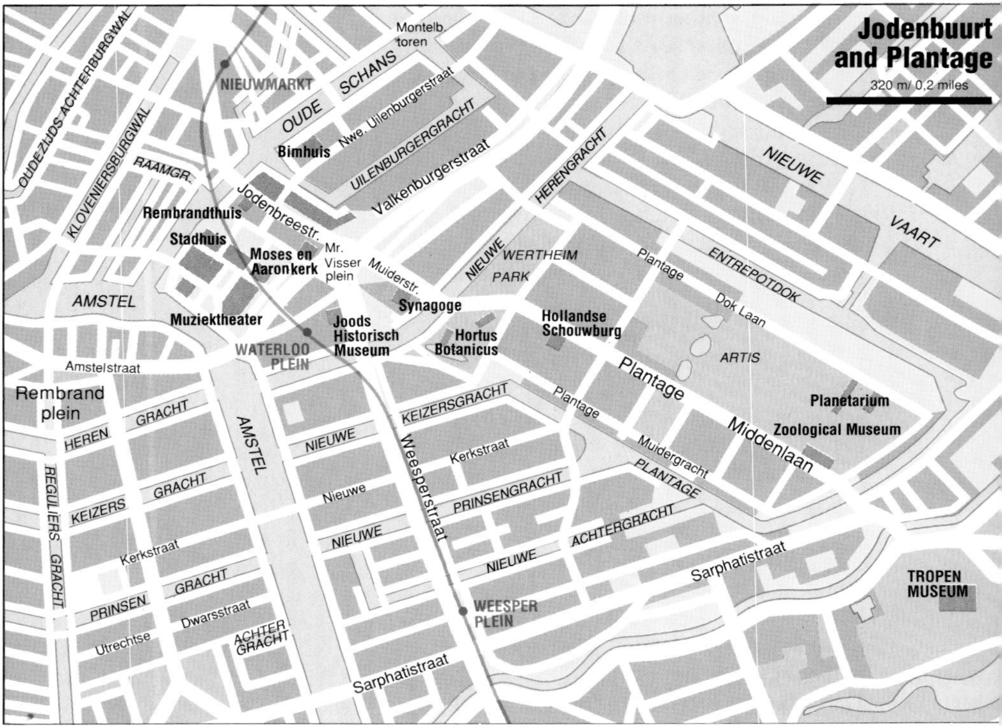

earned a place for the Muziektheater on the international opera and ballet circuit. Acclaimed guest performers have included Moscow's Bolshoi Ballet, London's Royal Ballet and New York's Martha Grahame Dance Company.

Rembrandt's home: The most-visited sight in the Jewish quarter is undoubtedly the **Rembrandthuis**, at Nos. 4–6 Jodenbreestraat. A former home of Rembrandt, this has been a museum since 1911. Of the 280 etchings known to have been made by Rembrandt, 245 can be viewed here. There is also an excellent display that explains the technique of etching. In summer, the Rembrandthuis is always—and justifiably—crowded.

Rembrandt Harmensz van Rijn, to give the artist his full name, was born in Leiden and came to Amsterdam in 1631 when he was in his mid-20s. Soon after arriving he took lodgings in what was then known simply as the Breestraat, or Broad Street, later to be known as Jodenbreestraat. In Rembrandt's day this was on the edge of the town; he used to walk out into the country, eastwards to the village of Diemen, now an Amsterdam suburb.

Because he lived in the fast-growing Jewish quarter, it is perhaps inevitable that Jewish life features so much in Rembrandt's work. His famous portrait of a leading rabbi, Menasseh ben Israel, who also lived in this vicinity, hangs in the museum. Many other prominent Jews commissioned him to paint their portraits and Rembrandt also liked local people to sit for him, with the result that a great many anonymous Jewish characters appear in his work.

Rembrandt purchased the house on Jodenbreestraat in 1639 by which time he was a celebrated artist, the recipient of important commissions. Even so, his comfortable new home (then just a two-storey building topped by a step gable) cost him dearly; he had incurred substantial debts to pay for it and the expense of furnishing and running it eventually contributed to his bankruptcy in

Waterlooplein flea market.

The Jews In Amsterdam

Jews first settled in the Netherlands in large numbers in the early 17th century. The 1579 Union of Utrecht, under which the northern provinces of the Netherlands agreed to assist each other against the Spanish, stipulated that no one should be persecuted for their religious beliefs. The rebellious provinces were reacting to Spain's repression of Protestantism and did not necessarily have the Jews in mind, though the principle was soon applied to them. At the end of the 16th century, the newly formed Republic of the United Netherlands offered Jews fundamental freedoms that they could not enjoy elsewhere in Europe.

The first Jews to settle in Amsterdam were Marranos—Sephardic Jews from Spain and Portugal. They were pseudo-Christians who had been forced to convert to Christianity. By the middle of the 17th century the pattern had changed. Most of the Jews coming to settle in Amsterdam were Ashkenazic—Jews of German or Polish origin.

Amsterdam's tolerance of its Jewish immigrants was not unbounded. In 1598 the city magistrates determined that the Portuguese merchants could purchase citizenship providing that they did not worship openly. A more serious restriction, dating from 1632, prohibited Jews from becoming members of the guilds. Since nearly all trades and crafts were conducted under the authority of the guilds, the Jews were in effect excluded from most occupations.

This influenced the way in which the Jewish community did eventually become part of the economic fabric of Amsterdam. The Jews had to pursue activities not overseen by the guilds: retail trading and the banking business. There were also new crafts—some introduced by the Jews themselves—such as diamond processing, sugar refining, silk manufacture, tobacco twisting and printing. Even so, further restrictions were put in the way of the Jews: they were forbidden to own shops and another measure, passed in 1661, decreed that Jews should not attempt to convert Christians or "have any physical communion with Christian wives or daughters in or outside the state of marriage even though these women themselves might be of bad reputation."

It is hardly surprising, therefore, that Jews were forced to settle in the poorest and least valued of the city's neighbourhoods. In 1795, after two centuries of Jewish immigration, while nearly 37 percent of the city's population as a whole received poor relief, the figure for Sephardic Jews was 54 percent and for Ashkenazic Jews 87 percent. A grain crisis in 1771 led to an increase in mortality in Amsterdam of 30 percent; for Jews, the increase was 100 percent.

One of the most important dates for the Jews in Amsterdam was 1796, a year of significant emancipation: Jews were free to settle anywhere; with the disappearance of the guilds all occupations were open to them; and Jews even obtained the right to vote—some were eligible for nomination to positions in government.

As a direct result, Amsterdam's Jewish community grew substantially in the 19th century but the essential "boundaries" of the city's Jewish quarter had by now largely been established: St Antoniebreestraat, Jodenbreestraat and the area east of the Oude Schans canal and Zwanenburgwaal, especially the Uilenburgergracht and Waterlooplein. When the second phase of the Grachtengordel was completed, some of the richer Jews moved to the new canals—of Nieuwe Herengracht, Nieuwe Keizersgracht and Nieuwe Prinsengracht. Their unfavourable location on the far side of the Amstel made houses here unpopular among Amsterdam's wealthier citizens. Finally, by the end of the 19th century, Plantage Middenlaan and the streets nearby became a more affluent extension of the Jewish quarter.

By the turn of the century, about 60,000 Jews were living in this quarter of the city—more than half the total number of Jews living in the Netherlands—and at the outbreak of World War II that number had grown to 80,000. By the end of the war there were a mere 5,000 survivors and the entire area of Jodenbuurt had suffered such destruction that it was now left in ruins.

1656. Forced by his creditors to sell the house and many of his possessions, Rembrandt was nevertheless allowed to stay on until 1660, when he made a new home across the city in the Jordaan.

On the opposite side of Jodenbreestraat from Rembrandt's house is another important part of the Jewish quarter, bounded by Oude Schans and Valkenburgerstraat. In the 17th century there were two islands here—Uilenburg and Marken—thick with shipyards and wharves. When shipbuilding transferred to the newly developed islands of Kattenburg, Wittenburg and Oostenburg, large numbers of poorer Jews settled here.

Jazz and diamonds: A Jewish success story, in the shape of the former diamond factory of the Boas company, was founded here in 1878 and the building still stands overlooking the Uilenburgergracht. The processing of diamonds was very much a Jewish occupation and skilled cutters and polishers earned high wages. Today the area's principal attraction, particularly for jazz fans, is the **Bimhuis**. Housed in a former warehouse on the eastern side of Oude Schans (Nos. 73–77), this is one of Amsterdam's best (and most modern) jazz venues.

While Waterlooplein was the embryo of Amsterdam's Jewish quarter, its heart today is a short walk away in the **Joods Historisch Museum** (Jewish Historical Museum), situated on Jonas Daniel Meijerplein. The museum occupies the Ashkenazi Synagogue Complex, which comprises four synagogues built during the 17th and 18th centuries. The museum had previously been housed in the Weigh House (Waag), on Nieuwmarkt. When it moved to the Ashkenazi complex in 1987, Amsterdam's Jewish community achieved a long-standing ambition to have this major collection on Jewish life in a building where something of the Jewish spirit would reign.

ft, ***The ockworker***, **nas Daniel eijerplein. ght, mbrandt-is.**

The Jewish Historical Museum's stated aim is to provide a "place of reference for those whose links with past generations were broken by the war." Be warned that it is an enormous, sober and serious collection. If you want to absorb it fully, you should give yourself a full morning here. On a lighter note, the café attached to the museum sells the best cheesecake in Amsterdam.

Past and present: The museum's detailed history of Zionism, collections of Jewish religious artefacts and insights into the lives of important Dutch Jewish personalities are part of a narrative that primarily appeals to practising Jews. This is counterbalanced, however, by exhibits of a more general interest: the story of Jewish settlement in Amsterdam and the Netherlands, explanations of Jewish dietary laws and photographs that depict Jewish life today.

The oldest synagogue in the museum complex, the Grote Schul, dates from 1671. Across the way, between Jonas Daniel Meijerplein and Muiderstraat, the **Portuguese-Israelite Synagogue**

was completed just four years earlier. Both buildings are important in that they were the first synagogues of any size to be built in Western Europe.

The Portuguese-Israelite Synagogue is so large, in fact, that it dominates the junction of Mr Visserplein even today; in the 17th century the effect would have been more pronounced still. When wealthier Jews went to live in the extensions to the Grachtengordel, the new canals to the east, this locality became the new centre of the Jewish quarter. Paintings of the scene soon after the synagogue was constructed depict tranquil scenes on the Muidergracht, a wide canal (now partly filled in; it re-emerges at the eastern end of Plantage Middenlaan), which passed through what is now Jonas Daniel Meijerplein.

Emancipation: This large triangular space, flanking the Portuguese-Israelite Synagogue, is named in honour of Jonas Daniel Meijer (1780–1834). He graduated as a Doctor of Law at the remarkably young age of 16 and that same year, 1796, became the first Jew to be admitted to the Bar. It proved to be an auspicious year for the Jewish community as a whole for in 1796 Jews were also granted equal rights of citizenship for the first time.

Ironically, the square named after Meijer is associated with the annihilation of most of the city's Jews during World War II; it was the scene of the first round-up of Jews for deportation to the death camps of Nazi Germany.

Arrests: Following the German invasion in May 1940, anti-Jewish measures had been introduced only gradually. The stakes were raised in early February 1941 when the Germans ordered the Jewish Council to be set up, supposedly to maintain order among the Jewish people. Following a disturbance on 19 February, the German chief of police decided to make an example and on Saturday 22 February, 425 young Jewish men were forcibly arrested, herded together on Jonas Daniel Meijerplein and taken away in trucks.

Jewish Historical Museum.

Memorial: What happened on Jonas Daniel Meijerplein sparked off the first organised Dutch resistance against the German Occupation. In the face of further round-ups by the Germans the following day, the Communists called for a general protest strike. The dockworkers were among the first to respond and the strike spread through Amsterdam, only to be broken up violently the following day. The bulky bronze statue of *The Dockworker* on Jonas Daniel Meijerplein, unveiled in 1952, is one of Amsterdam's most important war memorials and commemorates the February strike.

The strike merely delayed the inevitable. The German policy against the Jews gathered pace in 1942. In January of that year, Jews from Zaandam were the first to be moved from their home town and Amsterdam was used as the collection point. The Nazis used the Jewish Council (whose headquarters were at No. 58 Nieuwe Keizersgracht) to co-ordinate the deportations. The Nazis forestalled resistance to the anti-Jewish measures by pretending that the deportees were being sent to work in German factories. The task of administrating the deportation was placed in the hands of the Jews themselves.

The extent to which the Jewish Council contributed to the destruction of Dutch Jews is still intensely controversial. Did the Jewish Council know what would really happen to the Jews when they were taken east? Was it effectively collaborating? Could the Jewish Council have taken any other course of action under the circumstances?

Outspoken: One Jew, L.E. Visser, was of a clear mind on the matter. His name is written into the neighbourhood: **Mr Visserplein** is the name of the junction next to the Jewish Historical Museum. In 1939 Visser was President of the Supreme Court in the Netherlands but was dismissed the following year. He spent the final two years of his life in defiance of the Germans. He worked for the illegal newspaper *Het Parool*, protested against the implementation of separate Jewish education, and refused to wear the Star of David. He spoke out against the Jewish Council, saying: "I am quite overcome by the humiliation which you, who are well aware of the historical importance of these measures, have brought about." A few days later he died of natural causes.

A little further down Plantage Middenlaan is another sad reminder of the war. The facade of the **Hollandse Schouwburg** has not been preserved for architectural reasons but as a memorial. In October 1942, this theatre was appropriated by the Germans as an assembly point for Jews prior to deportation. Their length of stay varied but their route out was always the same: by train to Westerbork, the transit point for the death camps of Auschwitz and Sobibor.

Through the doorway of this building is a quiet courtyard and a stark obelisk that stands as a monument to the 104,000 Dutch Jews killed by the Nazis. The building opposite is today a college

edeveloped ewish uarter: St ntoniesbree-raat and uiderkerk. ollowing ages: nsterdam o.

but, during the occupation, housed a crèche for the children and babies of those who were being kept in the Hollandse Schouwburg awaiting deportation. A brave smuggling operation ensured that many Jewish children were saved from the fate of their parents and taken to safety. On the front of the Hollandse Schouwburg is a plaque dedicated to Walter Susskind, one of the people involved in this clandestine rescue operation.

Parks and gardens: The Hollandse Schouwburg is located in the district known as the **Plantage**. This leafy suburb grew up in the second half of the 19th century and among the people who made their homes here were the numerous Jews who made good profits out of the booming diamond industry. With the Hortus Botanicus and Wertheim Park (named after a leading 19th-century Jewish banker) at one end, and the welcome space of the Artis Zoological Gardens at the other, this was (and still is) a popular place to live, with broad streets and elegant houses that provided a contrast to the Jewish quarter proper.

The **Hortus Botanicus**, once a rather unkempt collection of tropical and semi-tropical trees and shrubs, is undergoing comprehensive restoration and will re-open with new greenhouses dedicated, respectively, to tropical and desert flora.

Further down Plantage Middenlaan is the **Artis Zoo**, which opened in 1838 when the Plantage was virtually undeveloped and is still a cornerstone of this neighbourhood. For such a relatively small area it houses a surprisingly rich collection of animals, including lions, tigers, gorillas, polar bears and seals, plus a reptile house, aviary and stunning aquarium. All this has made the zoo a great favourite with Amsterdammers, although the rather academic Zoological Museum, at the eastern end of the zoo, receives far fewer visitors. You should therefore avoid the zoo on Sundays in summer, unless you are fond of large crowds.

L PIRATA

INDE·OVDE·SC

WAREHOUSES OF THE EAST

Amsterdam has always been a port and in the late 16th and early 17th centuries the city's phenomenal growth was built on its role as a mighty centre for shipping and world trade. Dutch maritime supremacy was founded on the fishing industry. A Dutchman discovered a recipe for curing fish and pickled herring thus became an important export commodity. Dutch sailors subsequently opened up scores of new routes to the Far East and the Americas, and the port of Amsterdam became the biggest and busiest in the world.

The port did not die with the passing of the Golden Age. In 1824 the North Holland canal was opened, dug through the entire length of the province of North Holland to the naval base at Den Helder. In 1876 the North Sea canal followed. The latter is 887 ft (270 metres) wide, 45 ft (14 metres) deep and 10 miles (16 km) long, and is connected with the sea via the locks of Ijmuiden.

The port and its associated activities of shipbuilding and repair is still an important factor in the city's economy, not only providing jobs but making a significant contribution to the gross city product as well.

Docklands tour: The story of Amsterdam's role as a port can still be traced even if the surviving maritime sites—with the notable exception of the Netherlands Maritime Museum—hardly count as scenic corners of Amsterdam; Prins Hendrikkade, the Eastern Docks and Oostenburgstraat can look rather forlorn. No matter! Amsterdam's wealth came in on boats and you cannot hope to understand what made this city tick without knowing a little more about its nautical past.

A maritime tour proper of Amsterdam should start with the **Schreierstoren**, situated on Prins Hendrikkade and just a few minutes away from the Central Station. This is the oldest tower surviving in Amsterdam and was built in 1482 as part of the city walls. Tradition has it that sailors' wives and sweethearts bade their men a weepy farewell from here.

The Schreierstoren, today a shop selling maps and books, gives three clues to Amsterdam's nautical past. A tablet from Greenwich Village Historic Society commemorates Henry Hudson's departure from here in 1609, the beginning of a long voyage to the harbour of New York and the eponymous Hudson river. Another tablet, dating from 1569, shows a weeping woman and departing ships. Yet another was placed in 1945 and reads: *Eerste schipvaart naar oostindie 1595* (First voyage to the East Indies, 1595).

Beyond the walls: While the Schreierstoren was once part of the city walls, an important area known as the **Lastage**, the site of the earliest shipbuilding yards, remained outside these fortifications. You can pinpoint this locality by finding the **Montelbaanstoren** on Oude Schans. This tower was constructed in 1512 as a fortification to protect the Lastage. The decorative spire was added in 1606 by Hendrik de Keyser, the architect responsible for many of Amsterdam's other pinnacles.

Once a busy harbourside, Prins Hendrikkade is today a major route taking traffic in and out of Amsterdam via the IJ Tunnel. **Scheepvarthuis** (literally "ship voyage house") is an appropriate name for the building that overlooks Amsterdam's Oosterdok even if it doesn't date from the city's seagoing heyday. It was constructed in 1915 and was designed by Van der Mey, one of the architects associated with the Amsterdam school of architecture that flourished in the early part of this century. Internally and externally the building's motifs and decorations recount Amsterdam's maritime history in delightful detail, with ships, whales and mermaids ornamenting the facade and railings that ripple like the sea waves.

Admiral Michiel Adriaensz de Ruyter, the city's most famous nautical son and a man credited with making the Dutch fleet a strong enough force to withstand British and French attempts to destroy it, once lived at number **131 Prins Hendrikkade**. A frieze over the front door commemorates him.

There is no shortage of buildings surviving from the days when Amsterdam was a centre of world commerce. A walk along the **Entrepôt Dok** reveals a long line of warehouses, now under conversion to apartments, built by the East India Company.

New uses: At the western end, the grand gateway emblazoned with the words Entrepôt Dok looks sadly out of place surrounded by the seedy bars and cafés of **Kadijksplein**. But go through the gate and walk along the waterside and you will be able to picture just how many shiploads of eastern promise at one time used these waterways. Today these buildings have been turned into stylish offices and apartments. Tucked between them are quiet bars that pro-

Preceding pages: ship in Amsterdam harbou[r] old Amsterdam; plaqu[e] on Oude Schans canal. Left, Montelbaan storen and Oude Schan[s] canal.

vide welcome ports of call as you retrace the footprints of Amsterdam's seafaring heritage.

Just over half way along Hoogte Kadijk, which runs parallel with the Entrepôt Dok, the **Kromhout Shipyard**, one of 30 shipyards that were established here by the end of the 17th century, still survives as a museum.

Ships of iron: The name Kromhout was first mentioned in 1757 in relation to a forge located on the site of the present shipyard. A shipwright, Doede Jansen Kromhout, developed the site. In the 19th century, a new owner, Daniel Goedkoop, equipped the yard for building iron ships. His son turned it into one of the most modern shipyards of the area. One of his investments, an iron canopy over the slipway, stands today and is a protected monument.

Moves to preserve the shipyard for the future were first made in 1970 and later gained the support of the Netherlands Maritime Museum. The Kromhout shipyard was also subsequently placed on Amsterdam's list of protected monuments. Still an operating shipyard, it now restores and repairs historic vessels.

There is also a modest museum. The exhibits mostly consist of old ship's engines and pumps, along with models of old steamers, which really only appeal to people with a penchant for marine engineering, but some of the framed engravings on display, depicting the Nieuwe Vaart as a busy artery of floating repair platforms and tall ships at anchor, are interesting and serve only to emphasise that the docks have long been dead.

Shortage of funds: There are plans to create a new permanent exhibition here that will give a comprehensive picture of shipbuilding on the islands and of the people who lived here. The sad fact is that the Kromhout Shipyard currently lacks the money to do justice to the heritage of this sleepy corner of Amsterdam. At present the Kromhout Shipyard is really for *aficionados* only.

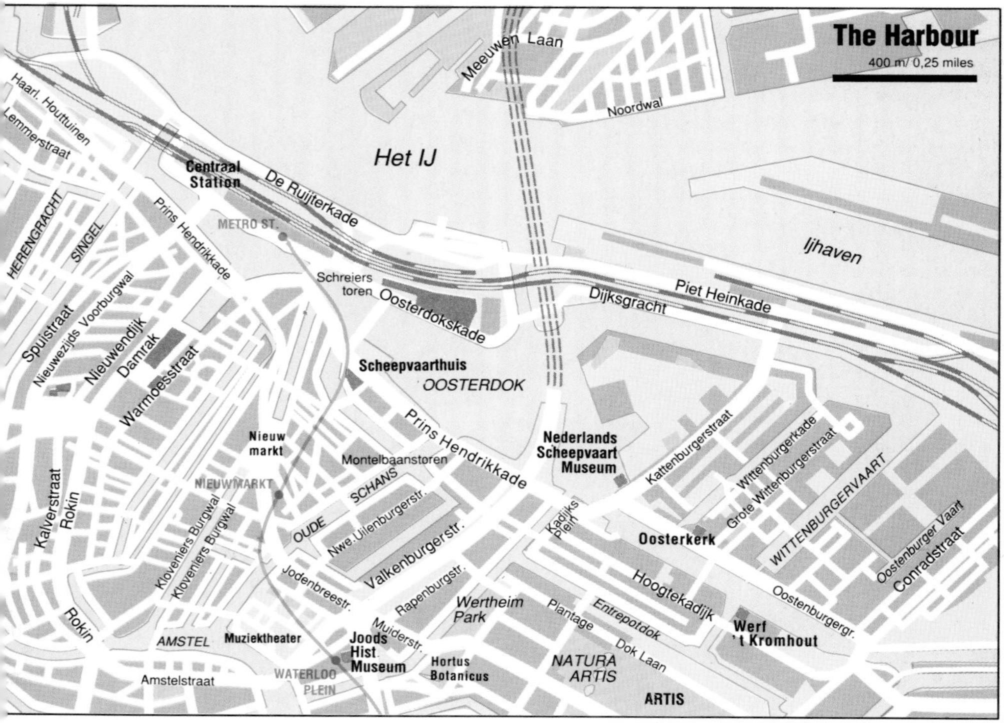

By contrast, the **Netherlands Scheepvaart (Maritime) Museum** is one of Amsterdam's highlights. Even the hardiest of landlubbers will consider an hour or two here well spent. This rich collection occupies Amsterdam's old Zeemagazijn, the arsenal of the Amsterdam Admiralty. From this building, constructed in 1656, sails, ropes, cannon, cutlasses, food and fresh water were supplied to the newly built ships, launched at the adjacent yard, and to the fleet moored in the port.

Change of use: In the 20th century the Dutch navy moved its facilities and installations to ports with direct access to the North Sea and the Zeemagazijn lost its original function. The building was renovated in the 1970s and a first-class museum was born. Its collection was assembled by the Society for the Netherlands Museum of Maritime History. The models and paintings are nearly all of the same period as the ships and events they represent.

The museum charts a detailed course through all of Amsterdam's, and Holland's, maritime achievements, starting with the V-shaped timber of a small medieval vessel found in the reclaimed land of the former Zuider Zee and finishing with glimpses into the lives of passengers cruising to South America, the United States, Asia and Australia in the luxurious liners of the early and mid-20th century.

Between those two points, the collection provides colourful insights into the development of the three-masted ships of the 16th century which opened the way to the uncharted oceans, the many naval wars in which the Dutch fought, and how, in the 17th century, Amsterdam was the world centre of cartography, producing the first sea-atlas.

So, if trailing round the islands doesn't appeal to you, or staring at warehouses doesn't inspire you, then you can let the Netherlands Maritime Museum alone remind you how Amsterdam made its own unforgettable mark on the map of Europe.

Below, canal boat art. Right, Kromhout Shipyard.

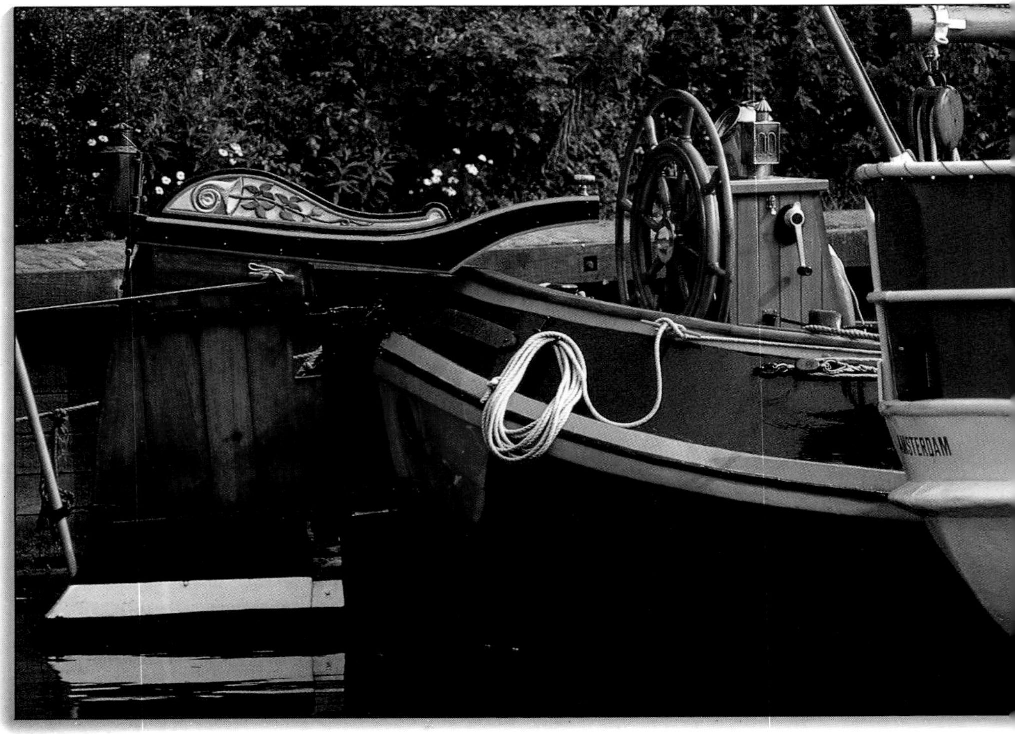

SUPREME ON THE SEAS

In 1597, a Dutch expedition reached the East Indies for the first time, travelling by way of the Cape of Good Hope and the Indian Ocean. There were merchants aplenty to exploit the trade potential of this new route. Voyaging as far as Australia and Tasmania, they opened up the legendary spice routes to the Far East and began to displace the Spanish and Portuguese as rulers of the waves. With the Dutch discovery of the route to the East Indies, better known today as Indonesia, the trade in tropical products became one of the largest sources of income for the city. In 1602, a number of small companies which had been trading in Asia united to form the famous East India Company, based on Amsterdam. Shares in the Company were traded in the Mercantile Exchange, built over the Rokin.

A West India Company was also founded, originally to maintain trade with New Amsterdam (New York) and Brazil. In 1609, when an exchange bank was established, Amsterdam was well on its way to becoming the biggest trade centre in the whole of Western Europe.

The East India Company's whole purpose and philosophy can be summed up in a single word: monopoly. Its aim was to secure absolute control of the East Indies spice trade, and for a long time it succeeded. On such secure foundations its rapid growth was inevitable. The Company established trading posts which eventually became colonies. By 1669, at the peak of the Dutch Golden Age, the Company owned 150 trading vessels and 40 warships. It employed 10,000 soldiers, and 1,000 shipbuilders worked in its yards at Amsterdam. The farthest outpost of the company was the Japanese island of Deshima in the Bay of Nagasaki.

By 1730 the East India Company was the world's largest trading enterprise and had even created its own coinage. Even though the Company gradually lost its leading position after 1750, its influence lasted much longer. The great empire of the Dutch East Indies remained intact until Indonesia achieved independence in 1949.

As carriers of trade, the Dutch were dominant in all parts of the world from the start of the 17th century and the Dutch fleet was by far the largest in existence. Dutch ship design was the envy of, first, Sir Walter Raleigh and then, later, Samuel Pepys. Tsar Peter the Great even came to live in Holland to acquire knowledge for building up a new Russian navy.

Warehouses are today the most visible legacy in Amsterdam of this 17th-century explosion in maritime trade and it is difficult to walk far without spotting chic warehouse conversions. There are also two sets of man-made islands dating back more than 300 years. These lay off the western and eastern coasts of the city, projecting into the IJ, and each still bears its original name.

The easterly islands—Kattenburg, Wittenburg and Oostenburg—were created to help Holland in the battles for maritime supremacy, which started around 1650, against Great Britain. Constructed to provide space for the building of warships, these islands were lined with harbours and bisected with wide canals. Houses, pubs and even a church were built here to provide a mini-community dedicated to maritime matters. Consecrated in 1670, and still protected as a monument, the Oosterkerk (East Church) stands near the old island harbour.

The three islands to the west of Amsterdam—known as Realeneiland, Bickerseiland and Prinseneiland—were specially constructed in the 17th century to provide more space for shipbuilding. The small shipyards based here profited greatly from the East India Company's policy of granting Dutch East India trading licences to companies that used ships built in the Netherlands. The westerly islands were also used for storing inflammables which the town fathers, fearful of fires, wanted well isolated from the business and residential centre.

Many of the imposing warehouses of the East India Company remain, some converted into comfortable and fashionable apartments. Unimproved warehouses, now becoming scarce, are favoured by artists, writers, designers and photographers because of their space and character.

Baby Kleuter Jongens
Meisjes Kleding

THE SUBURBS

Venture outside the semicircle traced by Singelgracht and you are already on your way into Amsterdam's suburbs. One of the best places to visit outside the city centre, however, is further afield. The **Amsterdam Bos**, on Amsterdam's southern fringes, is a product of the Great Depression. More countryside than park, it is a great splash of green that would be the envy of many another modern European city.

The decision to turn a group of polders on the city's southern edge into a park was made by the Amsterdam City Council in November 1928. A year previously, the world had seen Black Monday and was adjusting to the idea of mass unemployment. When work on the Amsterdam Bos started, it provided welcome jobs to many of the men who had become unemployed.

It was all too literally a man-made landscape—the work was done not by machine but by men and horses. Yet the Amsterdam Bos sprang to life quickly; the first tree was planted in 1936 and in 1937 the Bosbaan (rowing course) was officially declared open by Queen Wilhelmina.

receding ages: **msterdam chool rchitecture: embrug-traat. Left nd below, lbert uypstraat arket.**

To enable the trees to put down strong roots, the subsoil water level had to be lowered to 5 ft (1.5 metres) below the surface. This was achieved with thousands of porous pipes placed at intervals of between 50 and 80 ft (15 and 25 metres). Laid end to end, all these pipes would stretch a distance of nearly 200 miles (300 km). The result of this work was the creation of a 2,000-acre (800-hectare) park that draws people in their thousands all year round. With around 30 miles (48 km) of cycle paths and close to 100 miles (160 km) of footpaths, there is room for everybody.

Summer playground: There is also plenty to do and see. The rowing course, which exceeds the international competition length of 2,000 metres, also provides a venue for canoe, speedboat and swimming races. There's a 1,500-seat open-air theatre, a farm, playgrounds, a camping site and even an artificial hill to provide a focus to the landscape. The Forest Park Museum reels off the statistics of its flora and fauna with pride: hundreds of species of birds, trees, herbs and fungi. The Amsterdam Bos is also home to more than 700 different species of beetle.

In the summer at weekends a novel way of getting to the Amsterdam Bos is by catching an old-style tram from **Haarlemmermeerstation**, just north of the Olympic Stadium. The service is provided by the Electrische Museum Tramlijn (Electric Tramline Museum), which has collected and renovated antique trams from around Europe.

Another place that pulls the crowds is **Albert Cuypmarkt**, Amsterdam's busiest market and attracting upwards of 20,000 people on weekdays. One estimate puts the number of visitors on any Saturday at 50,000—more than 6 percent of Amsterdam's population!

Albert Cuypstraat takes its name from an important 17th-century Dutch landscape painter (one of his works can be seen in the Six Collection). The market starts at Ferdinand Bolstraat and stretches east to Van Woustraat. If you walk through this market, ponder the fact that it is the centre of Amsterdam's first suburb, an area that sprang up in the late 19th century.

Tenements: Development beyond the Singelgracht had begun around 1870. The City Council laid out the street plan but the construction of the houses themselves was in private hands. Cramped and often of low quality, this new neighbourhood—around Gerard Doustraat, Govert Flinckstraat and Albert Cuypstraat—was dubbed "De Pijp" (the pipe), after the long, narrow streets of three and four-storey tenements. It quickly earned a bad name; one commentator called it "a seedy district of dubious quality and dreary ugliness." Albert Cuypmarkt originated soon after the first streets of "De Pijp" had been built. It gained momentum in 1905 when a local law allowed a greater range of goods, including livestock, to be sold from market stalls.

The arrival of industry to Amsterdam in the 19th century brought with it thousands of immigrant workers, many of whom settled in "De Pijp". A second wave of foreign workers, after World War II, has widened the variety of ethnic groups represented here. Turkish and Surinamese restaurants point to the countries of origin of some of its inhabitants. The fortunes of Albert Cuypmarkt wavered in the early years but today it is a mile-long, crowded, noisy and fascinating market. If you want to rub shoulders with a sizeable proportion of Amsterdam's population, this is the place to come.

Cutting edge: Amsterdam, and this area in particular, can justifiably claim to be the "City of Diamonds"—diamonds have been processed here for four centuries. The "Cullinan" dia-

Artistic sign Albert Cuypstraat.

mond, the world's largest, was cut in Amsterdam in 1908 by the Asscher company. Several members of the Diamond Foundation of Amsterdam have an open-door policy; they allow you to see diamonds in the raw and learn something of how the cutting industry took root here. One of these, **A. Van Moppes & Zoon**, is conveniently located at Nos. 2–6 Albert Cuypstraat.

Growth: The Amsterdam diamond industry has always been dominated by Jews. When this business was new to Amsterdam, it was not governed by any of the guild regulations that would have disqualified Jews from becoming involved. It has been calculated that in 1748 around 600 Jewish families earned their living from diamond processing. The great boom came during the Kaapse Tijd (Cape Age) when, around 1870, the first raw diamonds began to arrive from South Africa. The resulting surge in the supply of diamonds broke the monopoly of the Diamond Cutting and Polishing Society. Soon there were more than 3,000 people working with diamonds in Amsterdam.

The firm of A. van Moppes was established on Plantage Middenlaan soon after the Kaapse Tijd, by David Levie van Moppes, the son of a diamond worker. Having taken refuge in Brazil during World War II, the Van Moppes family returned to Amsterdam and moved into their current premises at Albert Cuypstraat.

False hopes: This building had previously been used by the Germans as part of their bid to get a slice of the lucrative world diamond industry. They assumed that the conquest of Britain would mean that the supply of South African diamonds would be theirs for the taking. In 1940 they had founded a training school that would groom their own diamond cutters and polishers—Jewish skills in this business were deemed unsuitable. Britain was not conquered and the German entry into the industry was not to be. The Van Moppes' business meanwhile has flourished.

A few minutes to the northwest of Albert Cuypstraat, at the southern end of Museumplein, the **Concertgebouw** has the reputation of being acoustically among the best concert halls in the world. Built in 1888, it houses two halls: the Grote Zaal, seating 2,250, and the Kleine Zaal, which accommodates 450. Famous European and American orchestras have performed here alongside the lesser known Dutch orchestras, though the Concertgebouw's programme is not exclusively classical. Past performers have included Nana Mouskouri and Cleo Laine and John Dankworth. It is also home to the Koninklijk Concertgebouworkest (Royal Concertgebouw Orchestra), which takes its place among the top international orchestras.

Green lung: You do not have to go as far as the Amsterdam Bos if you are looking for green open spaces. One entrance to **Vondelpark**, the oldest of Amsterdam's municipal parks, is just a short walk from the crowds that congre-

hopping for
amonds.

gate in Leidseplein. Opened in 1865, the park's namesake is the 17th-century playwright Joost van den Vondel; though born in Cologne, he settled in the Netherlands and is popularly known as the Shakespeare of the Netherlands.

For such a relatively small city as Amsterdam, Vondelpark is a sizeable stretch of ponds, lawns and woods, equivalent in length to the distance between the Central Station and Leidseplein. A focal point is the striking form of Het Ronde Theehuis (The Round Tea House). The Nederlands Filmmuseum, on the northeast corner, is a resource centre that also shows a range of specialised films and documentaries.

Vondelpark's architects, J.D. and L.P. Zocher, made a deliberate move away from the symmetrical Dutch garden style when they drew up their plans in the 19th century and aimed instead for a romantic English garden.

Hippie heyday: The niceties of a style pioneered by England's Capability Brown were not the magnet of attraction, however, when in the heady days of the 1970s Vondelpark became an open-air dormitory. Under pressure to alleviate the housing problem, the City Council approved the use of Vondelpark as a sleeping area from May until September. Tents were prohibited and the playing of musical instruments past midnight was discouraged. Nevertheless, about one third of the park was set aside for sleeping. Toilets, a baggage depot, a shower area and a medical centre provided this mini-community with essential amenities.

The days of the hippie camping ground have gone but today's park buskers, flea markets and summer rock concerts are a direct legacy of that era. You can check with the VVV for specific events but strollers in Vondelpark on any summer weekend will always find something to entertain them.

Social architecture: If "De Pijp" shows Amsterdam pushing back its boundaries with little concern for visual style, elsewhere in the city's suburbs—espe-

Below and right, summer Sunday in Vondelpark.

cially in the Nieuw Zuid—there are strong examples of a much more inspirational kind of architecture. One of the best-known of the city's architectural movements was the Amsterdam school, which emerged in the early part of this century. The term was used for a group of socialist architects who developed a radically new style of building.

Author Adam Hopkins has described the work of the Amsterdam school as "solid but rather playful housing... a kind of domestic sculpture in brick." Even though the style lasted for just a decade it has become a well-known ingredient in Amsterdam's street scene. An important piece of legislation in 1901, which introduced municipal subsidies into the construction of working-class housing, paved the way for more buildings in the distinctive style of the Amsterdam school.

If you want to pursue suburban examples, go to **P.L. Takstraat**, a few minutes' walk south of Sarphatipark, to see apartment blocks designed by architect P.L. Kramer. Nearby, on **Henriette Ronnerplein** to the east, and on **Therese Schwartzeplein** to the west, are good examples of the work of M. de Klerk, another accomplished Amsterdam school architect.

Playful details: The very best examples of Amsterdam school architecture lie elsewhere in the city. The exuberant **Scheepvarthuis** on Prins Hendrikkade was not only the building that launched the style, it is also one of its best expressions, decorated with lively imaginative and humorous seafaring motifs.

Further out, the northwestern suburb of **Spaarndammerburt** is entirely a creation of Amsterdam school architects, working here from 1914 to 1923. The colourful buildings are modernistic and yet hark back to the medieval *hofjes* with their intimate courtyards. The architects who worked here, de Klerk, Maard, Walen Kamp and de Bozel, designed every last detail, even down to the letterboxes and the tiling.

Back in P.L. Takstraat you are within easy walking distance of the **Verzetsmuseum** (Resistance Museum), at No. 63 Lekstraat. The street names around here—Churchill Laan, Vrijheidslaan, Roosevelt Laan—are reminiscent of the themes of this collection; housed in a former Jewish synagogue, it covers the history of the Dutch Resistance between 1940–45. It is still collecting exhibits. A nationwide gun amnesty in late 1988, for example, unearthed a pistol which belonged to Hannie Schaft, a famous wartime figure.

Underground press: This is not, however, a war museum. It is concerned with resistance—active and passive, armed and unarmed. Booklets in English, French and German explain the fascinating story of the occupation from the day that Rotterdam was bombed in May 1940 to the last chaotic months before liberation. Between these two points you gain insights into how 1,200 clandestine publications came into being, how forged documents permeated every level of society, and how thousands of men sent to work in Germany on the Arbeitseinatz programme for the war economy managed to return secretly to the Netherlands.

Financial aid: The most common form of resistance was to go underground. By 1944 there were an estimated 300,000 people in hiding: Jews, students, those wishing to avoid the Arbeitseinatz, and active members of the Dutch Resistance. Those in hiding benefited from a massive loan operation administered by the NSF (National Relief Fund). This was guaranteed by the Dutch government in exile and supported in the Netherlands by Dutch tax inspectors who managed to channel around 5.4 million guilders of tax money into it.

Further to the east of the suburbs, just south of the Plantage district, there is another block of streets with evocative names. Madura Straat, Java Straat, Celebes Straat, and many others, call to mind the huge extent of the former Dutch colonies. The Dutch Empire in-

Concertgebou

cluded most of modern Indonesia, and at other times drew in territories in southern Africa, India, Australasia and South America.

Change of emphasis: At the centre of this district is the **Tropenmuseum** which started life earlier this century as the Dutch Colonial Institute. Then it was unashamedly a celebration of imperialism. That all changed in the 1970s when the museum was carefully sanitised. Today it shows a more liberal face as a showcase for the lifestyles, and some of the problems, found today in many Third World countries. On two floors there are reconstructions of typical streets and dwellings, rendered in astonishing detail, from South America, Africa, India, the Middle East and Southeast Asia.

These echoes of empire, inside the Tropenmuseum, in the terracotta friezes that decorate the facade of the building illustrating the peoples of the east, and in the names of the surrounding streets, seem out of place and out of time. The great, grey bulk of the Tropenmuseum itself, visible from afar, sits awkwardly just beyond the eastern end of Plantage Middenlaan, rather like a beached whale.

Yet inside, you encounter a thoroughly modern and often provocative museum, one in which you can lose yourself for hours, especially if you stop to watch the videotapes that show continuously in various rooms; these explain the Netherlands' current policy towards such vexed issues as the Indonesian migration programme, designed to relieve population pressure on Jakarta by colonising underpopulated islands. Frequent cultural performances are held in the museum's main hall, and if it happens to be a wet Monday, when most of the other museums of Amsterdam are shut and the city's streets seem uninviting, the sounds of gamalan music from Indonesia or South American panpipes gently floating through the Tropenmuseum conjure up a warmer, more colourful world.

ce planting: Tropen- useum eze.

DE KAT

JUST BEYOND

Amsterdam makes surprisingly few concessions to the worst kinds of commercialised tourism. With the exception of Madame Tussaud and the ubiquitous "city of diamond" coach tours, contrived tourist attractions are happily absent.

Clogs and cheese: Just beyond Amsterdam, however, the tourist machine is allowed occasionally to get into top gear as coach loads of visitors are herded daily to set-piece locations. The most popular places, and the nearest to Amsterdam, lie to the north: Alkmaar, Marken, Volendam, Zaanse Schans and Edam. Souvenir gift shops loom large. Demonstrations of cheese-making and clog-making are *de rigueur*.

Yet these are not the only options. Within a 15-mile (24-km) radius of Amsterdam are a number of places that make for excellent half-day or full-day excursions. Schiphol's Aviodome and Aalsmeer's flower auction both lie to the south. To the west is Haarlem, Zandvoort and the Keukenhof Gardens at Lisse. East of Amsterdam lie Muiden and Naarden.

Organised excursions: Some of these are served by package coach tours, though you can say no to these and find your own way, using bicycle, bus, train or rented car. All of the locations mentioned in this chapter can be reached by these methods; ask at Amsterdam's main VVV office for details. The Central Station has information on Dutch Railway day excursions to Zaanse Schans, Volendam and Marken, and the Keukenhof Gardens: these include a reduced train fare and often reduced admission charges, discounts on local buses or trams, and free coffee and cake.

If you want to get close to and learn more about Dutch windmills, head north to **Zaanse Schans**. This small community is a conservation project established in 1960 to illustrate how a

Dutch windmill village would have looked around the turn of the 18th century. The bright-green wooden houses here reflect the local Zaan style. More to the point, they are lived in and the windmills are authentic working mills. There's a bakery, a clock museum, an antique shop and cheese-maker as well as an oil mill, paint mill, saw mill and mustard mill. Tiny bridges and cobblestoned walkways make for a deliberately picturesque setting.

Decline: You can walk around the village for free but the windmills charge an admission fee. It is worth paying this to help preserve an aspect of the Dutch landscape that at one time was in danger of disappearing. Around 1850 there were over 9,000 windmills working in the Netherlands but by the turn of this century only 2,500 were left. Today just 900 are in good condition.

If you want the full story behind this decline, cross the bridge to the other side of the river. The small community of **Koog an de Zaan** has another group of old-style green-painted houses. Here, the Molenmuseum (Windmill Museum) tells the story of the rise and fall of the Netherlands' windmills.

World-famous cheeses: Within easy reach of Amsterdam there are four villages on or near the IJsselmeer: Edam, Volendam, Monnickendam and the island village of Marken. The northernmost, **Edam**, is still less than 15 miles (24 km) from Amsterdam. The distinctive red balls of cheese have spread the name of Edam to many parts of the world. With its picturesque canals, narrow bridges and tidy 17th-century exteriors, the village has done well not to give in to the worst excesses of tourism.

Edam was at one time a port and shipyard. Dutch maritime power faded but the village of Edam lived on. Today the **Kaasmarkt** (cheese market) and the 16th-century **Weighhouse** ensure Edam's continuing prosperity.

If cheese isn't enough to attract you, a number of historic buildings provide another reason for coming here. The

Preceding pages: Zaanse Schans windmills; Alkmaar, cheese market; Volendam harbour.

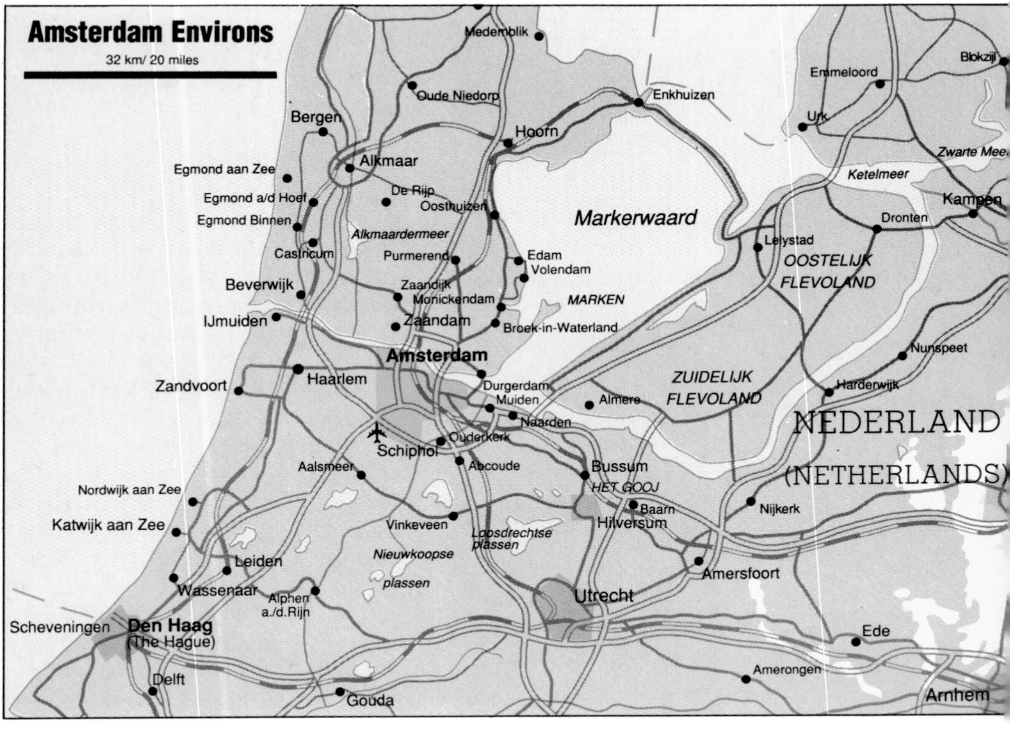

leaning **Speeltoren**, for example, is a remnant of Edam's 15th-century Kleine Kerk. The **Grote Kerk** (on Kerkstraat) also dates from the 15th century, though what you see today is the result of a reconstruction in 1602 following a fire.

In addition you will find 16th-century almshouses belonging to the Beguine sisterhood (the same group associated with Amsterdam's Begijnhof). There is a small museum housed in a 16th-century building, while overlooking the Damplein is the **Raadhuis** (Town Hall), built in 1737 and blessed with an elaborate stucco interior and some good antique furniture.

Tourist trap: Volendam could learn much from its neighbour Edam. Once a quiet fishing port, today it is the most commercialised village on the IJsselmeer. A few fishing boats still use the small harbour, but it does not take much to see that Volendam has now put all its money on the tourist trade. No doubt this provides a more reliable source of income than fishing ever did.

Volendam's greatest asset is its distinctive local style of costume, especially the winged lace caps of the women. On the seafront there are shops inviting you to dress up in traditional costume so that you can have your picture taken. Volendam is strictly for people who do not mind rubbing shoulders with coach parties.

Escape from the crowds: The boat service from Volendam to **Marken** takes you swiftly away from the crowds. At one time this village did not sit on the edge of the IJsselmeer—it was an offshore island in the Zuider Zee. Before 1957, when a short causeway was built, the only way in and out of the village was by boat. Then there were just 70 families living in Marken. Today the population is more than 2,000. Even so, Marken still hasn't lost its insularity and the inhabitants like to keep themselves to themselves.

One of the few concessions to tourism is a small house on the seafront billing itself as having a typical Marken

laarlem.

interior. This is the quietest—and the prettiest—of the Ijsselmeer villages and you can't help feeling that the people of Marken are going to keep it that way.

Monnickendam is equally unspoiled and, with Amsterdam just 8 miles (13 km) away, it makes for an easy excursion to the IJsselmeer. A 15th-century church, a 16th-century belltower, a 17th-century weighhouse (now a restaurant) and an 18th-century town hall account for just some of this village's charm.

If all you want out of aircraft is to be whisked in and out of Amsterdam safely and punctually, you won't head for Schiphol until your flight home. If you like aircraft for their own sake you should include the **Aviodome** on your excursions. A few minutes' walk from Schiphol train station, the Aviodome houses the Netherlands' National Aerospace Museum. With 20 aircraft (and a few spacecraft for good measure) squeezed under a 60-metre-wide dome, this is an excellent display, especially for aviation buffs and/or their children.

The Aviodome was established in 1969–70, the joint 50th anniversary of the founding of Fokker, KLM and Schiphol airport. The exhibits represent the progress of aviation and emphasise the Dutch contribution. KLM (Koninklyke Luchtvaart Maatschappij) was the world's first airline and, not surprisingly, features strongly. A heart-stirring exhibit is the sturdy bulk of the Fokker F VII, one of KLM's first passenger aircraft. This, coupled with a good selection of KLM memorabilia, including posters from the 1920s, brings back all the romance of flying—long since lost.

Castles and poets: There are two towns within easy reach of Amsterdam by car or bus to the east. At **Muiden**, you can take a guided tour of the red-brick Muiderslot, a moated castle built by Count Floris V of Holland. Floris was murdered here in 1296 by noblemen who were unimpressed by his efforts to help the common people. The castle as it stands today dates mainly from the

The island village of Marken.

14th century. The interior, however, is a recreation of the castle as it appeared when it was occupied by the poet and historian Pieter Hooft in the first half of the 17th century.

Spanish attack: The fortification theme continues at **Naarden**, a few miles further east. This town's impressive double line of ramparts was built at the end of the 17th century. Naarden had already suffered its worst attack a century earlier, when, in 1572, Spanish invaders massacred the town's inhabitants. One bastion of Naarden's fortifications houses the Vestingmuseum (Fortress Museum), complete with underground passages and cannon. Climb the tower of the Grote Kerk and you will get a bird's-eye view of the whole town.

Just 14 minutes west of Amsterdam by train, **Haarlem** is a large town steeped in history that merits a full day-trip. The suburbs of Amsterdam virtually merge into the suburbs of its neighbour but Haarlem is small and manageable; its many places of interest all lie close to the imposing **Grote Kerk**.

This church, dedicated to St Bavo, is the city's biggest landmark and was constructed during the 15th and 16th centuries. Inside, a magnificent vaulted cedar ceiling is supported by 28 columns. Equally grand is the famous Müller organ, with no less than 5,000 pipes, said to have been played by Handel and Mozart. Frans Hals is buried here as is Laurens Coster; Haarlemmers claim that Coster was the co-inventor, with Gutenberg, of printing in 1423. Outside, at the eastern end of the church, a statue of Coster pays another tribute to the man.

Outstanding artist: Top of the list for many visitors is the **Frans Hals Museum**. Frans Hals, one of the great Dutch portrait artists, lived most of his life in Haarlem and died here in 1666. He became a specialist in the group portraits commissioned by bodies such as the civic guards and the militia companies, arranging the subjects so that they each played an equally important

andvoort
oastal
esort.

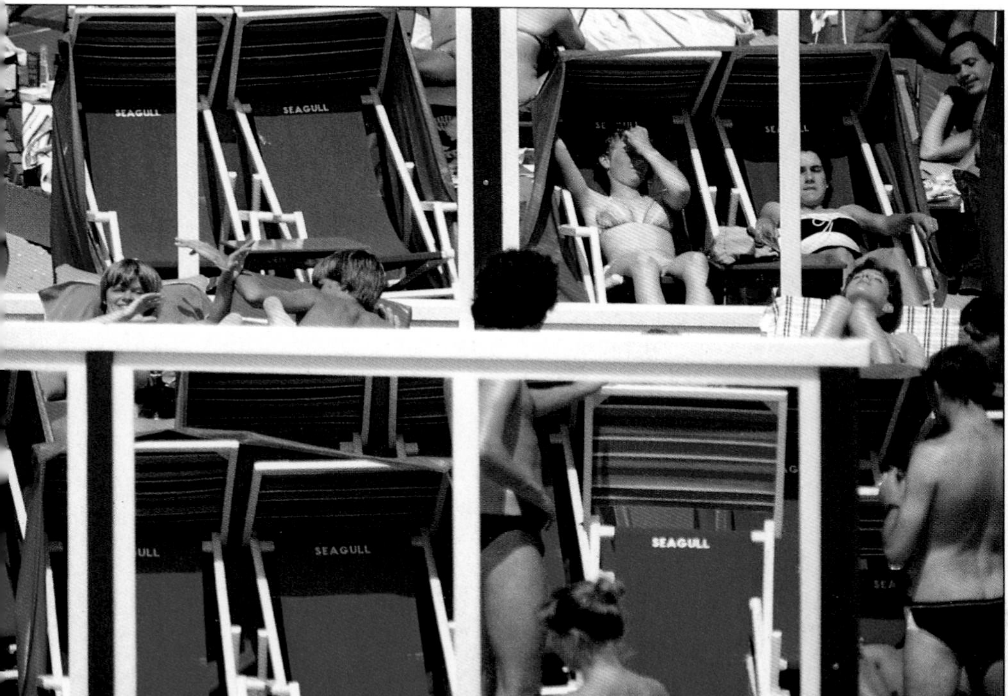

role in the finished work. He also painted individual portraits. Many of his works, including *The Laughing Cavalier* in London's Wallace Collection and *The Merry Drinker* in Amsterdam's Rijksmuseum, are world-famous.

Landscape painters: The Frans Hals Museum has the best collection of his work and other artists are represented here too. In particular, there are a number of important works that reflect the crucial role played by Haarlem in the development of Dutch landscape painting. Refugee Flemish landscape artists came here late in the 16th century, when conflict with Spain was at its peak. Before long, native Dutch painters came to the city to join them. The Haarlem landscape painters include Salomon van Ruysdael and his nephew Jacob van Ruisdael, both of whom are represented in the museum.

If you do visit Haarlem during the summer, bear in mind that you are only a short bus ride from **Zandvoort**. After Scheveningen, near The Hague, this is the most popular of the Netherlands' coastal resorts. In the summer months Amsterdammers flock here, but there is space enough for everybody. Behind the 5-mile (8-km) long beach is an extensive area of sand dunes called the Waterleidingduinen. More dunes, known as the Kennemerduinen, lie to the north of Zandvoort.

In the spring, the best second stop beyond Haarlem would be Lisse, where you can visit the **Keukenhof Gardens**. Special combined tickets, including rail/bus fare and admission, are issued at Amsterdam's Central Station from late March to late May, so you can make a visit during the flowering times. The gardens are laid out in a large tract of parkland planted with tulips, crocuses, narcissi, daffodils and hyacinths and complemented by ornamental gardens, ponds and glasshouses. When it comes to stepping out beyond Amsterdam at bulbtime, horticulturalists and garden lovers will see little sense in heading in any other direction.

Below, Keukenhof Gardens. Right, the products of Aalsmeer. Following page: fairground organ figure.

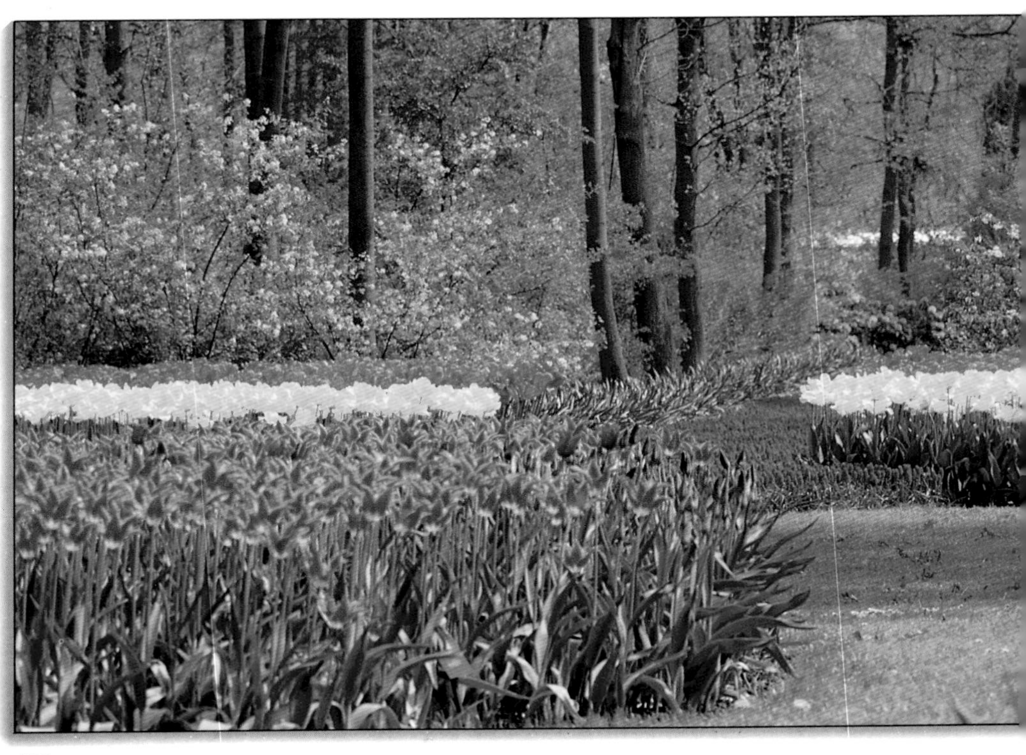

AALSMEER

Five days a week, at 6.30 a.m., millions of flowers and pot plants start their journey to destinations across the globe. Around 3.5 billion flowers and 400 million plants are sold annually. Annual turnover is nearly 2 billion guilders (£670 million/ $1.07 billion).

This is the Aalsmeer Flower Auction. Flowers have been sold at the Aalsmeer site since 1912. In 1968 two separate auction houses then based here merged to form the Verenigde Bloemenveilingen Aalsmeer (VBA). The first premises occupied an area of 88,000 sq. metres. Since then business has bloomed and the VBA is now the world's largest flower auction, occupying a building with an area of 600,000 sq. metres, equivalent to 90 soccer pitches—the largest commercial building in the world.

Aalsmeer is just a 45-minute bus ride from outside Amsterdam's Central Station. Accommodating an annual total of around 200,000 spectators is just a sideline for the VBA. There are no tour guides. You are free to walk around a long rectangular walkway that gives you a clear view over the whole complex and allows you to watch the lightning-fast transactions. Information points are used to deliver pre-recorded commentaries explaining how the VBA conducts business.

The VBA is a co-operative sales organisation made up of more than 5,000 growers, all of whom must sell their products at Aalsmeer. The growers pay an auction commission of about 5 percent and this money is used to finance the running of the building and staff costs.

The VBA auction is nocturnal and you'll need to be an early riser to be in at the kill. The flowers arrive at night pre-packed into boxes or containers and are examined early in the morning for quality and length by inspectors before the auction begins at 6.30 a.m. Arrive at this time if you can—most of the action is over by 9.00 a.m.

There are five auction rooms in all, each accommodating around 300 buyers, and a total of 13 clocks which control transactions. Each clock is used for the same sort of produce each day so that the buyers know where to go. The computer system is the key to everything. On registering, a buyer receives a computer card which has to be inserted into the desk at which he sits. This unlocks the "buy" button and links the customer into the computer.

Appropriately enough, Aalsmeer uses the "Dutch auction" system: the pointer of a large clock face marks decreasing prices as it turns back from 100 to 1. The clock gives the unit of currency in which the transaction is being offered, the number of flowers in each bunch or bucket put on display, the minimum purchase quantity, and the price per flower or plant.

By pressing the "buy" button each buyer can stop the pointer when it indicates a price he is prepared to pay for each individual flower or plant. The buyer can inform the auctioneer, via a microphone fixed near his seat, whether he wants the entire lot or just part. If a part-lot is sold the clock goes back to 100 and the process is repeated until the entire contents of each lot has been sold.

The system is kept busy processing an average of 50,000 transactions in just a few hours. All the transaction data from the auction floor is transferred directly to the central computer, which prepares the detailed invoices needed by the buyers and growers.

After each batch has been wheeled through the auction room and sold, it is driven out of the auction room to an area where VBA staff can divide up the flowers or plants according to each sale. More than 350 buyers rent spaces in the packing area and operate their businesses from here. Only 15 minutes elapse between the auctioning and the delivery of each consignment to the buyer.

More than 80 percent of everything sold at Aalsmeer is exported and, on average, 2,000 trucks leave the building daily. The close proximity of Schiphol airport means that flowers and plants auctioned in the morning are on sale in florists right around the world the same evening or the following day. Flowers are big business at Aalsmeer. And one couldn't hope for a sweeter-smelling start to the day.

TRAVEL TIPS

Getting There

BY AIR

Schiphol Airport, 9 miles (14 km) southwest of the city, is connected with 196 cities in 90 countries. With its huge range of duty-free goods, reputation for efficiency and easy access to the centre of Amsterdam, it is arguably the most popular international airport in Europe. Between them, British Airways, KLM (Royal Dutch Airlines) and British Midland operate an almost hourly service during the day from London Heathrow; British Airways, BAC 1-11 and Transavia Boeing 737 provide up to 11 services a day from London Gatwick.

Best value of the lot for British visitors is the Amsterdam Air Express from Gatwick, departing on Friday afternoons only and returning on Monday evenings. Services from major regional airports are covered by various British and Dutch airlines. Several airlines offer cut-price fares which work out little more than the cost of a standard rail ticket. These cheaper flights are usually dependent on you staying a Saturday night away.

Very regular flights link Schiphol with all major European airports and there are several flights a week from North America, Canada and Australia.

BY TRAIN

Day and night services operate from London (Liverpool Street) to Amsterdam via the Hook of Holland – journey time is around 12 hours by ferry, 10 hours by jetfoil. A quicker option is London (Victoria) to Ostend via Dover, but there are several transfers involved. You can also go via the Sheerness to Vlissengen rail ferry.

There are good rail connections to Amsterdam from the main ports of arrival. Amsterdam's railway station, the impressive Centraal Station at Stationsplein, has excellent connections to the rest of the country and a very regular service to Brussels, Paris, Antwerp, Cologne and Hanover. Facilities include the city's main tourist office, with hotel booking service, money changing facilities and (just outside the station) the GVB office will give you all the information you need on transport within Amsterdam. Trams radiate from the station to practically all parts of the city.

BY SEA

Sealink operates two sailings a day from Harwich to the Hook of Holland: crossing time 7 hours by day, 8 hours at night. North Sea Ferries has a daily sailing from Hull to Rotterdam, taking 14 hours, which could be useful if you live in the north of England. Olau Line, which has a reputation of offering the highest standards at the best prices, has two sailings a day from Sheerness to Vlissingen, taking 7 hours by day, 8 hours 30 minutes by night. It describes its newest ship as "the largest and most luxurious" ferry in the EC.

The fastest sea route is the jetfoil from Dover to Ostend, which takes 1 hour 45 minutes.

BY BUS

The cheapest deal is the Hoverspeed City Sprint, departing daily from Victoria. Journey time is roughly 10 hours. Details from Hoverspeed Ltd., Maybrook House, Queens Gardens, Dover.

BY CAR

Except for the jetfoil service, all the companies mentioned in the "By Sea" section offer a car ferry service. Advance bookings are advisable in summer.

From the Hook of Holland to Amsterdam, travel time is roughly 3 hours 30 minutes. If you don't mind a longer drive on the Continent you can, of course, take the shorter cross-Channel ferry routes: Ramsgate/Dunkirk (Sally Line, 2 hours 30 minutes), Dover/Ostend (P&O Ferries, 4 hours) or Dover/Calais (Sealink and P&O, 1 hour 15 minutes to 1 hour 30 minutes).

To drive in Holland, you must carry a current driving licence (an international licence is not necessary), vehicle registration document, Green Card insurance policy and a warning triangle for use in the event of an accident or breakdown. Holland has an excellent network of roads and signposting is good. But once you're in Amsterdam, a car is more of a hindrance than a help.

PACKAGES

Numerous companies offer 2 to 7-day packages by air or sea, which often (but not always) work out cheaper than fixing your own travel and accommodation. To qualify for the air packages you have to spend a Saturday night away. The packages range from all-inclusive (meals, excursions, welcome parties included) to basic travel and accommodation.

TRAVEL ESSENTIALS

VISAS

Visitors from the EC, US, Canada, Australia, New Zealand and most other European and Commonwealth countries require a passport only. Citizens of most other countries must obtain a visa in advance from Dutch embassies or consulates.

MONEY

Local currency is the *guilder* (f.), divided into 100 cents. There are notes of f.1,000, f.250, f.100, f.50, f.25, f.10 and f.5 (not many of these around) and coins of f.5, f.2.5, f.1, 25c, 10c and 5c. The safest way of carrying around large amounts of money is in travellers' cheques or Eurocheques, changeable at all banks and bureaux de change. The best rates of exchange are those of national banks; beware high rates of commission at hotels. Major credit cards and Eurocheques are accepted in all main hotels, restaurants and shops. The GWK bank office at Centraal Station is open 24 hours a day.

HEALTH TIPS

No health certificates or vaccinations are required for EC citizens. EC citizens who have obtained an E111 form from their local social security office before departure are entitled to free treatment by a doctor and free prescribed medicines. But the insurance is not comprehensive and won't cover you, for example, for cancellation or cost of repatriation. If you want full cover you should take out separate medical insurance.

WHAT TO WEAR

The unpredictability of the weather calls for a raincoat and/or umbrella at all times of the year. Light clothing should be sufficient in summer but take a jacket or light coat for the evenings. Very warm clothing is advisable for winter. Comfortable footwear is essential for sightseeing and pacing the cobbled streets. Casual dress is the norm, though some of the smarter hotels and restaurants require men to wear a jacket and tie.

ANIMAL QUARANTINE

An official certificate of vaccination is required for cats and dogs brought into the Netherlands from any country other than Belgium and Luxembourg.

CUSTOMS FORMALITIES

Personal possessions are not liable to duty and tax provided you are staying for less than six months and you intend to take them out again. There are no restrictions on the amount of currency that you can bring into the Netherlands. Among prohibited or restricted goods are plants, flowers, weapons and narcotic drugs.

Duty-free allowances vary according to where you bought the goods. Goods obtained duty and tax-paid within the EC: 300 cigarettes or 150 cigarillos or 75 cigars or 400g of tobacco; 1.5 litres of alcoholic drinks over 22 percent volume or 3 litres of alcoholic drinks under 22 percent volume plus 4 litres of still wine; 75g (3fl oz or 90 cc) of perfume and 375 cc (13 fl oz) of toilet water; 1,000g of coffee and 200g of tea. Goods bought duty-free or in non-EC countries: 200 cigarettes or 100 cigarillos or 50 cigars or 250g of tobacco; 1 litre of alcoholic drinks over 22 percent volume or 2 litres of alcoholic drinks under 22 percent volume plus 2 litres of still wine; 50g (2 fl oz or 60 cc) of perfume and 250cc (9fl oz) of toilet water; 500g of coffee and 100g of tea.

Getting Acquainted

TIME ZONES

Holland is one hour ahead of Greenwich Mean Time (GMT) in winter and two hours ahead in summer (last weekend of March to last weekend of September). During Standard Time periods, when it is 12 noon in Amsterdam, it is 12 noon in Bonn, Paris, Rome and Madrid; 1 p.m. in Athens and Cairo; 2 p.m. in Moscow and Istanbul; 4.30 p.m. in Bombay; 6 p.m. in Bangkok; 6.30 p.m. in Singapore; 7 p.m. in Hong Kong; 8 p.m. in Tokyo; 9 p.m. in Sydney; 1 a.m. in Honolulu; 8 a.m. in San Francisco and Los Angeles; 5 a.m. in Chicago; 6 a.m. in New York and Montreal; 8 a.m. in Rio de Janeiro; 11 a.m. in London.

CLIMATE

Amsterdam has much the same temperature as the UK but is wetter than London and marginally cooler in winter. Summers are generally warm but you can expect rain at any time of year. Spring is the driest time of year and a favourite time for tulip enthusiasts. Advantages of a visit in winter are the cut-price package deals and the fact that museums and galleries are pleasantly uncrowded.

CULTURE & CUSTOMS

The city has a reputation for being supremely tolerant. Foreigners, including minorities, are always welcome and as a tourist to Amsterdam you are likely to find the locals pleasant, polite and civilised. They may not be very demonstrative or vivacious but they are rarely inhospitable or unfriendly.

First-comers are frequently surprised at the leniency towards both drugs and prostition. Although there has been a crackdown on hard drugs, you can still buy dope in many cafés (distinguished by the marijuana plant sign on the door) and you may well be offered space cakes in the Vondelpark. Many locals argue that the drugs problem is no worse than in any other major city – just more open.

Tips are included in taxi fares and prices in restaurants and bars, so all that is required is some small change if you think the service warrants it. Porters and hairdressers will expect a small amount for their services.

LANGUAGE

There is no real need to try and master Dutch. Even the tram drivers speak English.

ELECTRICITY

The standard current is 220 volts AC. Plugs have two round pins, so British and American plugs need adaptors.

BUSINESS HOURS

Normal shopping hours are 8.30 a.m. or 9 a.m.–5.30 p.m. or 6 p.m. Late-night shopping is usually Thursday. Food stores close at 4 p.m. on Saturdays. All shops close for one half day a week, often Monday morning. Banks are open: 9 a.m.–4 p.m. Monday–Friday; 9 a.m.–7 p.m. Thursday.

HOLIDAYS

Banks and most shops are closed on the following days:

New Year's Day
Good Friday
Easter Sunday and Monday
30 April (Queen's Day)
Ascension Day
Whit Monday
Christmas Day
26 December

FESTIVALS

The following are the main events of the city:

25 February: Commemoration of the "February Strike", led by the dockers in 1941 against treatment of the Jews, held on J.D. Meijerplein.

March: Amsterdam Carnival; Blues Festival.

Late March: Art and Antiques fair in the Nieuwe Kerk.

30 April: Queen's birthday. Street markets, street parties, fireworks and festivities on Dam Square.

Late April: Keukenhof Floral Parade at Keukenhof Gardens, 19 miles (30 km) southwest of Amsterdam.

June: Holland Festival. Major theatrical, operatic and musical events, celebrating Dutch artists and performers, also held in The Hague and Rotterdam. Free concerts and theatre from early June to the end of August in the Vondelpark.

August/September: Jazz Festival.

Mid-September: Jordaan Arts Festival.

September: Flower parade from Aalsmeer to Amsterdam.

November: Parade of St Nicholas.

31 December: Fireworks on the Dam.

RELIGIOUS SERVICES

Services are held in English at:

Anglican Church/Episcopal Christ Church: Groenburgwal 42, tel: 248877.

Presbyterian English Reformed Church: Begijnhof 48, tel: 249665.

Roman Catholic Church of St John and St Ursula: Begijnhof 30, tel: 241048 or 221918.

COMMUNICATIONS

MEDIA

The main national newspapers are *De Volkskrant*, a serious left-of-centre heavyweight, and *De Telegraaf*, right wing, more popular and perhaps the most widely read. English newspapers arrive on the same day they are published and are widely available. The monthly English language *Holland Herald* gives listings and reviews of what's on in the city (and elsewhere in Holland). Brown café notice-boards are another good source of information on local events.

On cable TV you can watch BBC1, BBC2, Sky Channel and Superchannel. English-language films are frequently shown on Dutch TV channels, undubbed. On the radio you can tune into the World Service and Radio 4.

TELEPHONE

Telephone boxes are green and take 25c, f.1 and f.2.50 coins. You find them in post offices, large stores, cafés and in some streets. For international calls, it's easier to go to Telehuis, Raadhuisstraat 48 (open 24 hrs), where you can talk in a booth for as long as you like and pay later. If possible, avoid making long-distance calls from your hotel where rates may be double or even treble those of the post office or telephone boxes.

POSTAL SERVICES

The main office is at Nieuwezijds Voorburgwal 182, behind the Royal Palace. Open: Monday–Friday 8.30 a.m.–6 p.m; 8 p.m. on Thursday; Saturday 9 a.m.–12 noon. Parcels are handled at the post office at Oosterdokskade 3–5 p.m. Open: Monday–Friday 9.30 a.m.–9 p.m; Saturday 9 a.m.–12 noon. Stamps are available from post offices, tobacconists, news-stands and stamp machines attached to the red and grey letter boxes. *Poste restante* facilities are available at the main post office – you need a passport to collect your mail.

TELEGRAMS & TELEXES

The Telehuis at Raadhuisstraat 48 handles telegrams, telexes and fax.

EMERGENCIES

SECURITY & CRIME

Amsterdam is a major European centre for drugs and much crime here is drug-related. A major crackdown several years ago cleared the notorious heroin dealers' haunt, the Zeedijk (in the Red Light District) of its undesirables, but there is still a thriving cocaine and heroin trade and soft drugs are still sold openly in cafés.

As a tourist, you are unlikely to be affected directly by the drugs trade. But, as with any other major city, Amsterdam has its fair share of petty crime. Keep a careful watch on wallets, bags and other valuables, especially on public transport. Leave large amounts of cash and jewellery at your hotel. Deserted areas of the city should be avoided after dark. In the Red Light District, it is wise to keep to the main canals, Oude Zijde Voorburgwal and Oude Zijde Achterburgwal, and avoid the smaller, sleazy side streets.

MEDICAL SERVICES

In emergencies, call **Police** tel: 222222 or **Ambulance** tel: 555555.

For urgent medical or dental treatment, contact the Central Medical Service, tel: 642111 (SOS doctor) or 791821 (SOS dentist). Open: 24 hours.

The most central hospital is the Onze Lieve Vrouse Gasthuis, le Oosterparkstraat 179, tel: 5999111.

The main hospital is the Academisch Medisch Centrum, Meibergdreef 9, tel: 5669111. Both hospitals have an out-patients, and casualty ward.

Chemists or *Apotheek* are normally open Monday–Friday 9 a.m.–5.30 p.m. or 6 p.m. Late-night chemists operate on a rotating basis. For information, contact the Central Medical Service (see above).

LOSS OF BELONGINGS

You should report loss or theft of valuables to the local police immediately as most insurance policies insist on a police report. The main police station is at Elandsgracht 117, tel: 559111. For the recovery of items lost on public transport, contact the GVB Head Office, Prins Hendrikkade 108–114, tel: 5514911. Loss of passport should be reported immediately to the police and your consulate. The Lost Property Office is at Waterlooplein 11, tel: 5598005.

GETTING AROUND

FROM THE AIRPORT

Shuttle trains leave every 15 minutes for Amsterdam Centraal Station during the day, once an hour at night. Travel time is under 20 minutes. Trains also run to the RAI station and to Amsterdam Zuid for the World Trade Center, both in the south of the city. KLM operates a coach service to the city every half an hour, but it's over twice the price of the train. There is also a much cheaper public bus service linking the airport to the city.

ORIENTATION

Thanks to its size and layout, the centre of Amsterdam is easily covered on foot. Main streets radiate out from Centraal Station, crossing a more or less regular pattern of concentric canals. It all looks very simple on paper but the canal system can be tricky to negotiate if you are a first-time visitor. It is worth spending some time studying the map and mastering the relative positions of the main squares, streets and canals, bearing in mind that *plein* means square, *straat* street and *gracht* canal.

The most prominent landmarks are the three main squares, the Dam, Rembrandtsplein and Leidseplein. The most relaxing way to get your bearings is to take the tourist tram ride, starting at the station, or, better still, the canal-boat tour which lasts about 1 hour 15 minutes. After that, take to the streets on foot, or master the tram system – undoubtedly the quickest and most efficient way of getting around.

RECOMMENDED MAPS

The GVB transport office in front of Centraal Station provides free public transport route maps. The best general map is published by Falkplan and entitled *This is Amsterdam*.

PUBLIC TRANSPORT

Trams, Buses and Metro: Unless you are travelling out of the centre you are unlikely to need the buses or metro. Within the city the prominent yellow trams are easily the best means of getting around and not expensive as long as you master the ticket system. The GVB office outside the station has information on the system in English and sells the various types of tickets. You can either buy individual tickets (which is the most expensive way of travelling), Rover tickets, which are valid for 1, 2 or more days' travel, or *strippenkaart* – strip tickets, in multiples of 6, 10 or 15; the more you buy, the cheaper they come. These are valid for one hour's travel and the amount you use depends on the zones you cover.

As a tourist you are unlikely to travel beyond the Central Zone; for this, you'll need to stamp two strips, and these are valid for transfers to other trams within the hour in the Central Zone. Tickets must be stamped in the machines that are usually located at the rear of the tram. Inspectors make random checks and failure to purchase or punch the tickets can result in a substantial fine. If you have no ticket enter through the front door (doors open automatically if you press the *Deur Open* button), state your destination and buy a ticket from the driver.

You can also buy tickets at the GVB kiosk on Leidseplein, from post offices and from some tobacconists.

WATER TRANSPORT

Boats and Canal Bus: Modern glass-topped launches (equivalent to the Parisian *bateau mouche*) will pick you up at various points of the city and take you through some of the loveliest parts of Amsterdam. Day tickets with unlimited mileage are available. Be prepared to queue in summer.

The Museum Boat service stops at 9 major museums at 75-minute intervals – well worth considering if you intend doing a lot of sightseeing. You can buy a day ticket from the VVV office opposite Centraal Station, where the boat service starts. The latest addition to water transport is the "Canal Bus", a 52-seat cruiser that provides a regular service between Centraal Station and the Rijksmuseum, with three stops on the way.

Waterbikes: Canal pedaloes for two or four are fun for exploring the canals. Detailed maps and suggested routes are provided by the hire companies, located opposite Centraal Station and opposite the Rijksmuseum.

PRIVATE TRANSPORT

On Foot: The centre is well suited to walking provided you don't object to cobbled streets, chaotic cyclists and an inordinate amount of dog dirt. The major museums and galleries are conveniently located in the same area (Museumplein) to the southwest of centre. From here it is about 30 minutes' walk to Dam Square and Centraal Station. Most of the hotels are within walking distance of the centre – notable exceptions are the those in the southeast (eg the luxury Amstel) and the business hotels near the World Trade Center and RAI Congress Center.

Bicycle: Being a city of cyclists, Amsterdam has numerous bike lanes. Cycling is a fun way of getting around but bear in mind that there are 500,000 other cyclists in Amsterdam and a lot of chaotic traffic with which to contend.

Two of the main places for renting cycles are: Damstraat Rent-a-bike, Pieter Jacobsz Dwarsstraat 11, tel: 255029, and MacBike, Nieuwe Vilenburgerstraat 116, tel: 200985.

Bicycle theft is rife (hence high deposits on rentals), so lock up at all times, wherever possible attaching your bike to railings or some other immovable object.

Taxis: Cabs seldom cruise but you can hire them from main city squares or by dialling 777777. Meters are used and the cost is calculated according to the zone and the time of day. On longer journeys it is always wise to establish the cost before you set off.

By Car: Driving within the city is best avoided. If you do take a car, be prepared to contend with parking problems, a myriad of mad cyclists, narrow canal streets (often blocked by delivery vans), the complexity of the one-way systems and trams which always have right of way. If you arrive by car, the best thing to do is leave it in a car park and go by public transport. The multi-storey Europarking at Marnixstraat 250 usually has space and is within walking distance of the centre.

Car Hire: Renting a car is worth considering if you want to explore cities and regions beyond Amsterdam. Roads are good and signposting is clear.

Avis Rent-a-car: Nassaukade 380, tel: 836061.

Budget Rent-a-car: Overtoom 121, tel: 126066.

Europcar Rent-a-car: Overtoom 51–53, tel: 832123.

Hertz Rent-a-car: Overtoom 333, tel: 122441.

Kuperus BV: Middenweg 175, tel: 938790.

GETTING OUT OF AMSTERDAM

Amsterdam makes a good base for day trips. Distances to Dutch towns of interest are short: The Hague 33 miles (52 km), Utrecht 27 miles (43 km), Delft 39 miles (62 km), and easily covered.

A wide and very efficient network of rail services operates throughout the country. Fast electric trains link Amsterdam with most Dutch towns on an hourly or half-hourly basis. It is well worth finding out about excursion fares, which include entrance fees to museums and other attractions as well as the return rail fare.

Coach excursions are organised by Lindbergh Tours, Damrak 26, tel: 222766. Most popular are the bulb fields at Keukenhof, the traditional eel-fishing villages of Volendam and Marken, the cheese market at Alkmaar, the cheese-making centre of Edaam, the pretty town of Delft and the city of Den Haag (The Hague), seat of the Dutch government (see *Things to Do section* for more details).

WHERE TO STAY

For most visitors, the favourite overall location is the southwest quarter, close to the major museums and art galleries, to the large, green Vondelpark and to the popular square of Leidseplein. There are plenty of hotels to choose from in this area and most of them are quieter than those in the more central Dam/Damrak area.

Roughly half the total number of beds in Amsterdam are in deluxe or first-class hotels but tourists tend to go for the small, family-run hotels, which are not only cheaper and more charming but are often more centrally located. Many of these lower category hotels are converted from narrow old town houses overlooking canals, and the disadvantages are very small rooms and steep stairs – many hotels don't have a lift.

Prices in all categories are rather steep but bear in mind that, unlike most other European cities, breakfast is normally included in the price of the room, and the choice of cheeses, cold meats, cakes and rolls is usually ample to keep you going throughout the day.

Busiest times of year, when you need to book well in advance, are the flower season (April/May), Easter, the summer months and Christmas. Low season, when packages and hotel prices are at their cheapest, is from

October to March. The VVV publishes a useful guide called *Hotels in Holland*, available from their offices locally and abroad.

Reservations can be made via a travel agency or through the Netherlands Reservation Centre, P.O. Box 404, 2260 AK Leidschendam, The Netherlands, tel: 070-202500, telex 33755. The Reservation Centre offers special winter packages known as "Amsterdam, the Amsterdam Way", a deal which includes lower rate accommodation (from budget to luxury hotels) plus, for example, free entrance to the Rijksmuseum, free drinks in certain bars and a free canal cruise.

If you arrive in the city on spec there is a free telephone reservation service at the airport, or you can ask the VVV office at Centraal Station to make a reservation for you – a small booking fee will be charged. If you want to stay with a family in a private house – which works out a lot cheaper than opting for a hotel – the VVV will also be able to help you.

Immediately around Centraal Station you will find many so-called "Hotels" and "Youth Hostels" offering accommodation at rock-bottom prices, and in summer you may be approached by touts as you arrive at the station. Cheap they may be, but they are also fleapits, often located above a noisy all-night disco or café, and you will be expected to share rooms as well as the none-too-clean bathrooms. They are best avoided, but if you use them, never leave any of your valuables unattended.

HOTELS

DELUXE

Amstel: Professor Tulpplein 1, tel: 226060.

Lavishly furnished 19th-century hotel, on the banks of the River Amstel (20 minutes' walk from the centre). Popular among visiting celebrities. High-class cuisine in La Rive restaurant. Plush bedrooms and suites, efficient service, delightful terrace in summer. Part of the InterContinental chain.

Apollo: Appollolaan 2, tel: 730333.

Modern luxury hotel on the waterside, 2 miles (3 km) south of the centre; two restaurants with waterside terraces, buffet breakfast served in brasserie.

Europe: Nieuwe Doelenstraat 2–8, tel: 234836.

Grand late 19th-century hotel overlooking the River Amstel and the Mint Tower. Facilities include swimming pool (the only one in the city), open-air terrace, meeting rooms, fitness centre and two restaurants.

Golden Tulip Barbizon Palace: Prins Hendrikkade 59–72, tel: 5564564.

Nineteen old houses converted into a spanking new luxury hotel overlooking Centraal Station. Interior is a combination of the old Dutch, French and post-Modern styles. Many facilities, including health spa with sauna and fitness room.

Okura Amsterdam: Ferdinand Bolstraat 333, tel: 787111.

Essentially a hotel for business travellers, not far from the RAI building and with car parking space for guests and their visitors. Twenty-three floors with top-floor bar and restaurant. A good choice for gourmets – see Food section for Ciel Bleu (French cuisine) and Yamazato (Japanese).

Sonesta: Kattengat 1, tel: 212223.

Large, luxury hotel close to Centraal Station (but a few sleazy streets nearby). Numerous facilities, including fitness club, disco and Dutch café. Good collection of modern art. Restored Lutheran church opposite where conferences and concerts take place.

EXPENSIVE

American: Leidsekade 97, tel: 245322.

Outstanding Art Nouveau building on the lively Leidseplein. Comfortable well-equipped bedrooms, popular café famous for Tiffany-style decor and colourful clientele, Night Watch cocktail bar with converted terrace.

Ascot: Damrak 95–98, tel: 260066.

Efficient, ultra-modern Swiss-run hotel in city centre, very close to the Royal Palace and Dam Square. Sound-proofed rooms and suites, French cuisine in Le Bistro.

Krasnapolsky: Dam 9, tel: 5549111.

Spacious comfortable rooms on main Dam square facing the Royal Palace. Breakfasts are served in a glass-roofed winter garden.

Pulitzer: Prinsengracht 315–331, tel: 228333.

Terrace of 17th and 18th-century canal-side residences and warehouses, converted into a hotel of considerable charm and character. Exposed brick, old beams, antiques and beautiful furnishings. Sophisticated bedrooms overlooking canals or gardens.

MODERATE

The Beethoven, Holland, Museum, Terdam and Trianon are all part of the AMS Hotel group and, apart from location, differ very little in decor, prices and facilities.

Ambassade: Herengracht 341, tel: 262333.

Highly popular, very friendly B&B converted from a series of 17th and 18th-century canal-side houses. Lots of antiques, paintings, steep steps and spiral staircases. Book well in advance for this one.

Arthur Frommer: Noorderstraat 46, tel: 220328.

American-owned hotel in quiet location between art museums and Rembrandtsplein. Comfortable rooms built round private courtyard (where you can park free of charge).

Atlas: Van Eeghenstraat 64, tel: 766336.

Small Art Nouveau hotel in quiet leafy residental quarter close to the Vondelpark.

Beethoven: 43 Beethovenstraat, tel: 6644816.

On a smart shopping street, 2 miles (3 km) from the centre, with bar, restaurant and terrace. Tram stop outside.

Canal House: Keizersgracht 148, tel: 225182.

American-owned hotel, expertly converted from merchant houses on a quiet canal. Lots of antiques and a charming breakfast room.

Estherea: Singel 303–309, tel: 245146.

17th-century canal house, 2 minutes from Dam Square. Steep stairs but there is a lift.

Holland: P.C. Hoofstraat 162, tel: 764253.

Quiet location close to the Vondelpark and the Concertgebouw.

Jan Luyken: Jan Luykenstraat 58, tel: 764111.

Late 19th-century building close to major art museums, the Concertgebouw and the Municipal Theatre. Quiet rooms and bar/lounge with adjacent patio.

Museum: P.C. Hoofstraat 2, tel: 831811.

Busy spot, beside the Rijksmuseum. Own restaurant, coffee shop and bar.

Prinsen: Vondelstraat 38, tel: 162323.

Converted 19th-century houses in quiet street, 2 minutes from Leidseplein.

Owl: Roemer Visscherstraat 1, tel: 189484.

Friendly, with small but pleasant rooms, and quietly located by the Vondelpark, 5 minutes from Leidseplein.

Terdam: Tesselschadestraat 23, tel: 126876.

Best value of the AMS Hotel chain, 5 minutes' walk from Leidseplein.

Trianon: J.W. Brouwersstraat 3–7, tel: 732073.

On quiet road behind the Concertgebouw. Standard AMS group furnishings.

Weichman: Prinsengracht 328–330, tel: 263321.

Attractively located canal-side hotel, north of Leidseplein. Antique furnishings in the public rooms.

INEXPENSIVE

Acro: Jan Luykenstraat 44, tel: 662 0526.

One of the better value budget hotels close to the art museums and the Vondelpark. Pleasant modern furnishings, in good condition.

Cok Budget: Koninginneweg 34–36, tel: 664 6111.

Large, modern hotel-cum-hostel complex in the Vondelpark, with trams to the centre. Plenty of facilities, including games room, disco and shops.

Quentin: Leidsekade 89, tel: 262187.

Small, charming and well maintained, on a wide canal near Leidseplein. Popular with artists.

Wijnnobel: Vossiusstraat 9, tel: 622298.

Cheap and cheerful, with views of the Vondelpark. No private bathrooms.

YOUTH HOSTELS

Amsterdam has a good choice of hostels open to people of all ages. Most offer dormitory accommodation only but some provide private rooms and a few have family facilities such as childrens' menus. If you are not a member, a card can usually be issued on the spot. The two official YHA hostels in the city are:

NJHC-**City Hostel "Vondelpark"**: Zanpad 5, tel: 831744.

Quiet, well-equipped hostel in the Vondelpark. All rooms with shower and toilet; recreation rooms, meals and snacks, bar and family rooms.

NJHC-**Youth Hostel 2 Stadsdoelen**:

Kloveniersburgwal 97, tel: 246832.

On a canal, 10 minutes' walk from Dam Square and close to the Red Light District. Bar and snacks, recreation room.

CAMPING

Camping is only permitted on official campsites. The VVV office can provide a list of sites near the city but cannot make a reservation for you.

Most sites are easily accessible by bus from Centraal Station. Two of the closest to the city are **Amsterdam Ijsclub**, Ijsbaanpad 45, tel: 620916, near the Olympic Stadium, and **Amsterdamse Bos**, Kleine Noorddijk 1, Amstelveen, tel: 416868.

The two main youth camp-sites are **Vliegenbos**, Meeuwenlaan 138, tel: 368855, 10 minutes' bus ride from Centraal Station, and **Zeeburg**, Zuider Ijdijk 34a, tel: 944430, not so easy to get to.

FOOD DIGEST

WHAT TO EAT

Although the heavy, calorie-loaded typical Dutch dishes have gradually given way to the demands of diet-conscious Dutch, you can still find plenty of vegetable hotchpotches, thick pea soups, wholesome stews, apple pies and pancakes with lashings of cream. Dutch food may not be very exciting, but most of the time it is good and is sure to fill you up.

Typical Dutch breakfasts – consisting of a variety of cheeses, cold meats, sausages, breads and rolls along with coffee, tea or chocolate – are more than sufficient.

Amsterdam excels in delicious snacks: salted or pickled herrings served from street stalls (and traditionally swallowed whole on the spot), smoked eel, meat croquettes, sausages, french fries with mayonnaise, sweet and savoury pancakes, waffles and *proffertjes* (mini-pancakes coated with icing sugar). Even the *automatieken*, the food-dispensing machines, provide some surprisingly appetizing snacks such as meat and cheese croquettes, saté and egg-roll.

The local equivalent to sandwiches are *broodjes*, soft rolls loaded with fish, smoked sausage, spiced ground beef, roast beef, ham, cheese and an infinite variety of other savoury fillings.

A lunch in a café might comprise a *Koffietafel* ("coffee table"), similar to a Dutch breakfast, plus fruit and perhaps a hot dish in winter; *Uitsmijter*, an open sandwich, with roast beef, meat balls, ham or cheese on bread topped with fried egg; or *Erwtensoep*, a thick soup with peas and pork.

Dinner is the main meal of the day, usually taken early at 6 p.m. or 6.30 p.m. If you are on a tight budget, look out for the *Tourist Menu* sign, indicating a three-course main meal for an all-inclusive price. Restaurants displaying the sign *Neerland Dis* serve regional specialities.

You can find every type of cuisine in Amsterdam, from Argentinian to Thai, but, as far as most visitors are concerned, the city's gastronomic forte is Indonesian cuisine, a legacy of Dutch colonialism. The *pièce de résistance* is the *rijsttafel*, an exotic variety of meat, fish and vegetable dishes such as saté, spicey meatballs and *loempia* (a kind of egg roll), all served with steamed rice.

WHERE TO EAT

Bear in mind that 15 percent service charge and VAT are invariably included in bills, both for restaurants and bars, and there is no compulsion to tip.

DELUXE

Ciel Bleu: Okura Hotel, Ferdinand Bolstraat 333, tel: 787111. Closed: lunch. First-class French restaurant on top floor of 23-storey Japanese hotel.

La Rive: Amstel Hotel, Professor Tulpplein 1, tel: 226060. Closed: lunch. French cuisine in intimate and elegant hotel restaurant. Faultless service.

Trechter: Hobbemakada 63, tel: 711263. Closed: lunch, Sunday, Monday and mid-July to August. Very small, serving top quality *nouvelle cuisine*.

Yamazato: Okura Hotel, Ferdinand Bolstraat 333, tel: 787111. Best Japanese food in Holland (forming part of Japanese hotel).

EXPENSIVE

Dorrius: NZ Voorburgwal 336–342, tel: 235875. Solid Dutch fare served by white-aproned waiters in wood-panelled, typically Dutch restaurant. Quite smart, and popular with tourists.

Dynasty: Reguliersdwarsstraat 30, tel: 268400. Closed: lunch, Tuesday and one month at Christmas. Exquisite Chinese, Thai and Indonesian dishes. Oriental decor. Very fashionable and reservations are essential.

Tout Court: Runstraat 17, tel: 258637. Closed: lunch and Monday. Small, sought-after French restaurant with imaginative menu combining traditional and *nouvelle cuisine*.

d'Vijff Vlieghen (Five Flies): Spuistraat 294–302, tel: 248369. Closed: lunch. Something of a pricey tourist trap but very picturesque setting (with seven separate rooms, beams, tiles and candles) and authentic Dutch cooking.

MODERATE

Die Port van Cleve: Nieuwe Zijds Voorburgwal 178, tel: 244860. Hotel restaurant famous for steaks. Every thousandth one comes free. Nice place for lunch.

Golden Temple: Utrechtsestraat 126, tel: 268560. Small, serving excellent vegetarian food.

Indonesia: Singel 550, tel: 232035. One of the best spots to try *rijsttafel*; historic patrician house with rather grand decor, overlooking flower market and Mint Tower. Friendly service.

Sama Sebo: P.C. Hoofstraat 27, tel: 628146. Closed: Sunday and two weeks in July. Some of the best Indonesian food in town, located close to main museums and shops. Booking essential.

Sluizer: Utrechtsestraat 43–45, tel: 263557 for fish restaurant; tel: 226376 for Dutch restaurant. Two restaurants, the more sought-after serving a large selection of imaginative fish dishes, the other meat and Dutch food.

Umeno: Agamemnonstraat 27, tel: 766089. Closed: Wednesday. Good Japanese restaurant patronised by businessmen, fairly close to RAI exhibition center.

INEXPENSIVE

(see also *Cafés & Bars* below)

Bojo: Lange Leidsedwarsstraat 51, tel: 227434. Good value Indonesian food just off Leidseplein. Open all night.

Café de la Paix: Wolvenstraat 22–24. Lively and popular spot for a drink, snack or full meal.

De Blauwe Hollander: Leidsekruisstraat 28. Straightforward wholesome Dutch food in cosy setting.

Floreat: 502 Overtoom. Vegetarian specialities.

Speciaal: Nieuwe Leliestraat 142, tel: 249706. Unspecial street in the Jordaan district, but wonderful value Indonesian food, including *rijsttafel*, in semi-tropical setting.

DRINKING NOTES

The most popular drinks are fresh coffee and lager. Holland is the world's number one producer of beer and the local lager is served in cafés and restaurants throughout the city, usually in 25cl measures. Heineken is the most popular. Foreign brands are available at much higher prices. The native gin is *jenever*, drunk neat (and traditionally knocked back in one) or with a beer chaser. Various varieties include *oude* (old), which is the sweeter, and *jonge* (young), the more powerful. The place to try out the local spirits and liqueurs is a *proeflokaal* or tasting house, the best known being Wijnand Fockink (see below).

CAFÉS & BARS

There are numerous cafés throughout the city, serving invariably good coffee – often with apple tart or spicey biscuits. A typical brown café is an intimate, semi-bohemian bar with nicotine-stained walls (hence the name), rugs on tables, sawdust on the floor and newspapers to peruse. These are usually frequented by the locals (as well as tourists) and are places where you can often get good quality food at reasonable prices or linger over a drink and a book on a rainy afternoon.

In contrast are the new wave bars, with cool, whitewashed and mirrored walls, an abundance of greenery and a long list of cocktails. Some bars have live music, often jazz or blues. Cafés displaying a marijuana plant sign sell soft drugs as well as coffee.

Americain: American Hotel, Leidseplein 28. Splendid Art Nouveau café overlooking Leidseplein, very popular amongst fashionable locals. Mata Hari had her wedding reception here.

Berkhoff: Leidsestraat 46. Elegant café with pianist and wonderful pastries.

Eylders: Korte Leidsedwarsstraat. Former haunt of the literati, just by Leidseplein. Occasional modern art exhibitions.

Het Hok: Lange Leidsedwarsstraat 134. Specialises in chess, backgammon and draughts.

Hoppe: Spui 20. Smoke-filled and crowded bar, unremarkable except for the fact that the locals all love it. Crowds usually spill out on to the street.

Jan Heuvel: Prinsengracht 568. Traditional brown café close to the Rijksmuseum.

Oblomow: Reguliersdwarsstraat 40. Trendy 1980s establishment with bright white interior. Popular for drinks and reasonably priced meals in a separate restaurant.

De Prins: Prinsengracht 124. Charming 18th-century canal house, where you can linger over a drink or have a full breakfast, lunch or dinner.

Schiller: Rembrandtsplein 26. Splendid Art Deco interior; otherwise uninspiring.

Wijnand Fockink: Pijlsteeg 31. Picturesque old bar/tasting house off Dam Square where you can try out the local spirits and liqueurs.

THINGS TO DO

DIAMOND FACTORIES

Amsterdam is a major diamond centre with dozens of workshops where you can watch the cutting and polishing. Entrance is free and there is absolutely no obligation to buy. If you are tempted, bear in mind the import tax you will have to pay if you live in the EC.

The following give free guided tours:

Amsterdam Diamond Centre: Rokin 1.

AS Bonebakker & Zoon: Rokin 86/90.

Coster Diamonds: Paulus Potterstraat 2–4

Holshuysen-Stoeltie B.V: Wagenstraat 13–17

Van Moppes Diamonds: Albert Cuypstraat 2–6

Gassan Diamond House: Nieuwe Achtergracht 17–23

CITY WALKS

Brochures are available from the VVV and the Amsterdam Historical Museum detailing walks around the city and covering Jewish Amsterdam, famous shopping streets and Amsterdam School architecture, amongst other themes.

EXCURSIONS

Travel agents organise city bus tours, canal cruises and excursions further afield. Within the city the most popular excursions are daytime and evening canal cruises in modern glass-covered motor-launches. Normal trips last about 1 hour to 1 hour 30 minutes, taking in some of the prettiest and most interesting features of the city. You can also take an organised tram ride around the city, starting from Centraal Station. City sightseeing tours by coach take in the Royal Palace, the Rijksmuseum, a diamond-cutting factory and other places of interest. It is much cheaper to do these tours yourself but they are worth considering if time is limited and you don't know the city. For excursions out of the city, the main operator is Lindbergh Tours, Damrak 26.

The following are some of the most popular excursions:

Volendam and Marken: Traditional fishing villages with wooded houses and locals in traditional colourful costumes. Quaint but very touristy. The excursion also takes in a visit to a cheesemaker and perhaps a clogmaker too.

Aalsmeer: Venue of the world's biggest flower auction. The flower festival is held here on the first Saturday of September.

Alkmaar: On Fridays from April to September Alkmaar is the scene of a lively and very picturesque cheese market, with barrel organs, buskers and streets packed with stalls selling cheeses.

Delft: A picturesque little town of canals and white bridges, where you can watch craftsmen making genuine Delft pottery.

The Hague: Seat of the Dutch Parliament and home of Dutch royalty, less than an hour's journey from Amsterdam. A prosperous, somewhat sedate city of embassies, parks and palaces, well worth visiting for good museums and art galleries. The Maurithuis has an exceptional collection of Dutch masterpieces, including some of Rembrandt's finest works.

Haarlem: A well-preserved 17th-century city whose chief attraction is the Frans Hals Museum.

Utrecht: Historic religious centre which still preserves Gothic churches and old patrician houses. Also an international business/industrial centre.

Grand Holland Tour: A day's excursion taking in Aalsmeer, The Hague, the miniature town of Madurodam, Rotterdam and Delft.

CAFÉ-LOUNGING

Sitting and watching the world go by is one of the most entertaining ways of getting to know the city. Everything goes here so, from the vantage point of a pavement café, you will see plenty of way out get-ups as well as all the street entertainment, including barrel organs, buskers and fire-eaters. The best spot for people-watching is Leidseplein.

PARKS

The Vondelpark, close to Leidseplein, provides a welcome retreat from the narrow, traffic-filled streets of the city. Extensive lawns, flowerbeds, lakeside teas, free concerts in summer, Sunday afternoon pop groups, fire-eaters and jugglers and teas by the lakeside are all part of the attraction. For outdoor activities, there's nothing to beat the Amsterdamse Bos – a 2,200-acre (890-hectare) public park southwest of Amsterdam, with miles of walking and biking paths, and places for boating, riding and swimming.

CULTURE PLUS

MUSEUMS & ART GALLERIES

Amsterdam has 42 museums, ranging from some of Europe's finest art collections to a host of small, specialist museums reflecting the diversity of the city's culture. The top three attractions, the Rijksmuseum and the Van Gogh and Stedelijk museums, are all conveniently located round the Museumplein.

If you intend spending a large proportion of your time visiting museums, it may be worth buying a Museum Card (available at main museums and the VVV), valid for a year and entitling you to free entry to approximately 350 museums in Holland, 16 of them in Amsterdam. The price of the Museum Card is such that you need to visit at least 10 museums before you begin to make a saving, and to buy one you will need a passport-sized photograph. Most museums are closed on Sunday mornings and all day Monday.

KEY SIGHTS

Rijksmuseum: Stadhouderskade 42. Finest collection of Dutch paintings in existence, featuring famous Rembrandt paintings (the showpiece being *The Night Watch*). Also portraits by Hals, landscapes by Van Ruisdael, bawdy scenes by Jan Steen and peaceful domestic scenes by Vermeer. Also sections covering foreign art (Bellini, Tintoretto, Goya, Van Dyck, Rubens), Dutch history, sculpture, Delftware, furniture, prints, Asiatic art and a splendid collection of 17th-century dolls' houses. Impossible to do in one visit. Open: 10 a.m.–5 p.m., Sunday 1–5 p.m. Closed: Monday.

Stedelijk: Paulus Potterstraat 13. Municipal museum of modern and contemporary art. Whitewashed walls, huge windows and partially glassed roof form the setting for works by Picasso, Manet, Cezanne and Chagall, though greatest emphasis is placed on the post-war visual arts. Temporary exhibitions, featuring living artists, are frequently shown. Open: 11 a.m.–5 p.m.

Van Gogh: Paulus Potterstraat 7. Stunning collection of paintings and drawings by Van Gogh, from the dark colours and heavy forms of his early Dutch period, through the Impressionist paintings of his years in Paris to the vivid, writhing works of the later years in Arles. Also works by contemporaries such as Manet, Gauguin and Toulouse-Lautrec. Expect queues, especially on Sundays. Open: 10 a.m.–5 p.m., Sunday 1–5 p.m. Closed: Monday.

Royal Palace (Koninklijk Paleis): Dam. Original Town Hall of Amsterdam, converted to a Royal palace during the Napoleonic occupation. Grandiose halls decorated with fine sculpture, moralising murals and paintings and Empire-style furniture. Open: June–August 12.30–4 p.m. September–May by arrangement only.

Nederlands Scheepvaart (Maritime Museum): Kattenburgerplein 1. Models of ships, old maps, globes, prints and paintings, covering all aspects of the Netherlands' illustrious seafaring history. Housed in the former arsenal of the Amsterdam Admiralty. Open: 10 a.m.–5 p.m., Sunday 1–5 p.m. Closed: Monday.

Rembrandthuis: Jodenbreestraat 4–6. Drawings and prints by Rembrandt in the house where he once lived. Open: 10 a.m.–5 p.m., Sunday 1–5 p.m.

Six Collection: Amstel 218. Entrance only with a card of introduction from the Rijksmuseum information desk (passport needed). Outstanding collection of Dutch 17th-century paintings, including works by Rembrandt and Hals. The showpiece is Rembrandt's *Portrait of Jan Six*.

Amsterdam Historical Museum: Kalverstraat 92. The growth of Amsterdam, illustrated by prints, paintings, maps and documents, displayed in a splendid 17th-century converted orphanage. No English labelling, but guides, in several languages, are available on loan. Open: 11 a.m.–5 p.m.

Madame Tussaud: Kalverstraat 156. Waxwork figures of Dutch and international personalities. Open: 10 a.m.–6 p.m. July and August 9 a.m.– 7 p.m.

Anne Frank House: Prinsengracht 263. Hiding place in which Anne Frank wrote her famous diary. Documentation room illustrating the rise of the Nazis and the persecution of the Jews. Expect long queues, especially in summer. Open: 9 a.m.–5 p.m., Sunday 10 a.m.–5 p.m. June, July and August 9 a.m.–7 p.m., Sunday 10 a.m.–7 p.m.

Jewish Historical Museum (Joods Historisch Museum): Jonas Daniel Meijerplein 2–4. Four synagogues imaginatively converted and linked by the Shulglass, a glass-covered thoroughfare. Open: 11 a.m.–5 p.m.

Amstelkring Museum: Oude Zijds Voorburgwal 40. Seventeenth-century canal-side houses, the lofts of which were converted into a clandestine Catholic church. Open: 10 a.m.–5 p.m., Sunday 1–5 p.m.

Tropen Museum: Linnaeusstraat 2. Contemporary life in the Third World. Labelling and audio-visual material in Dutch only, but plenty of activities for children. Open: 10 a.m.–5 p.m., Saturday and Sunday 12 noon–5 p.m.

Artis Zoo, Aquarium and **Planetarium**: Plantage Kerklaan 40; Very large collection with reptile house, nocturnal house, farmyard and largest and oldest aquarium in the Netherlands. Zoo and Aquarium open: Monday–Sunday 9 a.m.–5 p.m. Planetarium: Monday 1–5 p.m., Tuesday–Sunday 9 a.m.–5 p.m.

Aviodome National Aeronautics and Space Travel Museum: Schiphol Airport. Display of some two dozen planes and space craft, including the Wright Brothers' 1903 *Flyer*. For enthusiasts only. Open: 10 a.m.–5 p.m. Closed: Mondays from November–March.

Nederlands Theater Instituut (Dutch Theatre Museum): Herengracht 168. History of Dutch theatre, temporary exhibitions on theatre, mime, film and dance, collection of theatre costumes, models of stage sets, all housed in splendid 17th-century canal house. Open: Tuesday–Sunday 11 a.m.–5 p.m.

National Spaarpotten Museum/Money Box Museum: Raadhuisstraat 20. Witty collection of piggy banks from all over the world. Children love it. Open: Monday–Friday 1–4 p.m.

Van Loon Museum: Keizersgracht 672. Grand but faded canal-side house full of Van Loon family portraits. Open: Monday only 10 a.m.–12 noon, 1–5 p.m.

Willet-Holthuysen Museum: Herengracht 605. Canal-side house entirely furnished in 17th and 18th-century style, featuring antiques, glass, paintings, porcelain and the original kitchen complete with copper pots. Open: 10 a.m.–5 p.m., Sunday 1–5 p.m. Closed: Monday.

MUSIC, OPERA & BALLET

For the majority of theatre, music, ballet and opera performances, seats can be booked in advance at the Amsterdam Uitburo on Leidseplein or from the Theater Bespreek Bureau at the VVV. For information on what's on, consult the English guide *Amsterdam This Week*, available from the tourist office and main hotels, or the monthly Uitburo publication, *Uitkrant*.

The chief venue for classical music is the Concertgebouw, Museumplein (tel: 718345), home of the leading Concertgebouw Orchestra. Chamber music is often performed in the city's historic churches – watch out for free lunch-time organ recitals. The impressive 1,600-seat Muziektheater, overlooking the River Amstel by Waterlooplein, is home of the National Ballet and Netherlands Opera. The Vondelpark is the venue in summer for free concerts, classical and pop. The main annual event is the summer Holland Festival, featuring international opera, theatre, music and dance.

THEATRE

Small venues all over the city host fringe performances. The following theatre groups put on English-language performances: the English Theatre Company of Amsterdam (tel: 247248), the American Repertory Theatre (tel: 259495), the Schaffy Theatre (tel: 231311) and the Theater De Suikerhof (tel: 227571). The Stadsschouwburg Theatre on Leidseplein puts on modern dance, drama and musicals.

CINEMA

There are 50 cinemas and film theatres and a large selection of the latest international releases, shown in the original language. Look for listings in cafés and bars or in *Amsterdam This Week*.

ARCHITECTURE

Begijnhof: Spui. The English church is often used for lunch-time recitals. Delightful, quiet courtyard encircled by 17th-century almshouses.

Nieuwe Kerk (New Church): Dam. Large Protestant church in which organ concerts and other cultural events are regularly held. Despite the name, the church was founded in the 15th century and only the spire was added in the 19th century. Dutch monarchs are crowned here.

Oude Kerk (Old Church): Ouderkerksplein 23. The oldest church in the city, incongruously close to strip clubs and sex shops. You can climb the tower during summer months.

Westerkerk (West Church): Prinsengracht 281. Built between 1620 and 1631. The tower, which can be climbed in summer, is decorated with the imperial crown of Emperor Maximilian of Austria.

Zuiderkerk (South Church): Zandstraat. Picturesque tower which you can climb in summer. Rembrandt sketched it from his window.

NIGHTLIFE

After dark, entertainment focuses on three main areas: Leidseplein, for lively discos and nightclubs; Rembrandtsplein for clubs, cabarets and strip shows pandering to older tastes; and the Red Light District, notorious for scantily dressed females sitting in windows and notice-boards saying "room to hire".

Strip shows, porn videos and sex shops centre on the main canals of Oude Zijde Voorburgwal and Oude Zijde Achterburgwal. The smaller, sleazier streets leading off these two canals are best avoided, and you are advised never to take photographs.

On an entirely different note, you could spend the evening on a candle-lit canal cruiser, with wine and cheese or full dinner provided, or try out one of the numerous brown cafés, some of which provide live music.

DISCOS & NIGHTCLUBS

Bamboo Bar: Lange Leidsedwarsstraat 64. Live jazz and blues in an exotic setting.

BIMhuis: Oudeschans 73. The in-place for jazz, both modern and classical.

Escape: Rembrandtsplein. Big new disco with variety of music, some live, and host to the weekly televised SKY channel Top Ten countdown.

Fizz: Nieuwe Zijds Vooburgwal 165. New wave club.

Mazzo: Rozengracht 114. Self-conscious new wave disco: dancing, videos and some live music.

Melkweg: Lijnbaansgracht 234a. Off-beat arts centre-cum-club near Leidseplein, with concert hall, disco, experimental plays (some in English) and art exhibitions. Dope and space cakes for sale.

Nijlpaardenhuis: Warmoesstraat 170. Roller skate disco, with skates for hire.

Odeon: Singel 460. Elegant 17th-century house, converted into disco and café, with suitably smart clientele.

Paradiso: Weteringschans 6–8, just off Leidseplein. The hot spot for rock, reggae and live pop concerts.

Zorba the Buddha: Oude Zijds Voorburgwal 216. Stylish Bhagwan-run club popular with trendy teenagers.

GAMBLING

Holland Casino Amsterdam, Hilton Hotel, Apollolaan 138–140. Passport or ID card necessary for entry.

SHOPPING

Bargains are a rarity but browsing is fun, particularly in the markets and the small specialist shops. For general shopping, the main streets are Kalverstraat and Nieuwendijk; for exclusive boutiques try P.C. Hoofstraat, and for the more off-beat shops, head to the Jordaan northwest of the centre where many of the local artists live. The VVV tourist office provides a series of useful shopping guides: *Art and Antiques*; *Beautiful and Chic*; *Open-air Markets* and *Between the Canals*. The leaflets give maps, route descriptions, places of interest and a list of addresses and shop specialities.

WHERE TO BUY

ANTIQUES

Nieuwe Spiegelstraat (starting opposite the Rijksmuseum) is lined with small and immaculate antique shops. The Amsterdam Antiques Gallery is at Number 34. Look out for old Dutch tiles, copper and brass, glass, pewter, snuff boxes, clocks and dolls. In markets, beware of imitation antique copper and brass, made in Tunisia.

ART & REPRODUCTIONS

The major museums and art galleries have excellent reproductions of paintings in their collections, particularly the Rijksmuseum and the Stedelijk. Numerous small commercial galleries sell original oil paintings, watercolours, drawings, engravings and sculpture. For old prints and engravings, try the Antiekmarkt de Looier, Elandsgracht 110.

BOOKS

The city has an exceptionally large choice of books, both new and second-hand. For second-hand English-language books, try the the English Open Book Exchange, Prinsengracht 42, or the American Discount Book Center, Kalverstraat 185. The Allert de Lange, Damrak 62, is strong on literature, travel and art; the Athenaeum Boekhandel & Nieuwscentrum, Spui 14–16, has a superb selection of literature in a splendid Art Nouveau setting.

CLOTHES

The major department stores are concentrated along Kalverstraat and Nieuwendijk, but the biggest and most prestigious is De Bijenkorf, Damrak 90. For designer labels, try P.C. Hoofstraat, Van Baerlestraat and Beethovenstraat; for less conventional boutiques, the Jordaan is the place to go.

JEWELLERY

Jewellery shops all over town have eyecatching displays of modern and traditional pieces, some original and designed on the spot. (See under *Things to Do* section for visits to diamond factories.) The fact that Amsterdam is a major diamond-cutting centre doesn't mean you'll get them cheap.

PORCELAIN

Cheap imitations of the familiar blue Delftware are sold all over town. The genuine article, always with a capital 'D', is made at Royal Delft's official retail branch, De Porceleyne Fles, Muntplein 12. You can visit their showrooms and watch painting demonstrations.

Focke & Meltzer, with branches at P.C. Hoofstraat 65–67 and the Okura Hotel, have a good choice of porcelain and glass, and some attractive reproduction Delft tiles. For a huge range of antique tiles, try Eduard Kramer, Nieuwe Spiegelstraat 64.

GIFTS

Tulips and bulbs are always popular. If you fail to get them at the flower market (see below) you can buy them at higher prices at Schiphol Airport. Other things typically Dutch are cigars (the best known shop is Hajenius, Rokin 92), chocolates (made by Van Houten, Verkade and Droste; Boots, at P.C. Hoofstraat 84, has a superb selection), Edam and Gouda cheeses and clogs. Excursions to Volendam and Marken usually take in a cheese farm and a visit to a craftsman making clogs – one pair can take as little as five minutes to make.

SCHIPOL AIRPORT

If there are any guilders left you will no doubt be tempted by the enormous range of goods at Schipol Airport. Apart from duty-free goods, there is an excellent food section, selling smoked Dutch eel and cheeses, and shops specialising in bulbs and seeds, flowers, Delftware, clothes and souvenirs. Although quite pricey, you can also find some unusual and affordable gifts here.

TAX REFUNDS

Non-EC residents are entitled to a refund of the 20 percent sales tax (VAT) levied on individual items costing in excess of f.300. The leaflet *Tax Free for Tourists*, available at Schiphol Airport and the VVV office, explains the procedure, and shopkeepers are always happy to help.

MARKETS

Held Monday to Saturday unless otherwise stated.

Flower Market: Singel. Dazzling displays of flowers, many sold from barges. Some stalls will pack and export bulbs for you. Reasonable prices and worth seeing, even if you don't intend to buy.

Albert Cuypstraat: Large bustling general market with a wide choice of food, household goods, clothes, etc.

Book Market: Oudemanhuispoort. Passageway with stalls selling antique books and prints.

Stamp Market: N.Z. Voorburgwal. Stamps and coins, held on Wednesday and Saturday.

Waterlooplein: Extensive flea market with a lot of junk and occasional bargains; clothes, books, records, animals and antiques.

SPORTS

SOCCER

You can watch matches at the Ajax Stadium, Middenweg 401, or at the Olympic Stadium, Stadionplein 20.

CYCLING

The Dutch are a nation of cyclists and the country is crisscrossed with cycle paths and routes. You can either hire a bike (see *Getting Around*) and set off independently, or opt for a bike excursion, which will include bike hire, a cheese farm visit and boat rides. Information from the VVV. The Amsterdamse Bos park, southwest of Amsterdam, offers several bike trails.

WATERSPORTS

Canoes, rowing boats and windsurfing boards can be hired in the Amsterdamse Bos. Canal bikes (similar to pedaloes) can be hired at various points in the city.

GOLF

The greens closest to the city centre are at the Amsterdamse Golf Club, Zwarte Laantje 4, and the Golf Club Olympus, 150 Ouderkerkerdijk.

SWIMMING

De Mirandabad, De Mirandalaan 9, has both indoor and outdoor pools and the Marnixbad, Marnixplein 9, is an indoor pool with slides.

SQUASH

Courts at Sportcentrum Borchland, Borchlandweg 8–12.

ICE SKATING

If it's cold enough, you can skate on the canals; otherwise, an outdoor rink is set up in Leidseplein every winter and there is year-round skating at the Jaap Edenbaan ice-skating rink, Radioweg 64.

SPECIAL INFORMATION

DOING BUSINESS

Amsterdam ranks eighth in the world as a congress centre, hosting more than 90 international congresses every year and 50 trade shows and exhibitions. The Dutch tend to be efficient and civilised when it comes to doing business and the wide knowledge of English is obviously a huge advantage.

CHILDREN

Tram trips, canal cruises, water pedaloes, barrel organs and mime shows are all likely to amuse the young. The Vondelpark has a playground, duck ponds and free entertainment in summer. The Amstelpark provides pony rides and the Amsterdamse Bos, reached in summer by vintage trams, provides a huge expanse of parkland with lakes, swimming, riding, fishing, biking and canoes.

Favourite childrens' attractions in the city are Madame Tussaud, the Spaarpotten (Money Box) Museum, TM Junior Museum at the Tropen Museum (a lively "hands-on" museum on the Third World), the Artis Zoo, the Maritime Museum and the delightful dolls' house section of the Rijksmuseum.

As an excursion for children, you can't beat Madurodam – a Dutch town in miniature complete with churches, castles, farms, ships and planes, followed, perhaps, by an afternoon on Scheveningen beach.

GAYS

Of all European cities, Amsterdam is the most welcoming towards gay men and women. There are special hotels, restaurants, bars, bookstores, shops, nightclubs, cinemas and plenty more. The *Best Guide to Amsterdam* is full of useful information.

DISABLED

The National Board of Tourism publishes the leaflet *Holland for the Handicapped*, which lists hotels, restaurants, museums and other places of interest with facilities for the disabled. Most of the major museums and art galleries have access for wheelchairs, although the city in general, with its narrow cobbled streets and wealth of steep narrow staircases, is not ideal, and you should check before booking into a hotel whether it has a lift; some staircases are almost as steep as ladders.

STUDENTS

Young people under 24 can get reduced-rate admissions to most museums, though you may need to produce a passport as proof of your age. The magazine *Use it*, available free in youth hostels, the VVV and camp sites, is crammed with practical information on cheap accommodation, bars and music. The local student campus restaurants are called *Mensas* and any one can eat there. Food is filling and cheap but served only Monday to Friday lunch times.

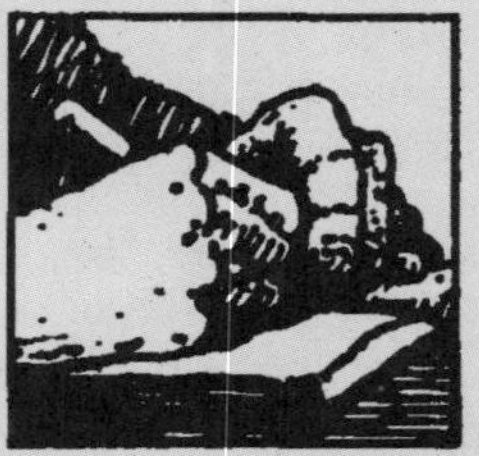

USEFUL ADDRESSES

CONSULATES

America: Museumplein 19, tel: 790321.
Austria: Weteringschans 106, tel: 268033.
Australia: Koninginnegracht 23, 2514 AB Den Haag, tel: 070-630983.
Belgium: Herengracht 541, tel: 248771.
Canada: Sophialaan 7, 2514 JP Den Haag, tel: 070-614111.
Denmark: De Ruyterkade 139, tel: 234145.
Finland: Herengracht 462, tel: 249090.
France: Vijzelgracht 2, tel: 248346.
Germany: De Lairessestraat 172, tel: 736245.
Great Britain: Koningslaan 44, tel: 764343.
Italy: Herengracht 609, tel: 240043.
Japan: Keizersgracht 634, tel: 243581.
Norway: De Ruyterkade 107, tel: 242331.
Spain: Jacob Obrechtstraat 51, tel: 796591.
Sweden: De Ruijterkade 107, tel: 242699.
Switzerland: Johannes Vermeerstraat 16, tel: 644231.

AIRLINES

KLM: Leidseplein 1, tel: 493633.
British Airways: Stadhouderskade 2, tel: 852211.

TRAVEL AGENTS

American Express: Damrak 66, tel: 262042.
Holland International: Rokin 54, tel: 5512812.
Lindbergh: Damrak 26, tel: 222766.

TOURIST INFORMATION

The main tourist office (VVV) is opposite Centraal Station at Stationsplein 10, tel: 266444. Open: Easter to June and September daily 9 a.m.–11 p.m., Sunday 9 a.m.–9 p.m. July and August Monday–Sunday 9 a.m.–11 p.m. October to Easter, Monday–

Saturday 9 a.m.–5 p.m., Sunday 10 a.m.–1 p.m., 2–5 p.m. There is also a VVV bureau at Leidsestraat 104.

There is a tourist information office at the airport, which is particularly useful if you have not already booked your accommodation. The free booklet *Amsterdam This Week* includes a small map and lists museums, events and other attractions. Other guides can be bought at the VVV.

The GVB office, also at Stationsplein, alongside the metro entrance, tel: 272727, provides information and ticket sales for local and city public transport. Open: Monday–Friday 7 a.m.–10.30 p.m.

FURTHER READING

There are surprisingly few books on Amsterdam that go beyond the practicalities of staying in the city. But there's plenty of choice for those who want to steep themselves in specific themes such as history, art and architecture.

A Short History of Amsterdam, by Dedalo Carasso (Amsterdam Historical Museum) is packed with historical information on the city and is available from the Amsterdam Historical Museum.

The Guide to Jewish Amsterdam, by Jan Stoutenbeek and Paul Vigeveno (Jewish Historical Museum) provides comprehensive coverage of the history of Amsterdam's Jews, the Jewish community, walking tours of the areas, and the shops and retaurants that are still the centre of Jewish daily life. No real competition, however, for the world-famous Diary of Anne Frank, still one of the most compelling reads of its time.

Amsterdam Architecture: A Guide, edited by Guus Kemme and published by Vitgeverij Thoth, is the most comprehensive guide to the city's buildings, new and old, and describes over 250 in detail, with lots of illustrations.

Rich Van Gogh freaks can buy the catalogue produced for the 1990 Centenary, the most comprehensive guide to Vincent's art ever published, along with extracts from his letters and reproductions of the pictures that influenced his own work.

Of the numerous books on Dutch art, R.H. Fuch's *Dutch Painting* (Thames & Hudson) is a useful introduction to the subject.

Dutch Art and Architecture 1600–1800 by Jakob Rosenberg, Seymour Slive and E.H. ter Kuile (The Pelican History of Art) is an admirable and highly detailed study by three of the greatest authorities on Dutch art.

Art/Photo Credits

Photographs	
29, 42, 184	**Amsterdam Historical Museum**
48, 138	**APA Archive**
20, 22, 60, 92, 106, 117, 125, 126, 144, 158, 162, 166, 196	**Bodo Bondzio**
79, 146	**K. Debnicki**
95, 176	**Lee Foster**
219	**Manfred Gottschalk**
46	**Hans Höfer**
198, 216	**D. & J. Heaton**
49	**Indonesian Department of Information**
37, 80, 160, 175, 177, 212	**Lyle Lawson**
16	**Kal Muller**
64, 84, 87, 104, 122, 123, 134, 135, 150, 223	**Christine Osborne**
28, 34, 41, 44, 72, 74, 75, 77, 85, 88, 90, 93, 97, 102, 103, 124, 132, 133, 141, 147, 148, 165, 173, 179, 180, 187, 192, 194, 201, 202, 204, 205, 209, 210	**Eddy Posthuma de Boer**
164	**G. P. Reichelt**
Cover, 3, 18, 30, 35, 39, 40, 45, 59, 62, 65, 67, 69, 70, 71, 76, 82, 83, 94, 100, 101, 115, 116, 118, 119, 120, 121, 125, 130, 131, 142, 153, 154, 155, 163, 178, 181, 182, 184, 188, 189, 190, 198, 207, 208, 211, 214, 221, 222, 224	**Paul van Riel**
26, 38, 47, 168, 170, 171, 172, 174	**Rijksmuseum**
86	**David Simson**
214	**Adina Tovey**
139	**Bill Wassman**
9, 14, 63, 68, 78, 96, 98, 108, 110, 129, 136, 143, 145, 151, 152, 156, 161, 185, 191, 200, 206	**George Wright**
Maps	**Berndtson & Berndtson**
Illustrations	**Klaus Geisler**
Visual Consultant	**V. Barl**

INDEX

I–J

K

L

M

N

O

P

R